More praise for *The Weight of the Yen*

"Aside from being a riveting tale of what has happened to the Japanese economic miracle, *The Weight of the Yen* is also the first serious book on what is crucial in the U.S.-Japan relationship."
—Karel van Wolferen, author of *The Enigma of Japanese Power*

"The writing is lucid, crisp and mercifully free of bankerspeak . . . [The book] is a powerful warning for two nations to get a grip on their relationship and face the future together. Do your part: Read *The Weight of the Yen*."
—Brad Glosserman, *The Japan Times*

"Murphy shows how the Reagan/Bush deficits were financed and the price we are paying. He illuminates the critical problems in our relationship with Japan. *The Weight of the Yen* is an explosive book that Americans who care about the future of their country will want to read and ponder."
—Richard A. Gephardt, House Democratic Leader

"Murphy provides the most valuable description to date of decision-making in Japan's powerful Ministry of Finance . . . [His] contrast of the U.S. and Japanese systems is so stark that it obviates unsophisticated debate about unfair Japanese and Americans who don't try hard enough."
—J. Douglas Johnson, *Far Eastern Economic Review*

"Murphy's criticism of the MOF is devastating . . . [His] book makes compelling reading, especially since his taut, vigorous prose gives the book the flavor of a suspense novel."
—John Vachon, *Asahi Evening News*

"*The Weight of the Yen* is mercifully free of the preconceptions that bedevil so much writing on Japan. Working from his own experiences and observations here, Murphy constructs a picture of the Japanese economy—and its intertwining with the American—that is utterly convincing."
—Akio Mikuni, president, Mikuni and Company

"Murphy's book is both a history lesson and a revelation . . . *The Weight of the Yen* reads much like a high-paced thriller with detailed characterizations of people and places, helped by Murphy's background as a financial analyst and long-time Japan resident. Anyone with an interest in Japan and its relationship with the States will find *The Weight of the Yen* a valuable and enlightening read."
—Mario di Simoine, *Mainichi Daily News*

"An astute analysis of the dangerously self-serving economic games Japan and the U.S. have been playing over the past 15 years . . . In mercifully jargon-free fashion, Murphy offers a critical interpretation of the events, strategies, miscalculations, and errors that have brought Tokyo as well as Washington ever closer to a day of financial reckoning."
—*Kirkus Reviews*

"Murphy brings a rare bicultural perspective to his enlightening and disturbing saga of how Japan became the world's largest creditor country while the U.S. became the world's biggest debtor." —*Publishers Weekly*

"An engaging and witty analysis of the forces that have permitted Japan to pile up cash and the policy blunders that have kept U.S. presidents from Nixon to Clinton in denial, as he puts it, about the challenges these forces represent."
—William Glasgall, *Business Week*

The Weight of the Yen

How Denial Imperils America's Future and Ruins an Alliance

R. TAGGART MURPHY

W · W · NORTON & COMPANY

NEW YORK · LONDON

To my mother and

the memory of my father

First published as a Norton paperback 1997

The text of this book is composed in Galliard with the display set in Galliard, Windsor Light, and Janson. Composition and manufacturing by the Maple Vail Book Manufacturing Group. Book design by Marjorie J. Flock.

Library of Congress Cataloging-in-Publication Data

Murphy, R. Taggart.
        The weight of the yen : how denial imperils America's future and
    ruins an alliance / by R. Taggart Murphy.
                p.   cm.
        Includes bibliographical references and index.
        ISBN 0-393-03832-7
        1. Investments, Japanese—United States.   2. Budget deficits—
    United   States.   3. Stocks—Prices—Japan.   4. Loans, Japanese—
    United States.   5. Japan—Economic conditions—1945–1989.
    6. United States—Foreign economic relations—Japan.   7. Japan—
    Foreign economic relations—United States.   I. Title.
    HG4910.M8695   1996
    337.52073—dc20   95-37461

                            ISBN 0-393-03832-7
                            ISBN 0-393-31657-2 pbk.

W. W. Norton & Company, Inc., 500 Fifth Avenue, New York, N.Y. 10110
    W. W. Norton & Company Ltd,. 10 Coptic Street, London WC1A 1PU

                        1 2 3 4 5 6 7 8 9 0

Contents

III
Paying the Price

Preface to the Paperback Edition

AMERICA'S jumble of conflicting impressions and misinformation about Japan has grown even more incoherent in the months since this book was published. The Japan that fades in and out of the American mass media sprawls supinely under the weight of falling stock markets, crumbling banks, an endless recession, and petty bureaucrats who perversely refuse to "deregulate." For decades, this Japan sneakily got away with defying "market forces"; today those implacable gods are said to exact a grim revenge. Meanwhile, a casual comment by a well known Wall Street banker that Japanese investors might sour on U.S. Treasury securities freezes the American stock and bond markets for several days. They resume their climb only after a chorus of reassurances from Tokyo and Washington that, no, the Japanese will keep buying U.S. Treasury bonds. Like a wise old abbot instructing a roomful of novitiates, Treasury Secretary Robert Rubin endlessly chants "a strong dollar is in America's interest," patiently denying repeated speculation that he cuts secret deals with Japan's Ministry of Finance (MOF) to prop up the U.S. bond market. A delegation of top Detroit executives visits Rubin's office, moaning that the Japanese will again drive them to the wall unless the dollar surge ends.

The Japanese economy has indeed been in the doldrums for some years now, but clearly not everyone has written the place off. The Robert Rubins of this world understand that far from being an occasion for a spasm of American schadenfreude, Japan's troubles ought to be a cause for concern. The last two years have shown Rubin to be the most impressive treasury secretary in a generation, with an unrivaled command of the nexus of politics, markets, and finance. Unlike any of his recent predecessors, Rubin grasps the almost incalculable benefits that accrue to the United States from its position as the issuer of the world's currency. And he also knows that Japan holds the key to the dollar's continued reign.

In 1956, the great Belgian economist Robert Triffen prophetically pointed out the contradiction that lay behind the dollar's hegemony and would, he believed, eventually end it: foreign countries needed the "world's currency." To get dollars, they would have to run trade surpluses with the United States; those surpluses—mirror images of American deficits—would ultimately undermine confidence in the dollar. The dollar reign would be over.

This book attempts to explain why the "Triffen dilemma" remains unresolved; why, despite decades of American trade deficits, the dollar still stands, bloodied but unbowed, as the world's currency. The year that has passed since the book's publication confirms for me my basic thesis: that heroic efforts on the part of Japan's administrators to preserve the essence of the Japanese economic system have forced them, willy nilly, to prop up the dollar, despite the transfer over the last two decades of hundreds of billions of dollars' worth of purchasing power from Japan to the United States.

The combined efforts of Mr. Rubin and the MOF in August, 1995 to boost the dollar—described in Chapter Ten—have been an unqualified success. The strong dollar undergirds a robust American economy—complete with low interest rates, low inflation, and a booming stock market—that helped put President Clinton back in the White House.

Meanwhile, the breathing room it gave Japan's manufacturers permitted a recovery in corporate profits there that greatly helped the MOF to pull the Japanese banking system away from the abyss.

Alas, the Triffen dilemma cannot be banished so easily. Despite a robust American economy, the red ink in America's external accounts flows unstaunched. Long-term stability for the dollar can only come from a convincing demonstration that American trade deficits are dwindling. But deficits do not exist without surpluses; if American deficits decline, then so must someone else's surpluses. There is only one "someone else": Japan. Collectively, Europe's external accounts with the U.S. are roughly in balance. Latin American and African nations are too troubled or small to counterbalance shrinking U.S. deficits. The Asian nations other than Japan are mostly at a stage of economic development where they need to generate high domestic savings and thus external surpluses. That leaves Japan.

But today's high dollar/weak yen regime is being used by entrenched powerholders in Japan not to change the Japanese system but to preserve it—at whatever cost. This may seem bizarre to Americans, and from a strictly economic point of view it probably is. A policy revolution to create a Japanese economy driven by surging domestic demand instead of forced savings and exports would give most Japanese people richer lives, strengthen sectors of Japanese industry, revive the stock market, help end the banking crisis, and lead to that Japanese trade deficit needed to balance the global economy and stabilize the dollar. But describing such outcomes will not make them happen. Far from it: in April, the MOF will saddle a Japan enduring its longest postwar recession with heavy additional taxes. One has to go back to the 1930s to find policymaking quite this perverse.

Perverse, that is, if one evaluates policy purely by economic considerations—always a mistake when considering Japan. The MOF's tax hikes make perfect sense in the light of their real purpose: to preserve the MOF's hegemony over Japanese finance. Evidence suggests that even as sophisticated and subtle a policymaker as Robert Rubin finds it hard to accept this, to grasp that the roots of the "Japan problem" are institutional, not economic. The entire weight of Japan's modern history has led to institutional structures of extraordinary resistance to radical change and extraordinary resiliency in the face of challenge. A Japanese system that preserved its essential character through the catastrophic Second World War and an American occupation determined to dismantle it will not be derailed by a stock market collapse, a banking crisis, or a decade of no growth.

I re-emphasize the conclusion of this book: American policymakers cannot avoid dealing with Japan. Japan will continue to loom very large in the landscape of finance, business, trade, and international relations.

February 1997
New York City

Preface

LIKE MANY *gaijin* who end up here, I first came to Japan because of an accident. The accident wasn't mine; it happened to my little brother, struck by a glandular infection that nearly killed him. We were ten and eight, living in Laramie, Wyoming, and the doctor told my parents he needed a year in a warm climate to make a complete recovery. In Laramie you walk to school if the temperature climbs above minus fifteen, you wear a windbreaker instead of an overcoat if it gets into the twenties, and two consecutive daily highs of seventy-five qualify as a heat wave. So my father left the University of Wyoming for the University of Hawaii.

In addition to the requisite year-round warm weather, the latter place had strong links with Japan. Visiting Japanese scholars there became interested in my father's work; he was a geographer, and indeed, his system of landform classifications is still used in many Japanese geography textbooks. Thanks partly to the contacts made in Honolulu, an invitation arrived a few years later for him to spend a term teaching at Tohoku University in Sendai. The whole family went over, and my brother and I (we were by then fourteen and sixteen) enrolled in a Japanese high school. My mother said we looked like refugees from the Spanish-American War in our black serge uniforms, complete with gold buttons, celluloid collars, and military hats.

Japan hooked me. We hadn't been there more than a few weeks before I decided that I didn't want to go to any college where I couldn't major in Asian studies. Japan's appeal to Westerners such as this moody loner of an adolescent has never been fully analyzed, although Donald Richie came the closest to it for me in his haunting travelogue-cum-diary *The Inland Sea*. The physical beauty and sensuality of the country certainly account for part of it; the fundamental humanity and decency of ordinary Japanese people—their sensitivity to the feelings of others—explain even more. Of course, the country has more than its share of arrogant martinets, but anyone who has lived in Japan for any length of time discovers that Japanese people can become extraordinary friends. Short-term visitors often fail to realize this because the Japanese don't make friends easily or casually; they take human relationships very, very seriously and thus can hesitate before making the kind of commitment that to them friendship implies. But real friendship in Japan is the payoff for whatever frustrations may accompany life here; it carries with it the kind of closeness and loyalty that is rarely found in the United States—at least after adolescence—outside the family.

Harvard's reputation in Asian studies lured me to Cambridge in the fall of 1970. Fewer than twenty of us enrolled in first-year Japanese. I can't recall anyone in the class having much interest in business or finance or thinking that by learning Japanese we were making a "smart career move" in the way those words would be used by the M.B.A.'s of the 1980s. Japan didn't seem a very important country at the time. To be sure, every year it posted stunning growth rates and had made a miraculous recovery from the devastation of the Second World War, but wasn't that all due to cheap labor, low defense spending, and help given by the Americans during the occupation? In the late sixties a young person planning a business career—and there weren't that many such folks back then at Harvard to begin with—or a budding intellectual drawn to economics or political science would not have considered wasting time with a minor country like Japan. People who studied Japan were interested in its wonderfully exotic culture, in Zen Buddhism and aikido, in flower arrangement and tea ceremony, in the Nō theater and the diaries of court ladies who lived a thousand years ago. I was no different; I wanted to read *The Tale of Genji* and Mishima Yukio in the original. At some point during my junior year, however, I realized to my dismay that becoming an academic specialist in Japanese literature meant not so much daily immersion in the far-off melodies and perfumes of the tenth-century Heian court as the unending drudgery of spending most of the next decade memorizing tens of thousands of kanji—the Chinese characters used to write Japanese. I lacked the necessary resolve.

I couldn't think of anything to do after I graduated. It was the midst of the 1974–75 recession, and after hanging around on the fringes of Harvard for a few months, I thought I might as well go back to Japan. I taught English for a while, remembered why it was I had fallen in love with the country in the first place, and then, concerned that my life wasn't going anywhere, resolved to get a "real job." I found it working at the Tokyo office of what was then the largest and most profitable bank in the world, Bank of America.

By this time—the late 1970s—Japan had begun to register on the American radar screen. The country had gone from dominating low-value-added, intensive-labor businesses such as textiles to global supremacy in consumer electronics, shipbuilding, and steel. The American television industry had been destroyed. Japanese automakers could clearly produce higher-quality cars more cheaply than their American competitors; Chrysler teetered on the brink of bankruptcy. At the time of the first oil shock of 1973 many had confidently predicted the end of the Japanese economic boom. But by 1976 Japan had briskly recovered. Its trade surpluses swelled while the yen began a long, steady march from 300 to the dollar, where it had been through much of the first half of the decade, to an unbelievable high by mid-1978 of 177 to the dollar.

The standard explanations for Japan's success had worn thin. Labor costs had closed in on Western levels. American aid during the occupation and procurement during the Korean War were distant memories. The people I worked with in the Tokyo office understood what was happening in Japan and what it could do to "BofA." In San Francisco, however, anyone suggesting that within ten years Bank of America would lose its premier standing and be going hat in hand to its Japanese counterparts for subordinated debt in order to survive would have been regarded as a lunatic.

At the Harvard Business School, where I matriculated in 1979, much of the faculty had started thinking about Japan. Although the M.B.A.'s golden era had only recently dawned, one could sense the beginnings of defensiveness at HBS—and Japan played a part in that. The school stood accused of sharing the blame for America's decline by its instrumental role in the creation of a rootless class of "professional managers" who disdained nitty-gritty decades-long involvement in the particulars of specific industries. Even more embarrassing, the school had to confront in Japan the implications of a country beating the United States *without the benefit of M.B.A.'s*. But to give credit where credit is due—more than can be given, for example, to the typical Anglo-American economics department—the school at least grasped Japan's importance. First-year students sat through nine case study sessions devoted to modern Japanese economic history as part of the required curriculum.

Even if the Harvard Business School had begun—however uncomfortably—to notice Japan, recruiters for the investment banking industry had not. Like a good half of my classmates, I found this glamorous industry offering a cool $40,000 a year to newly minted M.B.A.'s awfully attractive. I naïvely assumed that with Japan's emergence as an economic powerhouse, investment banks would be falling all over themselves to recruit people with some expertise in that country. But when I started talking about Japan to interviewers from Goldman Sachs, Morgan Stanley, and First Boston, I could see in their eyes the pencil crossing off my name. I might as well have spoken of my close study and critical understanding of the operas of Monteverdi.

Within two years things had changed dramatically. Coming out of business school, I had managed to land a spot with an investment bank, albeit a second-tier house partly owned by Europeans. But when the firm got into trouble in 1983, it was quickly abandoned by its European partners, and I found myself back on the street looking for a job. To my surprise, however, I discovered that without really having done anything, I had become a hot property on the job market. Still smarting from the rejections of two years earlier, I hadn't even bothered to approach the famous Wall Street houses again and, anxious to get back to Japan, had accepted a position with Chase Manhattan's operations there. Then suddenly Morgan Stanley, which had been particularly snooty back at Harvard, approached me about joining its Tokyo office. I had already made a commitment to Chase and couldn't take it up, but I was stunned by the change in attitude.

Once I got back to Tokyo in the fall of 1983, I immediately understood why the attitude had changed. As bankers we were sitting in the midst—often as middlemen—of the greatest transfer of wealth in history. Matters had gone far beyond temporary trade surpluses, slowly strengthening currencies, and a few uncompetitive American companies whining about foreign competition. Japanese companies had achieved a superior cost position in almost any key manufacturing industry one cared to mention. Thanks to this position, the companies were inevitably accumulating vast cash hordes, and these cash hordes in turn were swelling the vaults of Japan's banks and insurance companies. But Japan's financial system had not been designed to handle cash in those quantities.

Ronald Reagan provided a solution. Just as the Japanese emerged with large quantities of excess cash, the American government enacted a series of laws that suppressed taxes, did little to control aggregate spending, and made only token gestures to raise the savings rate. The predictable result: a ballooning federal deficit. Doomsayers expected a crash, but the U.S. Treasury found a brand-new source of funds with hundreds of billions of dollars to lend: Japan.

The Treasury was only the first in line. Reagan administration policies unleashed a wave of debt-financed restructuring of American industry. American firms that had long been content to borrow from local banks found the Japanese offering lower rates. American municipalities discovered that Japanese banks charged less for guarantees than American banks. Corporate treasurers began routinely to check conditions in the Japanese market. And owners of corporations quickly learned to offer their companies in Tokyo if they wanted to sell; that's where you got the most money.

Americans formed only part of the queue at the Japanese honeypot. Corporations and governments in Southeast Asia, Europe, Canada, and Australia soon realized that the Americans rarely offered the best deals anymore. American banks might still lead-manage many syndicated loans, but the Japanese formed the heart of the syndicate. Traders in the Eurobond market got into the habit of talking to the Japanese first, and Japanese firms muscled their way into the top of the league tables.

My colleagues, competitors, and I had great seats for this game. We knew where to find the Japanese investors, and our institutions were in the business of helping people locate the money they needed. Investment banking had always been a matter of matching investors and borrowers. But from Tokyo the capital moved in only one direction: out. The Japanese authorities tried to control the whole process, but the amount of capital that had to get recirculated was so enormous they really couldn't keep track of all of it. We Americans might have lost our touch at making things, but we could still devise the best legal structures to allow buyers and sellers (or, in this case, non-Japanese borrowers and Japanese lenders) to do what they wanted to do, even if the authorities weren't too happy about it.

As a banker I felt like a child in a candy store. But as someone who cared about Japan I grew uneasy, and as an American, I was really bothered. I loved Japan, but I also loved my own country. I make no apologies for it; love of country is one of the most natural and, when uncorrupted, decent of emotions. A man who turns on the sights and sounds in which he grew up, rejecting those who nurtured him, is in a fundamental sense inhuman. People are right to regard traitors with instinctive contempt, no matter where they come from.

Like most Americans, I believed the United States had a claim on its citizens beyond that of a natural patriotism. As ethnic and religious hatreds tear the world apart, it is blindingly clear—to me, anyway—that the core American political principles—freedom of speech, press, and religion; equality before the law; accountability of the governors to the governed—are the only principles that hold out any hope for humanity's political future. And I tend to believe, with Lincoln, that the fate of these principles is probably bound up with the fate of the United States.

That is why I became increasingly disturbed as the 1980s proceeded. I had been raised a liberal Democrat. One of my earliest childhood memories is election day, 1956. I couldn't understand why my mother was weeping in front of a television screen that showed bands playing and crowds cheering. I proudly wore Kennedy/Johnson buttons to school in the third grade. I vividly remember the devastation that swept my family and my school when President Kennedy was shot. Nearly as vivid in memory is the exultation we felt over Lyndon Johnson's landslide victory in 1964, which seemed a partial redemption.

But by 1980 my childhood enthusiasm for liberal politics had entirely disappeared. I accepted most of the conservative critique of the liberal hegemony: Heavy government spending and capricious interference in markets had crippled the economy; taxes were too high; welfare, perhaps enacted initially with laudable motives, had ended up destroying neighborhoods and spawning new armies of make-work bureaucrats; and pork barrel spending in Congress had slipped completely out of control. Inflation, deficits, and the energy crisis, far from being inevitable, were the creatures of deceitful and cowardly politicians trying to finance vote-buying programs on the sly by gunning the money supply and hiding costs from beneficiaries.

With all their "social conservative," Moral Majority baggage, I couldn't bring myself to vote for Republicans. I nonetheless quietly rejoiced at Reagan's 1980 victory—particularly when it became clear the new administration intended to put "social" issues on the back burner and focus on rolling back taxes, inflation, and the government. But as the deadly combination of tax cuts, tight money, soaring defense spending, and no real cuts in entitlements took hold in the years following Reagan's inauguration, deficits exploded.

Like most responsible Americans, I worried about these deficits. Unlike most Americans, I also knew how and why they were being financed. I didn't congratulate myself on my special insight; it was obvious every morning when I came into work.

It all came together for me on a business trip to Europe in 1987, when I picked up the British edition of David Stockman's *The Triumph of Politics*. I had admired Stockman enormously— I still do—seeing him as the real hero of the Reagan administration's early days. I sat up on the flight back to Tokyo mesmerized by Stockman's account of how the Reagan administration had almost accidentally implanted annual deficits in the hundreds of billions into the American body politic. But reading Stockman's book was like reading the first three quarters of a well-designed thriller. Every clue is carefully brought out for the reader's inspection and put into place. The outlines of the scenario become clear. The pace quickens. You're all ready for the catastrophic resolution—and then suddenly the book ends.

I was on my way back from closing another garden-variety Japanese deal, a ¥20 billion ($140 million) insurance company financing with a swap attached for a Spanish government bank. While in Europe, I had also made some dozen calls organized by colleagues at Chase's offices in London, Paris, and Madrid on borrowers jostling for a place on the gravy train of Japanese finance. Japanese money had transformed the parameters of lending and borrowing; this was no more remarkable to me or any of the people I worked with than the telephone or the personal computer. But reading Stockman's book, I suddenly understood: *They hadn't seen it coming in Washington.*

Washington's policy elite clearly didn't grasp the political realities behind Japanese finance; if it had, it would never have allowed the United States to become so dependent on Japan. Nor did I think the United States was doing Japan any favor. All the fashionable talk about burden sharing and baton passing made little sense to me. Others drew parallels between the 1980s and the passage of financial hegemony from Britain to the United States a half century earlier; I couldn't see them. All I could discern in both Tokyo and Washington were layers of mutual deception and denial.

I wanted a chance to work out these ideas, maybe even stake a bit of a claim. The first stirrings of the 1988 presidential campaigns were under way, and one of my college roommates had long been in Michael Dukakis's inner circle. I sought the advice of Ezra Vogel. The high point of business school for me had been Professor Vogel's seminar "Japanese Business and Society," and we had kept in touch since I left Harvard. Professor Vogel was then living in Guangzhou doing research for his book *One Step Ahead in China.* On the way back from closing another deal—this one a ¥18 billion ($128 million) nonbank financing for Malaysia's government-owned cement company—I stopped in Hong Kong, took the three-hour train trip to Guangzhou, and spent most of a Saturday afternoon with Professor Vogel in the coffee shop of the China Hotel. He encouraged me to write an article or a book and offered to make arrangements for me to spend time at Harvard's Program for U.S.-Japan Relations. I owe Professor Vogel much, not just for arranging that and a subsequent sojourn at the program but for the support he has given me over the years. He is a great teacher and valued friend.

I spent six weeks in Cambridge the following summer doing the research and writing the article that became the germ of this book. The article, "Power without Purpose: The Crisis of Japan's Global Financial Dominance," did not see the light of day until well past the 1988 election, but I am grateful to the *Harvard Business Review* and to Alan Webber, then its managing editor, for turning the work of an unknown banker into the magazine's lead article in its March–April 1989 edition.

The spring of 1989 saw further upheavals for me. Goldman, Sachs approached me about joining its capital markets group, and unhappy with some recent management changes at Chase, I accepted the offer. Goldman asked me to spend a year split between New York and London learning about the firm and getting to know the people I would be working with over the telephone. I called it my Occidentation.

Shortly after I joined Goldman came a more critical event for me and for this book: the publication of Karel van Wolferen's *The Enigma of Japanese Power*. I had never met van Wolferen, although it turned out we had lived within shouting distance of each other for five years, and knew of him only as the author of a brilliant article for *Foreign Affairs*. I grabbed the book as soon as it came out, sat up much of the night reading it, went to sleep for a few hours, and then started all over again. I found later my reaction common among businessmen, bankers, journalists, and diplomats involved with Japan; van Wolferen had given us the conceptual framework to come to grips with the ultimate reality of Japan's institutions: the lack of a center of accountability.

Anyone who has dealt with Japanese institutions confronts the difficulty in locating a *responsible* center, in finding out who makes decisions and the process by which they are made. This is a fairly commonplace observation, and no one has written of it more eloquently in the context of Japan's modern history than the Japanese philosopher Maruyama Masao.

But van Wolferen's point was more subtle and more profound. He discussed the lack of *accountability*. Accountability consists in being required to explain what one is doing—if not to a congressional committee, a board of directors, or a group of voters, then at least to oneself. An entrepreneur or a tyrant is accountable because he must ask himself for what purpose he is doing things. *Enigma* is ultimately a long meditation on the consequences to a country when its institutions are not accountable.

I had been groping toward these ideas in "Power without Purpose" in the context of what I saw as the fatal flaws in assuming the United States could easily pass hegemony over global finance to Japan. *Enigma* brought them into focus for me.

I subsequently came to know van Wolferen, and I owe him my deepest gratitude for the help he has given me with this book. He encouraged me to write it, he has rescued me several times from despair over finishing it, I have tried his patience with draft after draft, and he has never failed to give criticism of the highest value. I count meeting him and becoming his friend among the most significant events in my life.

I got back to Tokyo in the summer of 1990 from my "Occidentation," but by that point Japan's "bubble" economy—fuel for so many of the deals I had been involved in—had started to implode. Pickings were slim, and the business wasn't much fun anymore. Nonetheless, if it had not been for the encouragement of people like Karel van Wolferen and Ezra Vogel, I would never have had the confidence to throw over my investment banking career for this project. Several other people also encouraged me to develop the ideas in "Power without Purpose," and I would like to thank Patrick Smith, Kenneth Courtis, Robert Neff, James Fallows, and Chalmers Johnson for their help in giving me the confidence to take the plunge. Any student of the Japanese bureaucracy is in Chalmers Johnson's debt, and I have admired his writing for many years. He has said nice things about me in print, read and commented on portions of the manuscript, and recommended me to my publisher. I am grateful for all this. James Fallows read the entire manuscript, made helpful suggestions, and offered encouragement when I thought I would never finish. I also benefited from reading his important book *Looking at the Sun*.

I want to offer special thanks to Mikuni Akio. Mikunisensei read the manuscript, gave freely of his time and knowledge in helping me understand the "big picture" of Japanese finance, and helped clear up many confusions. I count it a high honor to be his friend.

A number of other people read drafts at various stages of completion, offered comments, and made for a better book. I thank Eric Hayden, who first taught me how to write when I worked for him at Bank of America, Frank Packer, Michael Zavelle, Tanuma Toshiyuki, Hayakawa Kazuo, Mike Verretto, Tait Ratcliffe, Mark Callahan, F. John Adams, Tom Alexander.

During the early stages of work I had valuable research help from Asano Mikio. Later on Okubo Yoshino gave me critical support.

I thank Clyde Prestowitz and the Economic Strategy Institute for providing office space and support on an extended trip to Washington for research. On a second extended trip I benefited from similar support by Pat Choate and the Manufacturing Policy Project. I thank the Institute for Independent Japanese Studies for allowing me to use Ms. Okubo's time and for help with some research materials.

None of the people mentioned here have any responsibility for the conclusion or implications of the book, and any errors are solely mine. But I have debts of gratitude to many others. They include: Aritake Toshio, David Asher, Hasan Askari, Barbara Buhl, David Bussmann, Josephine Chesterton, Bob Cutts, Tom Dickson, Eleanor Dornon, Ivan Dornon, Eamonn Fingleton, Fukuhara Toshio, Glen Fukushima, Funaki Katsumi, Andy Gordon, Eric Gower, Ivan Hall, Hosomi Takashi, Jeremy Hovland, Jim Impoco, John Judis, Kevin Kearns, Komatsubara Yoshihiko, Kuriyama Yutaka, Mike Levitas, Jack Loughran, Makihara Jun, Makihara Kumiko, Joseph Massey, Matsuura Hitoshi, Nakamura Jinichi, Niimi Yoshiro, Nicolas Ollivant, Bill Powell, Bill Rapp, Saito Satoru, Phil Sheldon, David Stockman, Patrick Sun, Alan Tonelson, and Bruce Wymore. All of them helped one way or another. Like so many others—most significantly the American semiconductor industry—I owe much to the late Michael Jablow. He prodded and inspired me for a decade and is sorely missed.

A number of additional individuals gave of their time but asked not to be acknowledged. I thank them here.

I have tried the patience of Ed Barber and Don Lamm at Norton as an eighteen-month project stretched out over several years, and I appreciate their willingness to stick with me at a time when there was little to show for it. Ed Barber in particular made numerous editorial suggestions that have resulted in a stronger book.

Two other people in very different ways have given me such support that I could not have written the book without them. They are Kawada Osamu and Monden Akihiro. They know what they are to me.

Finally, I would like to thank members of my family. My late aunt Marjory Heckelman and my uncle Jack Heckelman, who met in Tokyo during the occupation, first told me when I was a small boy of a mysterious and beautiful country called Japan where people sat on the floor and ate with little sticks. Their son—my cousin—Charles Heckelman provided periodic and much-needed reality checks on the state of the world in finance. My aunts Mary Murphy and Ethel Goolsby and my uncle Hal Goolsby made a home for me on several extended stays in Washington.

My sister, Caroline K. Murphy, is the best editor one could want. As a veteran of the publishing wars herself she gave much valuable advice on the mechanics of the whole process and made numerous helpful editorial suggestions. In addition to getting sick at an opportune time and thus starting the chain of events that led to this book, my brother, Alexander B. Murphy, has been a source of support and intellectual stimulation as far back as I can remember. My admiration and love for him grow with each passing year. Both he and my mother read drafts and offered useful comments.

Back in 1963, shortly after the move to Hawaii, we all visited Honolulu's Punchbowl, where thousands of American dead from the Second World War are buried. Alec and I were horsing around, shouting and generally acting like brats. Our parents quite properly read our titles clear, pointing out that this was a sacred and solemn place, and the least we could do was act with some measure of respect toward those who had died so that we might have decent lives. Suddenly my father did something that shut me up more thoroughly than any conceivable threat or punishment he might have administered. He started crying. He had never done that before in front of me; I was awestruck and deeply troubled. My father saw action in the Pacific, but he didn't talk about it; he didn't sit around boasting or telling war stories. Only at that moment did I get some inkling of what the war had been to him.

This book is written in the last analysis as a plea for leadership in both countries I have loved, so that other fathers need not break down in front of other sons on the fields of the dead. That I could write it is ultimately due to what I learned, intellectually and morally, from my parents. It is thus to my mother and to the memory of my father that I dedicate this book.

September 1995
O-Namase, Daigo-Machi
Japan

Note on Terms

On Exchange Rates

SOME WILL FIND THIS BOOK a bit of a horror story. But I have at least one burden Stephen King or Anne Rice need not carry. They can write about small boys reborn as ghouls, elegant gay vampires, oversexed suicides coming to life in bathtubs. I have to write about exchange rates. Exchange rates are of great interest to exporters, importers, foreign currency traders, and tourists. They tend to bore everyone else. I have done my best to make the subject as unboring as possible. But it will help to keep in mind that in this book the yen is always quoted in terms of the dollar—360 yen per dollar, 85 yen per dollar. You can do it the other way around, but after fifteen years or so of living in Japan and working in finance for ten of those, I still have a hard time figuring it out when I walk into a bank or open a newspaper and see the rate quoted as 0.011765. If you say the yen has gone from 0.011628 to 0.011905, no one but a computer knows what you're talking about. But if you say it has gone from 86 to 84, then it is—I trust—a lot clearer. It means that while yesterday it cost 86 yen to buy a dollar, today it costs only 84 yen. It takes more dollars to buy a given amount of yen; it takes fewer yen to buy a given amount of dollars. The dollar has weakened—gone down—the yen has strengthened, gone up. The *smaller* the number used for the yen/dollar rate, the *stronger* the yen, the *weaker* the dollar.

When I first came to Japan in 1968, the rate was 360. Now it's around 95. In those days it cost ¥100 to get into a taxi—and

100 divided by 360 is about 28 cents. Today it costs ¥650—a six-and-one-half–fold increase in yen terms. But in dollar terms, you have to divide that 650 not by 360 but by 95, to give you a dollar price of $6.84. So in dollar terms, the cost of a short taxi ride in Tokyo has risen twenty-four–fold. Periodically I try to provide the dollar equivalents of yen amounts. Whenever I do this, I use the exchange rate prevailing at the time.

On the Administrators

I needed a term to label the men who collectively manage Japan's core economic and political institutions both in the "public" and the "private" sectors. "Bureaucrats" will do for those who staff the official ministries, although it should be kept in mind that these elite bureaucrats are not of the pencil-pushing, go-by-the-rules sort. Japan's governing class is not limited, however, to these bureaucrats. It also includes the men who manage the great established corporations, major financial institutions, and business federations. To describe the men who run Japan as "bureaucrats and business leaders" not only is unwieldy but fails to capture the reality of Japan's ruling elite. In seeking to refer to these men in their institutional capacity in a way that is both concise and descriptive, I have found that I could do no better than use Karel van Wolferen's apt term "administrators." The administrators are the men who run—administrate—Japan's important, established economic and political institutions. They are not the only powerful people in Japan, and they certainly have no monopoly on wealth, but collectively they run the country.

On Personal Names

I have followed the Japanese practice of putting Japanese family names before given names—Miyazawa Kiichi, not Kiichi Miyazawa.

Introduction

The West Wing and the MOF

THE WEST WING OF THE WHITE HOUSE is not so much a wing as a separate structure, connected to the president's home by a covered corridor. It is a smallish, vaguely neo-Georgian edifice, whose architect obviously had no greater ambition for it than that it blend quietly into the surroundings. But it is a pleasant place, set well back from the bustle of Pennsylvania Avenue, and on a nice spring day, banked by flowers and shaded by lovely old elms and oaks, the West Wing can seem quite beautiful.

No visitor, however, will mistake this setting for the English country retreats after which it was modeled. Aside from the permanent banks of television lights and cameras on the lawn, security is exhaustive; the guardhouse will have your Social Security number and birth date well in advance of your arrival. But the illusion of a civilized manor is nonetheless bravely maintained as you pass through the Grecian portico and the double doors into the spacious bright yellow reception room. You are asked—politely—your destination. You are almost certainly requested to take a seat on one of the comfortable couches to the receptionist's right and wait a few minutes; people with offices in the West Wing of the White House are busy. But eventually someone will fetch you and lead you through a labyrinth of narrow halls and up a very narrow staircase. You note the carpeted floor, handsome framed pictures on the walls, and clean white wainscoting. The offices you pass bulge with file cabinets and computer terminals, but they are well lit and open. You arrive at your destination. The person you have come to see rises to greet you, apologizes for the delay, offers you a cup of coffee, says something to his or her secretary about it, closes the door, and the meeting begins.

A visit to Japan's Ministry of Finance—generally called the MOF—is a different experience. This shabby slate gray affair stands right in the midst of central Tokyo's urban roar, looking for all the world like a medium-security prison. You pass a lone policeman, walk through a concrete courtyard packed with black limousines, and peer into a dim entryway. You search in vain for the information desk, uniformed pretty receptionists, or large well-lit building directory of most important Tokyo office buildings; a small board at the side is the only help you will get. You walk down wide, gloomy hallways searching for the appropriate room. Occasionally a pallid young man, tie askew and sleeves rolled up, will pad by in slippers, carrying a stack of documents, or perhaps it will be an older cleaning lady bearing a mop. At the appointed place none of the attractive young women who usually rise to greet the visitor to a Japanese firm is visible anywhere. Only a small sign above the door confirms the location.

Inside, you stand at the edge of a large room crowded with youngish men working at small gunmetal gray desks. The desks are jammed right next to one another except for a row of slightly spaced desks on the far side of the room under the windows. The men sitting at these desks are a bit older, and several of the younger men are running back and forth between these desks and their own. Each desk and the floor space around it are piled high with papers. No computer terminals are visible anywhere. The walls—surely unpainted for decades—are decorated solely with large calendars featuring pinup girls in tiny bikinis. You squint against the harsh fluorescent lighting after the gloom of the halls. You look around the room trying to spot the right man. You are almost surely not the only banker lined up against the wall, and there may also be two distinguished-looking older visitors sitting on the edges of chairs in front of one of the far desks. They listen intently to a man older than most of his colleagues in the room but still a decade or two younger than the men he is lecturing.

Your man notices you and motions you to wait a few minutes while he takes a telephone call. Finally he waves you over to the one available chair. Any colleague has to stand. Over the din you try to explain what you have come for. The noise is too much even for your host, and he suggests going to a meeting room. You go back out with him into the hall and spend five minutes looking for an unused room. When you finally find one, it has clearly just emptied. The table is covered with half-full teacups and overflowing ashtrays. Your host clears a space on the table and motions you to sit. He is cheerful and pleasant, but when you propose something that he doesn't approve of, he sucks in air through his teeth and suggests your idea is going to be "difficult" as if that were the end of the matter. Despite his obvious competence, he occasionally says something that leads you to realize he has never had to deal with common business problems, such as finding affordable office space in Tokyo's overcrowded commercial real estate market.

The differences between the West Wing of the White House and the Japanese Ministry of Finance do not, of course, end with their settings and their procedures. The West Wing of the White House contains the Office of the President of the United States; thus by law and in practice it forms the locus of power in the American political system. The Ministry of Finance, by contrast, enjoys no legal status beyond that of agent of Japan's elected legislature, the Diet. In theory the MOF has no say-so over policy; on paper it exists simply to carry out the wishes of its political superiors.

But the MOF is, in fact, the most powerful entity in Japan and in this one very important respect, if in no other, resembles the American presidency. The MOF controls the government's budgets. It largely determines Japan's fiscal and monetary policies and both sets and collects taxes. It not only supervises banks, brokers, and insurers but in a very real sense manages them as well, establishing parameters for credit, asset values, capitalization, and lending. It is ultimately responsible for financing Japanese industry and seeing to the security and use of the country's savings. It controls economic information to such an extent that it need not bother much about informed external scrutiny from politicians, economists, or journalists. Day to day it answers to no one for its actions—to no elected representative or independent judiciary.

Americans find this difficult to grasp. Americans are used to dealing with democracies or dictatorships. Most governments are either answerable to voters, or they hold power through repression and coercive control. In either case it is clear where ultimate authority lies and where one must direct attempts at influencing decisions. But Japan fits neither category.

Its Ministry of Finance is not subject to effective political oversight, and thus Americans cannot influence its policies by appealing to Japan's voters to put pressure on their government. Washington has, in fact, tried this tactic, urging on the Japanese media and the Japanese electorate the notion that changes the United States wants in the management of Japan's economy would benefit ordinary Japanese households. These efforts may have contributed something toward the political upheavals of 1993 that split the "ruling" Liberal Democratic party. But they were of no use whatsoever in securing any change in the policies of the Finance Ministry.

Direct appeals to the MOF have had no greater impact. When American officials dealt with the Soviet Union, they addressed representatives of the Central Committee of the Communist party, attempting to persuade them with logic, diplomacy, and the threat of force to shift policies. Sometimes Americans were successful; sometimes not. In either case, however, the Americans were talking to people in Moscow who had the power and the will to act if they could be convinced to do so. But the MOF is not all-powerful in this manner, nor does it see itself thus. Its officials regard themselves as an elite mandarinate, charged with protecting the fiscal integrity of the Japanese government from rapacious politicians, a "selfish," ignorant electorate, and the pleaders for special interests at the other ministries.* They believe they are responsible for the financial system and treat banks, brokers, and insurance companies as charges entrusted to their care—wayward children who, if left to their own devices, would quickly destroy themselves and the country. They hold the interests of the MOF and the interests of Japan to be identical and are thus obsessive about maintaining their instruments of control. Appeals from foreigners that the MOF reflect on its policies therefore fall largely on deaf ears; such appeals are weighed solely in terms of the possible impact on the ministry's reputation and its instruments of control and are accordingly effective only if backed by credible threats. A MOF can be convinced to permit foreign brokers to trade derivatives in Japan because the U.S. Treasury has the power to deny Japanese brokers primary dealer status in the huge and lucrative American government bond market. But arguments that the MOF use Keynesian stimulus to lift Japan out of a dangerously long recession do not register; foreigners have no power to force such stimulus, and it would result in a diminution of MOF control over the other ministries. Any possible benefit to Japan of such stimulus is irrelevant.

However difficult or elusive it may be, getting a conceptual grip on the MOF and on the Japanese institutions it controls and finances is essential for Americans. It is essential because the American presidency now depends on these institutions. How this dependence happened and the price it exacts, both in the United States and in Japan, are the subjects of this book.

At heart the story is a simple one. In order to maintain his country's place in the world while avoiding the political discomfort of hard trade-offs, an American president led the

---

* An exception is the Ministry of International Trade and Industry (MITI), the only other ministry seen by the MOF as concerned with Japan's general interest.

United States into an unacknowledged program of borrowing money. And in order to maintain its levers of control over Japanese finance, a Ministry of Finance would see to it that the money was lent.

The story has its roots well back in the past—in the measures taken by the Japanese elite in the late nineteenth century to "catch up" with the West, in the progressive erosion over the past seventy years in Washington of the aura of danger and even immorality traditionally attached to a government that did not pay its way.

But for our purposes the story begins in 1980 with the election of Ronald Reagan. What happened initially is so well known it seems hardly worth going over except as a reminder of its importance. In its opening months the Reagan administration pushed one of the greatest tax cuts in history through Congress. Administration officials also cut back government outlays in a number of areas—federal support for school lunches being only the most notorious example—but these spending reductions amounted to small change when measured against the extent of the tax cuts. Attempts to tackle the great middle-class entitlement programs—Social Security, Medicare, veterans' benefits—that form the core of nondefense spending were abandoned at the first whiff of political trouble, while defense allocations soared. The deficit exploded.

Ronald Reagan's critics have argued that the tax cuts were profoundly irresponsible, mortgaging the future of the country to pay for current consumption. Reagan's defenders label them an essential first step in an unfinished revolution aimed at rolling back the welfare state. The supply-siders who constructed the intellectual foundations for the tax cuts maintain that events bore out their contention that lower tax rates would bring in more revenue; it was just that government spending was to grow even faster than tax receipts.

At the time, however, no one—supply-sider, fire-breathing conservative, white-shoe Republican, "new" or old Democrat—believed that the United States could sustain fifteen years of deficits on the order of $150 to $200 billion annually. True, the supply-siders who sincerely thought the tax cuts would spark an economic boom sufficient to wipe out the deficit were greatly outnumbered, even in the Reagan White House, by those who regarded the idea as "voodoo economics." But Republican fiscal moderates came to see monstrous deficits as a useful, temporary bogey to scare Congress into finally shrinking the government. Meanwhile, House Speaker Thomas P. ("Tip") O'Neill had no intention of saving the administration's bacon by amicably agreeing to Social Security cutbacks.

It turned out, however, that the bacon was in no danger. The political game of chicken played between the White House and the congressional leadership in the wake of the summer 1981 tax cuts did not end in any financial crash when neither side would swerve into being the first to ax popular entitlements. Instead, once the U.S. economy emerged in late 1982 from the recessionary wringer Paul Volcker's Federal Reserve had been putting it through, the deficit largely disappeared as an issue.

This is what makes the events of 1981 so important. A fundamental political discipline broke down; the fear of the consequences of allowing government spending greatly to outstrip revenues melted away. Conventional wisdom had suggested that when the financial markets got wind of the witches' stew that the Fed, the White House, the Congress, and the Pentagon were preparing, the reaction would be catastrophic. Bond markets—believing the United States unable to raise the taxes necessary to pay off these levels of debt—would surely judge this deficit unfinanceable. They would see the only resolution in a return to inflation, allowing the debt to be paid off in cheapening dollars. And any sign of renewed inflation would cause investors to demand economy-flattening interest rates lest the United States follow in the steps of countries such as Brazil and Weimar Germany, printing more and more paper money to cover debts, leading finally to hyperinflation and a worthless currency.

But none of this occurred. For it did not matter if Americans themselves were not saving enough to fund the deficit, provided someone else was. It did not matter if Americans distrusted their government's promises not to inflate its way out of the deficit—not as long as people somewhere were willing for their own reasons to ignore the disastrous American record over the previous decade of maintaining its currency as a store of value.

Grasping what happened requires an understanding of how Japan works and wariness over the labels applied to institutions. A seemingly untroubled concept like the "private sector," for example, can utterly blur the reality of what actually goes on in Japan. We think we know what the "private sector" means: the area of economic life ruled by the market where the role of government is limited to the maintenance of a regulatory framework and the enforcement of contracts. We also define it by what it is not: the public sector—i.e., government and those institutions it directly funds and controls. Yet in Japan we encounter a group of core economic entities—financial institutions, large corporations—that are obviously not in the "public sector" as we understand it and are thus unthinkingly assigned to the private. But these institutions are not ruled by the market, and the role of the government in this sector goes far beyond that of providing a regulatory framework.

I discuss these institutions in the first two chapters. Large Japanese companies earned dollars with their exports; financial institutions lent them back to the Americans. I describe the incentive structure within which they operate, the factors that determine investment and credit decisions. In the subsequent two chapters I turn to the financing of the Japanese economic miracle and the obsessive attention paid to the two variables of its economic system Japan's administrators could not wholly control: exports and the exchange rate. Overall the first four chapters, Part I of the book, represent an attempt to explain the near inevitability of the surge of Japanese money into the

United States once the U.S. Treasury found itself having to finance annual deficits in excess of $100 billion.

Part II—Chapters 5 through 8—provides an account of the financing itself: the coming of Japanese money and the rise in the dollar's value; the Plaza Accord and its all-too-successful attempts to bring down the dollar; the creation of the "bubble economy" in Japan in response to the soaring of the yen; the New York stock market crash of 1987 and the successful efforts by the Ministry of Finance to contain the damage. The last two chapters—Part III—tally up the costs: the collapse of Japan's "bubble economy"; the return—more insistently and more dangerously—of the contradictions postponed and pasted over by twelve years of borrowing from Japan.

This may seem an economics story—a tale of dollars and yen, of banks and brokerages, of finance ministries and treasuries—but it is really a political story. By propping up American buying power for a decade and a half, Japan's administrators managed to sidestep the contradiction at the heart of their methods: that they depended upon the security and monetary arrangements provided by a foreign country whose strength was being undermined by Japan's success. As the buying power of the United States shrinks—measured by the fourfold increase in the value of the yen since 1971—Japan will be forced into a fundamental shift in the structure of its economy. And such shifts can be carried out only through the political process.

Similarly, the events of 1981 had, for the United States, the greatest effect on its political process. Democracy's fatal flaw lies in the ease with which the expedient can triumph over the necessary, the good, or the right. This flaw has troubled political philosophers at least since the time of Plato. It certainly troubled the founders of the United States, who deliberately created a complex system to check the politically expedient, to ensure that the political passions of the moment would not be allowed to overwhelm the fundamental legal framework protecting the rights of individuals. They saw to it that radical change could be effected only through the long and difficult process of constitutional amendment.

The founders could not, however, have anticipated at the time of the Constitutional Convention the politicization of economic life over the following two centuries. They could not have imagined a world in which money would be a matter of government fiat rather than an independent store of value, a world where the populace would look to government to ensure economic livelihood and hold it so accountable, a world where taxation and expenditures would become instruments that governments used to achieve macroeconomic outcomes that had nothing to do with paying the governments' bills. The Constitution calls for no institution either to guard against the harmful-but-expedient or to ensure the necessary in the area of economic policy making. The president is supposed to seek the approval of Congress for a declaration of war, but no legal obstacle stands in the way of a Federal Reserve pursuing an irresponsibly inflationary monetary policy or a Congress that chooses to legislate enormous deficits.

In the absence of legal sanctions or obstacles, what has kept the politically expedient from wholly driving out the necessary is the threat of economic catastrophe—catastrophe that in a democracy results in electoral defeat. The 1932 election, one of the great watersheds of American political history, saw an angry electorate hold the Republicans accountable for the Great Depression. The legacy of the depression has kept the Republicans to this day from returning to the full control of the American government they enjoyed for most of the seventy-five years following the Civil War. That election, and the consequences of allowing deflation and its concomitant unemployment to spin out of control, seared itself into the memory of a generation of politicians.

The experience of the Great Depression and the immense prestige of a half-understood Keynesian economics loosened a key restraint on political behavior, the idea that government expenditures should not exceed revenues. Until the experience of the 1930s most assumed that catastrophe would soon arise if the government spent more than it took in in taxes; indeed, in the 1932 election campaign Franklin Roosevelt and Herbert Hoover tried to outdo each other in their commitments to avoid any deficit spending. The political fallout of the Great Depression, however, removed much of the stigma that had historically attended deficits.

Between 1945 and 1981 the American political establishment was nonetheless held in check by the idea that one could overdo it. Yes, deficit spending to a certain degree was acceptable and even welcome—just as "a little inflation" appeared to be politically tolerable—but until 1981 no one had been willing to test such spending on a vast level outside wartime.

But since that fateful year, when the American political establishment closed its eyes, borrowed vast sums, and waited for the crash that never came, it has become impossible to do anything about the deficit. Politicians like Walter Mondale who suggest raising taxes condemn themselves to crushing defeat. Any attempt to rein in the core entitlement programs is instantly squashed. A Clinton administration that initially chose to pursue modest deficit reduction instead of meeting its "invest in America" campaign promises suffered the worst midterm loss of an incumbent party since 1946. A politician cannot be fiscally responsible and expect to remain in office. It is not just a matter of its being politically easier, in effect, to vote for deficits. It is the only way one can be reelected.

America's electorate and its representatives no longer believe in financial catastrophe. Warnings have been made and have not come to pass. The deficit proved easily financeable at levels that would have been regarded as economic suicide just a few brief months before Reagan was elected president. Ultimately, however, there is a price—and it is much greater than the current interest rates on government bonds.

I

Lender

1. The Japanese Company
Ownership, Control, and Competition

JAPANESE EXPORTS come with names attached—Sony radios, Toyota cars, Komatsu earthmovers, Canon copiers, Yamaha pianos, Honda motorcycles, Toshiba fax machines, Panasonic VCRs, Casio calculators, Seiko watches. What sorts of entities lie behind these names? Why are they able to do business the way they do? How can they set prices that would bankrupt any Western competitor that tried to follow suit and hold those prices for years?

If you look up *kaisha* in a Japanese-English dictionary, you will see it translated as "company, corporation." And these *kaisha* do play a comparable role in Japanese society to that of American firms in the United States. They are engaged in many of the same activities: manufacturing and services, production and marketing, finance and trade. Outwardly they have the same structures—boards of directors and CEO's, managers and work forces, stockholders and creditors, affiliates and subsidiaries. Like American firms, they issue annual reports and raise money through stock offerings, bond issues, or bank loans.

As a matter of course, then, Toyota is seen as the Japanese equivalent of General Motors. Komatsu is paired with Caterpillar, Fuji Film with Kodak, NEC with IBM, and Dai-Ichi Kangyo Bank with Bank of America. Indeed, most of these pairs of firms do compete with each other; a market share gain by one is likely to come at the expense of the other. But in drawing parallels, Americans assume an equivalence that is not there.

Take the idea of ownership, very straightforward for Americans. Companies are owned by their shareholders. Each shareholder holds a pro rata stake in the assets of a company. If you own 2 percent of a company, you own 2 percent of its factories, land, accounts receivable, cash, and intangible "goodwill" from the company's reputation and trademarks. Similarly, you have a right to 2 percent of the company's profits. You have a 2 percent say-so in the composition of the company's board of directors.

Or take the idea of purpose. Again, very straightforward. Companies exist to make profits for their owners, the shareholders. Governance? Companies are governed by boards of directors elected by shareholders. Control? Corporate control is determined solely by who owns the majority of the common shares. If someone buys up more than 50 percent of the shares of a company, he can fire all the managers and hire new ones more to his liking. Boards of directors must legally consider the interests of all shareholders, not just the majority, in a public company. Majority owners can install their own management teams, but they cannot deprive minority shareholders of representation or a pro rata share of profits.

Not one of these notions applies easily to a Japanese company. Japanese companies are not "owned" by their shareholders in any concrete sense of the term. The Tokyo stock market is not a market for corporate control. Shareholders do not, in effect, elect a board of directors; the board is appointed by management. The "rights" of minority shareholders are routinely ignored, as a number of foreign investors have found to their cost. Shareholders have, in practice, no pro rata claim to corporate profits; at most they are entitled to a small dividend stream. In fact, the status of a common shareholder in a Japanese company is equivalent to that of a preferred shareholder*

* Preferred stock gives the holder the right to receive fixed dividends before any payout is made to the holder of common shares. The preferred shareholder also has

in an American firm. If the company makes enough money, one can look forward to a predictable dividend stream, and that's it. The Tokyo stock market should properly be regarded as the world's largest market for preferred shares.

Concern with profits has historically been regarded in Japan as "selfish." In the 1930s both the militarists and the so-called reform bureaucrats who managed the war effort upbraided companies for being too profit-oriented and deaf to the needs of the nation. An influential reform bureaucrat, Hoashi Kei, wrote admiringly in 1941 of the "economic guidance"—as opposed to mere planning—practiced by the Nazis. While acknowledging that businesses needed a degree of independence, he thundered against the idea of a "free economy based on the principle of private profit-making."[1] Hoashi subsequently led Japan's most important postwar economic think tank, the Keizai Dōyūkai (Committee for Economic Development), which in a 1956 manifesto emphasized that contributions to Japan's national economic welfare must take precedence over profit making.

Even today only a rare Japanese CEO would describe his corporate mission as producing a high return for shareholders. The public relations emphasis has shifted from building a strong nation to feel-good contributions to harmony, global peace, and "beautiful human life,"* but it does not include profits. Japanese companies take deliberate steps to lower their reported earnings. This makes some economic sense. Japanese companies, unlike their American counterparts, must submit the same profit numbers to the tax authorities that they do to the investment community. The lower the reported profit, the lower the tax. But lowering reported profits is also driven by concerns that a company not appear too "selfish" or "un-Japanese."

Economists, business school students, and stock analysts

---

first claim on the companies' assets—thus the term—but has no ownership rights beyond this.

*The slogan of a major Japanese cosmetics firm.

trying to understand the behavior of an American company start from the assumption that the company's management is trying to increase at least short-term profits. They know that management worries how the stock market will react to its decisions. They understand that corporate officers and directors live under the constant threat of litigation.

But, again, there is little correspondence in Japan. Japanese semiconductor companies build so much capacity no one can make money in the business. A CEO announces his firm's intention to dominate a critical new electronics sector, even if this means a decade of losses. Japan's car makers spend billions reducing the amount of time it takes to produce a completely new automobile, wiping out much of the profitability in the industry. Japanese electronics firms pay huge premiums for American entertainment companies while Hollywood and Wall Street snicker.

One encounters various explanations: Japanese companies are said to be irrational, "excessively" competitive with one another (this one is popular inside Japan), involved in dark conspiracies to dominate the world (this one is more common outside Japan). Emotionally satisfying as they may be, these "explanations" explain little. Japanese managers are no less irrational than their counterparts in other countries. But they do have different priorities.

The assumptions that underlie American academic writing on finance and corporate governance—companies are contractual entities; shareholders bear residual risk—are thus next to useless in understanding Japanese corporate behavior. What about Japanese scholarship? Historically much of Japanese scholarship was in the thrall of a hidebound academic Marxism that attempted to squeeze Japanese companies into Marxist categories of "monopoly capital." The gradual collapse of the Marxist model demoralized Marxist scholarship, however, and replaced it in Japan with a new generation of Japanese intellectuals grappling with the question of what the Japanese corporation is and, by extension, what Japanese capitalism is. Their answers typically settle on one or another variant of employee sovereignty, the idea that the ultimate risk takers in a Japanese corporation, the real owners, are not the shareholders but the people who work there.

Itami Hiroyuki has coined the term "peopleism" (*jinpon-shugi*), arguing that this diffusion of managerial power, as he defines it, within the corporation has been the central unchanging principle of Japanese management since the end of the Second World War, despite upheaval in the external environment.[2] Matsumoto Kōji discusses "corporatism" (*kigyō shugi*). He writes of the absolute autonomy of Japanese management and the shift in postwar Japan to a new form of capitalism in which fundamental corporate risks are taken by managers and permanent employees rather than shareholders.[3] Okumura Hiroshi uses the term "corporate capitalism" (*Hōjin shihon shugi*) to describe the Japanese economic system and contrasts it with the individualist orientation of the Western.[4] Imai Masaaki holds out *kaizen* (improvement) as the guiding principle of Japanese management, measuring it against the "innovation" worship of Western business. He notes that "KAIZEN is people-oriented, whereas innovation is technology- and money-oriented."[5] Nakatani Iwao has written of "network capitalism."[6] Sakakibara Eisuke, the MOF's leading in-house intellectual, writes: "The fundamental principle underlying the Japanese model of mixed economy is anthropocentrism. . . ."[7] The naturalized American Japanologist Robert Ozaki synthesized many of these concepts with the term "human capitalism," popularizing them in the United States with a book of that title.[8]

Much of this scholarship is more boosterism than analysis. The old generation of Marxists rarely had anything good to say about Japan's economic enterprises. Today's analysts err in the opposite direction. There are far too many unexamined portrayals of Japanese companies as warm, supportive humanistic enterprises in direct descent from the traditional *ie* (extended family household) characteristic of premodern, agricultural Japan.[9] But while a lot of this writing may read like tiresome, narcissistic *Nihonjinron*—(theory of the Japanese)—or the notion repeated in an unending stream of Japanese books and articles that the Japanese are a race apart[10]—there are some useful concepts. One of them—that the working people in a Japanese corporation are both its ultimate risk takers and its ultimate beneficiaries—helps explain many elements of Japanese corporate behavior. If a Japanese manager, for example, sees it as his task to ensure workers' salaries twenty years off, he will take a different approach to investment and marketing decisions from that followed by an American edgy about quarterly earnings.

An even more powerful idea is Nakatani's network capitalism—that what really matters for a Japanese company are the strength and credibility of its network. Its "capital" consists less of yen than the number and quality of its relationships. Such relationships would begin with the bureaucracy, with other firms in the same *keiretsu*—the large business alliances that dominate the Japanese economy—and with the industrial associations. But they would also include lines of access to Japan's oligopolistic advertising industry, ties to important politicians who can run interference with the bureaucracy and help land big contracts, and contacts with university professors, ensuring a stream of quality recruits.* They would certainly comprise banking and brokerage house relationships. They can even include ties to organized crime, especially *sokaiya,* racketeers who disrupt shareholder meetings or, when paid off, keep others from doing so. Network capitalism tells us that it is the quality of these links that really constitutes a Japanese firm's "capital."

A Japanese firm with a solid network can withstand a lot. It can contemplate levels of investment regarded as reckless by Western competitors. Similarly, the occasional large firm that is

---

* An important responsibility of Japanese professors is securing employment for their students. The senior year in a Japanese university is spent almost entirely in a *zemi* (seminar) under a full professor who will be expected to arrange introductions to potential employers. Professors who are good at this have their pick of *zemi* students; in a mutually reinforcing arrangement, companies and ministries cultivate professors who get good students.

casual about network building may find itself unable to obtain credit at any price. A case in point is the bankruptcy of Sanko Steamship in 1985. Led by the autocratic Komoto Toshio, Sanko had several times defied the bureaucracy and the standards of "acceptable practice" in its industry. In 1964 the company had withstood efforts by the Ministry of International Trade and Industry to impose consolidation on the Japanese shipping industry.[11] Then, in 1973, it had attempted something unheard of for a big company: the hostile take-over of a competitor. The take-over was halted by the direct intervention of MITI.[12] Komoto himself made no secret of his political ambitions and attempted twice to buy his way into the prime ministership.[13] The second time, in 1982, he offended two of the most powerful politicians in Japan, Nakasone Yasuhiro and Takeshita Noboru. When Sanko ran into trouble in 1985 after the worldwide downturn in the shipping market, its access to credit was suddenly cut off, and the firm became one of Japan's rare cases of a big-company bankruptcy.

An American executive must lavish attention on his firm's share price and balance sheet health; his Japanese counterpart nurtures the company's network. Indeed, this largely constitutes the job of Japan's CEOs. It is why a strong liver is essential to reaching the top rungs of a Japanese corporate hierarchy. The day-to-day conduct of business is the responsibility of middle management, and the overseeing of the firm's finances—an obsession with the American executive suite, properly so given the rules of American business life—is, in Japan, a matter for the *zaimubu* (finance department).

Useful as it is, however, the concept of network capitalism glosses over another critical feature of Japanese corporate life, the two-tier structure of the economy. The distinction between the two tiers in Japan transcends the familiar dichotomy between large end product manufacturers (so-called original equipment manufacturers [OEMs]) and smaller suppliers. Rather, the crucial difference is security. Firms in the first tier rarely fail. In cases where they would otherwise go bankrupt, they are restructured—usually by institutions such as MITI and the Industrial Bank of Japan (IBJ)—or merged. Examples abound: the Japan Line of the mid-1980s; Prince Motors and Yamaichi Securities in the mid-1960s; the great names of Japanese banking that have been folded into one another over the past two decades—the Dai-Ichi and Kangyo banks, the Kyowa Bank, Saitama Bank, Mitsui Bank, Taiyo Kobe Bank, Mitsubishi Bank, Bank of Tokyo. No creditor or supplier was ruined, no permanent employee *(seisha-in)* was sacked in these large companies.

The situation in the second tier is radically different. Companies are started in the thousands every year and go bankrupt in the thousands. Workers are sacked or leave for higher-paying jobs elsewhere. Companies compete desperately for markets and for financing. The second tier of the Japanese economy is as ruthless a laissez-faire system as can be found anywhere—with the crucial distinction that disputes are generally resolved outside the legal system, often by resorting to the services of gangsters *(yakuza)*.[14] Close to two thirds of the Japanese work force are employed in the second tier. Jobs there are unstable, often feature fairly brutal working conditions, and lack status. Starting one's working life in the second tier largely precludes rising to a first-tier position. This fact alone explains the desperate competition for slots in Japan's leading universities. Diplomas from such institutions are the only sure tickets of admission to a first-tier organization.

The second tier serves a critical function as a shock absorber for the overall economy. It cushions the fluctuations of the business cycle. Acting something like Marx's reserve army of the unemployed for those who do not toe the line in the first tier, the second tier enables Japanese industry to lower costs quickly, thanks to the nature of power relations between the first and second tiers. Once in a while second-tier companies hit on an important technology and manage, thanks to unusually gifted managers, to "graduate" into the first tier. A good example is the ceramics firm Kyocera, an upstart outfit with no ties to an established Japanese company. Kyocera had to demonstrate its quality by selling its ceramic wrappings for semiconductors to American firms like Texas Instruments before leading Japanese manufacturers would even let its salesmen in the door. Kyocera is now a well-respected member of the Japanese business establishment, but it remains a rare case. Much more common is the pattern which sees a successful second-tier company manage to ally itself to a first-tier company, to join the latter's so-called vertical *keiretsu*.

Consider Koito, the Toyota group company made famous in the United States by T. Boone Pickens when he attempted to muscle into a cozy first-tier–second-tier relationship. Koito, founded in 1920, originally made lenses for railroad signals and diversified into headlights for automobiles in 1932. By the 1960s Koito had become the leading manufacturer of headlights in Japan, both the largest and the most technologically sophisticated. In the early 1970s Toyota made a crucial 19.2 percent investment in Koito. Such an investment in the United States would suggest an impending take-over, a joint venture, or a simple financial stake. In the absence of a formal equity relationship, two American firms could not enter into cozy marketing, pricing, or supply agreements without violating the law. But the stake Toyota took in Koito was fundamentally ceremonial in nature; it functioned as the seal of a done deal, an irrevocable announcement to the Japanese business community that Koito had become a Toyota group company. Once Koito joined the Toyota group, Toyota naturally began to supply much of Koito's senior management and to coordinate investment, financing, and R&D programs. Koito's current chairman, Matsuura Takao, is from Toyota. So are the president, Nagamura Yoshio, and much of the rest of the senior management. Toyota is, of course, Koito's principal customer.

Joining a vertical *keiretsu* like Toyota's protects the second-tier firm from the dog-eat-dog world of its tier and offers its work force lifetime employment. The second-tier firm can also look forward to a guaranteed market, help with financing, and often technology and personnel transfers. In return, the second-tier firm loses its independence. Its ability to sell outside the *keiretsu* is at the discretion of the top firm. It must often buy inside the *keiretsu*. Most important, it is subject to relentless pressure to reduce costs. Typically, first-tier firms negotiate annual cost reduction targets with their second-tier affiliates. The demands on the second-tier work force are thus very heavy. When one reads reports in the press of forty-hour five-day weeks becoming the "norm" in Japan, one should think only of the first tier and then only of the "official" hours.*

The ability to squeeze constant cost reductions out of second-tier firms has historically given leading Japanese manufacturers a cost advantage that cannot be matched. According to one of Japan's leading independent automotive experts, General Motors supplies approximately 70 percent of the value-added in a finished automobile, while the figure for Toyota is less than 30 percent.[15] This makes direct comparisons of compensation and other costs between the two automakers nearly worthless in analyzing Toyota's cost advantage. Toyota presses its own work force hard enough,[16] but the true secret of its success can be found only in its constellation of suppliers.

At issue here are more than Dickensian working conditions. Toyota can skim most of the potential profits from a captive supplier in the form of reduced costs. The supplier gets a guaranteed market in return and thus enjoys lower financing costs, passed through in reducing the final price of the car. Banks would look to Toyota to bail out a supplier in trouble.

T. Boone Pickens took on this system in 1988. He accumulated a 23 percent stake in Koito and was accused of acting as a front for a notorious Japanese greenmailer. Pickens denied the charge, arguing with impeccable American logic that with less than 20 percent of the equity, Toyota was robbing the other

---

* Official Japanese statistics on working hours do not tell the real story. To circumvent the legal requirement that overtime be compensated, employees of Japanese companies are pressured to put in many hours of so-called *sabiisu zangyo* (service, or free overtime) that are neither reported nor compensated. The normal workday in an established Japanese company is closer to twelve than to eight hours.

shareholders of their rightful profits by forcing Koito to sell to it at low prices. Pickens became a bigger shareholder in Koito than Toyota with the intention of muscling his way onto the board of directors and then changing Koito's sales and pricing policies to make it a more "profitable" company—run for the interests of all the shareholders, not just one.

But Pickens did not understand* that Koito's "equity structure" was meaningless in terms of real ownership and control. If by some miracle Pickens had gained control of Koito, he would have destroyed it. The company would have lost its market, financing, and work force.

A Toyota controls a Koito without any legal trappings. So-called main banks can act as quasi owners of companies, even though their equity stakes are less than 5 percent. Bureaucrats intervene in corporate affairs all the time without any clear formal right to do so. In the absence of formal mechanisms, how are disputes settled?

Recourse to the courts makes little sense when relationships among corporations are not defined contractually. Litigation is, in any case, impractical in light of the deliberately induced scarcity of lawyers and the huge backlog of cases before Japan's judiciary. The government itself rarely pursues legal remedies even when Japanese companies are in clear violation of the law. One of the most astounding aspects of the summer 1991 securities scandals to foreign observers was the absence of any government-instigated legal initiative against the putative miscreants.[17] As a prominent American scholar of the Japanese legal system put it, "The identification of litigation as a threat to the political and social status quo is implicit in all writing on Japanese law and society, and recent scholarship argues persuasively that self-interest has led the Japanese elite to take deliberate steps to discourage litigation."[18]

* Or at least he pretended not to understand. It was never clear just how firm the links were between Pickens and the greenmailer Watanabe Kitaro, from whom he bought his shares and who bought them back later. Watanabe may have hoped Pickens would attract unwelcome foreign publicity to the incident and thus put greater pressure on Koito and Toyota to come to terms.

Japanese companies may not need to take the potential for litigation into account when making at least domestic business decisions. But a society without checks on institutional behavior is headed for disaster. In American society that check is the threat of litigation. In Japan it is the network that keeps firms in line. The crucial difference between the two is the transparent, formal nature of America's system, the opaque informality of Japan's.

The tie that binds Toyota and Koito is only one strand of the web. Other strands are of equal importance. The institution of the so-called horizontal *keiretsu* or, as it is more commonly known in Japan, *guruppu gaisha*—groups of firms clustered around banks and trading companies all holding shares in one another—is now well understood outside Japan.[19] Leading examples are Mitsubishi, Sumitomo, and Mitsui. Less well known abroad are the industrial associations, made up of all firms in a particular industry. The industrial associations help keep firms in line. They discipline recalcitrant members and set—usually informal—standards within an industry, and they also communicate "guidance" from the relevant bureaucracy. The industrial associations themselves are further organized into nationwide groupings, the biggest and most important the Keidanren, (Federation of Economic Organizations). While not explicitly required by law, if a Japanese firm wants to do business, it must join the appropriate industrial association.

The tightness and intimacy of the webs binding a Japanese firm are often praised for fostering the sensitivity to technological change and constant industrial structure upgrading so characteristic of the Japanese economy.[20] Just as often these webs are condemned for their collusive, anticonsumer, antioutsider character.[21] But usually overlooked is the implicit coercion behind the networks.[22] Japanese companies cannot sustain opposition to the "collective" decisions of their webs.

Consider the exceptional case of one that attempted this: Sumitomo Metals. In 1965 it attempted to defy a MITI- and industrial association (Nihon Tekko Renmei, or Japan Iron and

Steel Association)—mandated production cutback. Sumitomo Metals found itself facing the full weight of opposition from Japan's elite, all of which came down hard: MITI, the Keizai Dōyūkai, IBJ, the Sumitomo Bank, even the Fair Trade Commission, which should theoretically have been on the company's side since the cartel was a flagrant violation of the elementary principles of market economics.[23] Another case in point is the maverick firm Kyocera that we met above. It was indoctrinated in proper Japanese behavior in 1985, when its president was publicly humiliated by the Ministry of Health and Welfare for failing to fill out an obscure form.[24] A year earlier Lion Petroleum had attempted, as it was legally entitled to do, to import refined gasoline from Singapore and was crushed by MITI, the petroleum industry, and Japanese banks' Singapore branches, which refused to handle remittances.

In January 1993 at an off-the-record briefing for foreign journalists, one reporter asked how the Ministry of Finance might deal with a bank that failed to cooperate with MOF restructuring plans to bail out the banking industry. The senior MOF official giving the briefing replied that such a bank would be "asked if it were Japanese."[25] Significantly, the briefing was for foreign journalists; no Japanese reporter would bother with such a naïve question.

The great strength and flexibility of the Japanese system lie in its very informality. When Korean steelmakers challenged the Japanese industry in the early 1980s as the Japanese had the Americans two decades before—by selling high-quality steel at lower prices than the domestic industry could manage—the Japanese steelmakers working through their networks could deal quietly and informally with the threat. They did not need the laborious petitions, hearings, press coverage, court cases, and legislative wheelings and dealings American companies had been forced to use. The steelmakers simply

applied "pressure" (their word) to distributors handling foreign steel. These firms were made to understand that if they continued to do so, their names would be stricken from the list of traders used by the Japanese producers.

There are reports of delivery trucks carrying Korean steel followed by agents of the Japanese producers to ascertain who was using the foreign steel, forcing importers to virtually smuggle Korean steel into the country. . . . At length, the smaller traders who handled most foreign steel were formed into an association, the Japan Iron and Steel Institute, whose purpose was to ensure "orderly marketing" of steel in Japan. The Institute now regulates the volume and price of imports so as not to disturb the output and price arrangements of the Japanese producers.[26]

Meanwhile, Japanese trade negotiators could smugly assert that Japan had the lowest formal trade barriers of any country in the world, and Japanese commentators could suggest that perhaps foreigners just didn't try hard enough or didn't make products that "we Japanese want to buy."

The masked coercion of Japanese business life—masked because it is not usually necessary to make the sorts of open threats used to discipline Sumitomo Metals, Kyocera, the importers of Korean steel—also applies to individual employees. A Japanese worker starts his or her first job fully socialized. The Japanese school system is admirably equipped to endow routine workers with the literacy and numeracy necessary for life in industrial society. But school in Japan is also a twelve-year experience in submission. The formal standards can be found in the plethora of school rules prompted by the policies of the Ministry of Education. These rules seem designed to curb individuality or nonconformism and are achieved most effectively through humiliation and making it impossible, in the words of one distraught mother speaking of her child, "to be good." Middle school boys are in some schools forced to strip in front of teachers to ensure their underwear is regulation white.* Girls with brown or naturally curly hair, instead of the more common straight black, dye or have their hair "ironed" lest they be ridiculed by teachers and students for being "different" and breaking school rules on hair treatment. Informal group consensus is achieved through the widespread bullying of children who are unusual or odd in any way, like the schoolgirl who spoke En-

---

*I have seen this on Japanese television.

glish too well because she had spent three years in the States with her father or the schoolboy who showed up with a book bag of the wrong color. The bullying is pervasive and often encouraged or even instigated by teachers.[27] Maturity is achieved when one endures uncomplainingly *(gaman suru)* any demands by any authority.

Conditioned to accept the right of the group or the boss to make limitless demands, a Japanese worker is already psychologically unprepared to resist even the most extreme orders from management—the reason why the Japanese have had to coin a word, *karoshi,* to describe the phenomenon of death from overwork. And the economic alternatives to one's current job are generally harsh. Unwritten agreements prevent companies from hiring those who have worked for direct competitors; you will find no ex-Sumitomo bankers at Mitsubishi Bank, no ex-Nippon Steel men at NKK or ex-Hitachi managers at Fujitsu. Thus a departing employee cannot take his skills to places where they would be the most valuable. While work of some kind is probably available, changing jobs usually means a heavy loss of income and status, at least for someone leaving a first-tier firm.

Life within the Japanese firm is also subtly underscored by coercion. In the 1950s and 1960s companies like Toshiba used secret organizations of favored blue-collar workers to spy on their colleagues. A report to management might include such "unusual" activities as taking the fully allotted number of vacation days. Farther up the corporate hierarchy, the constant late-night drinking with colleagues and the sacrifice of family life are not simply a matter of coping with crushing workloads in a difficult market. Any Japanese who aspires to an executive position must exhibit a sort of never-ending zealotry toward his job and his employer. He dare not show any outside interest beyond a handful of conformist hobbies such as golf or karaoke practiced with colleagues and customers.

The late American business consultant Michael Jablow, who worked with the Japanese semiconductor and electronics industries for twenty years, once suggested that if one had to summarize Japanese management practice with a single phrase, far better to call it Theory F—*F* standing for "fear"—than smarmy notions like human capitalism and Theory Z. "Theory Z-type theories don't talk about how the system actually works. It is actually fear that moves those managers," Jablow said.[28] The Japanese themselves describe their system as *genten shugi* (minus pointism, or the idea that only demerits are possible); he who accumulates the fewest wins. A close friend of mine in a major Japanese company calls Japanese business life more simply a jail.

Such informal networks and masked coercion give Japanese competition a surreal, theatrical aspect. Ferocious rivalry among Japanese firms is often noted, but it is equally often misinterpreted because there are two kinds of competition. That found among second-tier firms is familiar to Westerners. Competitors slug it out until one side gives up. But competition among first-tier firms is different. It leads to no real losers, no empty-handed creditors or unemployed managers. Year after year the same companies go through all the motions of competing—massive advertising campaigns and blizzards of new products—yet at the end of the year the relative standing of the major firms remains unchanged.

Mikuni Akio has described this sort of competition as "sword fighting with bamboo swords"—practice rounds for the real battles in foreign markets.[29] It is intense competition, but the stakes, if not predetermined, are about status and clout in the Japanese pecking order, not about profitability and corporate survival. It is the difference between sports and war.

Examples abound. In 1988 Asahi Beer, the traditional number three of the Japanese brewing industry, dislodged Sapporo from the number two spot with its cleverly marketed new Asahi Super Dry. The resulting beer wars saw each of the major companies bringing out a dizzying array of new brands. Yet at no point did the price of a bottle of beer vary by one yen from company to company. Nor did any of the brewers have to contend with the upmarket microbreweries that have been nipping at the heels of the American majors in the past decade. Sapporo lost its number two slot, but at no point did it, unlike, say, Schlitz, face a threat to its survival.

James Abegglen and George Stalk in their book *Kaisha* describe two episodes in the corporate history of Honda to illustrate their contention that competition with foreign firms is largely a by-product of brutal encounters among Japanese corporations.[30] The book is a useful guide to the how of Japanese corporate behavior, but it is less convincing on the why. The first story concerns Honda's wresting of leadership in the Japanese motorcycle industry from Tōhatsu in the late 1950s. Back then motorcycle manufacturing was not a mature or strategic industry. More than fifty players crowded the industry, with no well-established firm among them. The industry was on the verge of becoming important with annual growth rates of 40 percent per year. This type of cutthroat competition is sometimes encountered when second-tier firms go at each other in emerging industries, because the stakes are so high—the potential for membership in the Japanese establishment and first-tier status. Tōhatsu was driven into bankruptcy and Honda became one of the great names of Japanese business.

Twenty years later Yamaha, another established maker and first-tier firm, attempted to do in Honda as Honda had done in Tōhatsu. Honda beat back the attempt by product proliferation. Abegglen and Stalk provide a riveting account of the battle, but they miss the significance of the outcome: Although Honda won, Yamaha did not go bankrupt. Instead it re-resigned itself to its number two status. By a certain reckoning, the stakes were high—had Yamaha won the battle, it could have increased its heft in the Japanese power structure—but the stakes were deliberately limited. Creditors on both sides knew that pressure would be allowed to go only so far and were thus willing to fund levels of investment that no Western firm could have commanded, enabling Yamaha to mount its attack, Honda to beat it back, and both firms to strengthen the Japanese motorcycle industry as a whole. This is fighting with bamboo swords.

The risk of failure among large Japanese firms is eliminated by informal guidelines within each major industry. Breweries until recently could not compete on price, but liquor stores would stock every brand of beer. Consumer electronics firms can compete on price but not for dealers; try finding a Sony component in a Toshiba store. The result is a frenzied contained competition.

In the 1950s Westerners laughed at Japanese exports of trashy little radios and cars. Thirty years later they would hoot at the "inflated" prices Japanese companies were paying for overseas assets. Los Angeles office buildings and banks, industrial firms such as Firestone, entertainment conglomerates like MCA were snapped up by the Japanese at "ridiculous" levels. And indeed, many of these "investments" proved mistakes by such conventional Wall Street criteria as return on investment. But the purpose of these investments was not to earn more money for shareholders. These acquisitions wrote another chapter in the ceaseless struggle by Japanese companies to increase their weight and stature.

In the late 1970s Japanese companies began to accumulate large amounts of cash, an inevitable by-product of a slowing domestic economy still generating very high savings. The Japanese system would not permit companies to raise their dividends or award their CEOs stock options worth millions of dollars, even if they had wanted to. Armed with some grasp of Japanese corporate governance, American policy makers might have anticipated where Japanese companies would start putting their money.

But they were not so armed. Notions of sameness ruled. In a shrinking world, the argument went, the nationality of a company meant little. Liberals and conservatives might differ on everything else, but their most articulate spokesmen agreed on this fundamental analysis. Take Robert Bartley of the *Wall*

Street Journal, whose editorial page became the intellectual sounding board for the Reagan Revolution. Bartley's 301-page triumphal ode to the Reagan era contains eight brief references to Japan. In fact, he goes out of his way to stress the essential sameness of Japanese and American firms. In his introduction he sneers at the "liberal prophets of decline" finding they "could count on rhetorical support from the likes of Motorola and Chrysler, transnational corporations headquartered in the United States, who found they couldn't keep up with Sony and Toyota, transnational corporations headquartered in Japan."[31]

But what do the liberal prophets of decline actually say? Robert Reich, President Clinton's labor secretary, asks this in his book *The Work of Nations:* "What's the difference between an 'American' corporation that makes or buys abroad much of what it sells around the world and a 'foreign' corporation that makes or buys in the United States much of what it sells? . . . Who is Ford? Nissan? Mazda?"[32] Reich quickly provides an answer: "National champions [by which Reich means big famous companies; he uses NTT, Ford, Nissan, Mitsubishi, Daimler-Benz, Mazda, Northern Telecom, and Volvo as examples] everywhere are becoming global webs with no particular connection to any single nation."[33]

We hear this message in many quarters. Most companies, however, continue to find that nationality matters a great deal, particularly if their competitors are Japanese. These companies know their businesses well—they know what it costs to produce a color television set, a car, a sheet of steel, or a semiconductor chip; they know how to set the terms of a loan or a bond issue—but their Japanese counterparts do business at prices that seem to make no sense. So a company with its back to the wall gropes for an explanation: Japanese firms are dumping; they have incredibly low capital costs; they have mysterious Oriental management secrets; they receive covert government assistance. Or, in the words of one IBM executive, they have "no understanding of the need for profit."

Some of these explanations contain grains of truth. Ultimately, however, the behavior of the Japanese firm, like that of any institution, is driven by its sociopolitical role—what it does for its members and how it fits into the wider society. Japanese firms are often seen to prefer size to profitability, market share to earnings, but the significance of this observation is usually overlooked.

Japanese companies are best understood as alliances for mutual protection in a world where nothing is certain. The usual criteria of profitability provide no meaningful yardstick. The question of who owns what has no answer. To survive and thrive in such a world, an individual who alone counts for nothing seeks protection and security by affiliating with the largest and most powerful institution he can find. He pledges loyalty and submission to institutional goals and in return is promised the security and protection he seeks. The institution—mindful of its promise and knowing its continued existence depends on its ability to keep a myriad of such promises—is forever trying to increase its status and weight and seeks constantly to bind other institutions to it. To outsiders, this looks like a drive for market share. But the drive for market share is not an option that can be replaced next year with a different goal, such as higher profits, as many foreign observers urge. It is the essence of the Japanese corporation.

2. The Credit Decision

SOMEONE JOINING a big American "money center" bank—a Chase Manhattan, a Citibank, a J. P. Morgan—right out of college or business school is almost sure to start his or her career in the bank's training program. This program will cover a number of topics from the mechanics of funds' flows to the bank's organizational structure. Mostly, however, it is an exercise in teaching would-be bankers credit analysis—how to assess borrowers. If the bank lends money to a company, the instructor will ask, how can we bankers be sure we will get it back? How do we measure the health of a company? What are the right questions to ask the company's managers?

Trainees spend their days in class, their evenings doing homework. They analyze balance sheet after balance sheet, from that of a motel manager to that of a steelmaker. They learn why the finances of a bourbon distiller differ from those of a grain wholesaler. They also learn that making a simple yes or no credit decision is not enough. They need to understand what kind of loan is right for the borrower—why the bourbon distiller gets a well-secured, long-term loan while the grain wholesaler requires an annual line of credit with a lot of flexibility.

They are taught how to price loans. They probably already know that banks make most of their money on the difference between the cost of funds—primarily what banks pay depositors—and the interest they charge borrowers. Bankers call that crucial difference the spread. But trainees must understand that deposit rates, overhead, and expenses are not the only costs a banker needs to consider. Any loan must be priced high enough to permit the bank to maintain its capital cushion.

No matter how careful it is, a bank will make a few bad loans. When a loan goes bad, the deposits and other obligations the bank incurred to fund the loan must still be honored. It is the bank's capital cushion—paid-in stock, retained earnings, subordinated debt—that makes it possible to honor those obligations and prevent the bank itself from failing. Take a bank that is $100 million in size and has $10 million in capital.* Its $100 million of loans is *funded* with $90 million worth of deposits and other obligations and $10 million in capital. This bank can afford to see 10 percent of its loans go bad before unable to pay depositors, it has to close its doors. Now suppose the bank gets an aggressive new president and goes out and books $100 million of new loans, doubling in size to $200 million. If it funds these loans by the simple expedient of taking in $100 million in new deposits without raising the amount of its capital, it will be able to tolerate only 5 percent of its loans' going bad before it fails. Its capital cushion will have shrunk by half.† To minimize this risk of failure, regulators in most countries require banks to maintain capital cushions at a certain proportion of their loans. The best and most prudently managed banks generally exceed the minimum regulation.

Going outside to buy that capital cushion is expensive. Issuing new stock reduces the value of existing stock. Subordinated debt carries a high interest rate because the debt holders waive their right to receive interest in certain circumstances and must

---

* Basically this means the bank has $100 million of loans outstanding. There are other assets, of course, like buildings and computer systems and cash in the vaults, but we'll ignore them to keep it simple.

† In capsule form, this is what happened to the U.S. savings and loans industry in the 1980s. Thanks to deposit insurance, it was very easy for S&Ls to fund new loans. Before the Reagan years S&Ls had been effectively permitted to make only mortgage loans. In the early 1980s, with deposit rates rising, they were allowed to make any kind of loan they wished, but new rules were not issued on how the loans should be funded.

be compensated in return. Thus any bank will prefer to build capital by earning profits and putting them into the capital account as retained earnings. But to do this, the bank must charge enough on loans not just to cover funding and overhead costs but to increase capital. If our $100 million bank with a $10 million capital cushion makes a $1 million loan, it must earn at least $100,000 and add it to the cushion to keep that capital ratio at 10 percent.

The typical first assignment for training program graduates is the credit department, where young bankers spend a year or so helping to process loan applications. Skills acquired in the training course are honed and refined as classroom knowledge is applied to actual credit judgments. A young credit analyst learns to take periodic abuse from loan officers anxious to serve customers, edge out competitors, and book loans. He or she will feel the tension in most banks between loan officers eager to do more business and credit analysts held accountable for any mistakes the bank makes.

The next step up the career ladder is likely to be a line position directly under the supervision of senior lending officers. Fledgling bankers will learn how to talk to the finance departments of corporate customers, getting practice in pitching the bank's products and understanding clients' needs. And having worked as credit analysts, they should have a good feel for what the bank will approve. They will know it's a waste of time to submit loan applications for a young designer who has leveraged his company to the hilt, betting everything on the success of a new fall line of sweaters. But in chasing business the bank wants—say, a mortgage loan for a stable, successful chain of family restaurants to finance a new facility—they will almost surely encounter competition.

Competition is a fact of life in a market economy. Like every other kind of company, banks must cope with it. In competing for a piece of business, a bank must weigh its need to make money against the danger of eroding its capital cushion from pricing too cheaply. Banks keep a watchful eye on their competitors: How much are they paying for deposits? How well capitalized are they? How solid is their loan portfolio? What kinds of business are they likely to walk away from? A good fix on the answers gives insight into pricing, a key competitive edge.

But in the mid-1970s American bankers began running into competition they could not understand. They encountered groups of banks that priced loans and extended credit in ways that made no sense. They were Japanese banks.

For some American institutions, the Japanese were competitors from hell, systematically underbidding and underpricing in market after market. For others—often for different departments of the same banks—the Japanese were a boon. The big money center banks run a substantial business organizing syndicates of other banks to lend large sums to corporations and governments. The profits to the organizers come not so much from the spread on a bank's own portion of the loan as from the fees paid to manage the deals. The fee may be as little as one quarter of 1 percent, but on a $100 million syndicated loan, that is $250,000. Beginning in the late 1970s, Japanese banks became critical subscribers to big-ticket, syndicated loans. Indeed, after a deal had been signed and "put to bed," the American lead managers often turned around and sold most of their participation in the loan to a Japanese institution.

It wasn't just syndicated loans. Money center banks found across the board they could make more money at lower risk acting as arrangers of financing rather than as providers. A bright young banker began more often to find him- or herself assigned to private placements or asset sales rather than to the traditional loan department. Being an arranger enables a bank to maintain relationships its credit department might otherwise terminate. The bank earns money without risking its capital cushion.

The Japanese were crucial to these businesses. A private placements officer seeking financing for a corporate client might start out talking to insurance companies, smaller regional banks, S&Ls, and the large community of foreign banks with offices in New York. But in the 1980s the officer almost invariably found the best price from the Japanese.

Dealing with the Japanese was, however, an odd experience for American bankers who had come up through the traditional credit-focused career track. It started with the ambiance. Doing business with the Japanese in New York, for example, generally means discovering a whole hidden world of Japanese restaurants, karaoke clubs, and piano bars. There are two kinds of Japanese restaurants in New York: famous establishments catering to a typical, upscale cosmopolitan Manhattan clientele and lesser-known places that do not advertise but are nevertheless packed every night with an almost exclusively male Japanese crowd. The only non-Japanese are guests of the Japanese customers. The prices are high, and the sushi is excellent. Then there are the piano bars. Scores of these establishments dot midtown, although with their tiny pink or lavender Japanese signs they are almost invisible. Most of them feature karaoke machines and employ young women who act as hostesses. The clientele is, again, exclusively male and exclusively Japanese. The only Americans—aside from a few of the hostesses—are guests of the Japanese. The women who work in such places can be Japanese, Koreans, or Americans. They are not prostitutes but are employed simply to entertain and chat with the customers. At least one graduate student in Japanese literature at Columbia financed her Ph.D. with her earnings from piano bars.

Learning to enjoy sushi, singing off-key into microphones, and indulging in risqué give-and-take with attractive women were not difficult assignments for ambitious young bankers. But figuring out the Japanese approach to credit could be. American bankers approaching the Japanese for a deal were often startled to find themselves asked endless questions. Few of the questions, however, pointed to the rigorous, quantitative review of the borrower's financial statements complete with worst-case cash flow projections with which they were familiar. Instead there would be a great deal of attention to things the

Americans might have regarded as fairly irrelevant: where the potential borrower was located; the educational background of its senior management, how well known the company was, who else was lending to it. It helped if the company had its headquarters in Manhattan or downtown Los Angeles; it was even more helpful if the company was a household name. The clincher was likely to be the stance of other Japanese banks.

The credit decision seemed very much yes or no. If the decision was yes, pricing was less a function of the borrower's quality than what it took simply to get the deal. Private placements officers confronted the same puzzle as their colleagues in the loan department losing business to the Japanese: The Japanese were always cheaper. The ready answer that Japanese enjoyed access to artificially cheap deposits at home was no explanation in New York. There they paid at least as much as Americans for dollars.

The training young Japanese bankers receive offers some clues. The American college or business school graduate joining Chemical Bank, Bank of America, or First Chicago has his or her counterpart in a Japanese man* joining the Sumitomo Bank, Dai-Ichi Kangyo, or Industrial Bank of Japan. These banks hire a hundred to two hundred young men a year right out of such prestigious colleges as Tokyo University, Waseda, or Hitotsubashi; no business school graduates need apply. The banks do hire a comparable number of women, but they are mostly high school and junior college graduates on different career paths.

The young men do not go into a formal training course. Rather they spend their first three years in a series of rotations at branches in and around Tokyo, Osaka, or Nagoya, where the banks are headquartered. Most of the work done in these branches is clerical—the physical processing of payment orders, letters of credit, and the like. To succeed in these early rotations, a man needs to be on good terms with the more senior women

---

*The handful of managerial-track female hires in Japanese banks are so few that they are hardly worth mentioning. See discussion in Chapter 3.

in the branches. These "senior" women are, in fact, the same age as the young male recruits, but they will have been working at the bank for five or six years. They are the ones who really know the ropes, and it is from them a man learns what it is he is supposed to do.

The rotations vary—some men will find themselves doing foreign exchange, some credit, some loan processing—but they all have to pass one particular and widely loathed rotation: deposit collecting. It involves going from house to house begging housewives to open accounts with the bank. The assignment is a difficult one because there is no actual basis by which Japan's households can differentiate one bank from another. They all pay exactly the same low interest rates—except for the postal savings system, which offers a bit more interest and therefore holds more in deposits than all of Japan's commercial banks combined. Expanding the bank's deposit base comes down to the charm and sales skill of the young men sent around to raise money.

It is an important activity. The more deposits the bank brings in, the less it depends on funding from the Bank of Japan; the bigger the bank, the more influence it has. In many Japanese banks the mundane business of deposit collecting is something close to its top priority. Deposits are, if not an afterthought, way down the list at American counterparts, and no managerial track hire would be caught near such a boring, down-market job as hawking deposits. But in Japan good deposit collectors are heroes, their futures assured. They can relatively quickly become heads of important suburban branches and will devote much of their careers to it.

For the rest of the class, collecting deposits serves as a kind of boot camp, designed to break down the "selfishness" of college students, to teach them how dependent they are on the organization. There are few things that deflate the ego more quickly than begging a haughty fifty-year-old matron to open a bank account she doesn't need.

American bankers will have up to six months of formal

training before their first real assignments. Japanese get only a few days. They may be taken off-site for lectures by university professors and ex-bureaucrats on such things as the overall workings of the financial system, credit, and balance sheet analysis. Many banks contract with outside firms for independent study courses that involve reading books on finance and submitting papers. The banks don't take these courses very seriously, however, and the young bankers often crib one another's papers.

Real credit training in Japan is almost entirely on the job, watching supervisors deal with and process credit. A Japanese learns that what counts is collateral. Americans are taught to do pro forma cash flows for a project: If the bank lends a company $100,000 for a new store, how much in additional revenues will the store bring in? Will there be other expenses? What happens if the economy turns sour? What are the conditions in the neighborhood where the store is opening? Is anyone else planning a store that could eat into revenues? The American applicant must demonstrate that even under a worst-case scenario the cash flows stemming from the store will be sufficient to allow the company to pay off the additional debt. But Japanese bankers care about the company's assets, the collateral the company can put up to secure the loan. Japanese banks rarely extend domestic loans of any but the shortest maturity without collateral. And the collateral that really matters is real estate. Whether the store makes money or not is at most a side issue because the value of the land on which the store sits is bound to be worth far more than the store building or the present value of the store's earnings.

Credit is at the heart of not just banking but business itself. Every kind of transaction except, maybe, cash on delivery—from billion-dollar issues of securities to getting paid next week for work done today—involves a credit judgment. The strength and extent of a firm's credit are the ultimate criteria of corporate health. Credit decisions are made all the time in every type of economy—statist or laissez-faire, developmental or regulatory. Economic life is inconceivable without them.

Credit in some ways is like love or power; it cannot ultimately be measured because it is a matter of risk, trust, an
assessment of how flawed human beings and their institutions
will perform. But the effort of pinning it down, formalizing it,
is woven into the very structure of American business. Business
school students learn to put a number on that elusive chimera,
a firm's cost of capital, with the work of Nobel prizewinning
economists distilled into formulas like the Capital Assets Pricing Model. Then they are taught how to discount every potential investment with the resultant number. Analysts at ratings
agencies apply tests and ratios to firms so as to label them. Bond
sellers can then call a firm AA or B+, investment banks can
confidently "price" the firm's securities, and all hope to reassure
buyers about the risks of their investments.

The need to make resulting credit decisions—whether or
how much to lend or invest—as impersonal and objective as
possible has spawned rules and institutions that appear in
American eyes to be an immutable part of a proper capitalist
economy. While they may not always work, they are specifically
intended to override the natural inclination of managers to
reveal as little as possible, and then only the good news. They
include the so-called Generally Accepted Accounting Principles
(GAAP); accurate, timely, and comprehensive reporting of a
firm's financial condition; prohibitions on insider trading; the
existence of such independent, objective, and ideally incorrupt-
ible institutions as an accounting profession, ratings agencies,
and the legal system. Cases of accountants who may have mis-
represented corporate health are treated as grave signs of the
most serious sort of disorder.[1] If it were suspected that a Standard and Poor's or a Moody's were accepting bribes—or, in a
comparison more meaningful in the Japanese context, responding to activist government prodding by doctoring ratings—their credibility as institutions would be destroyed and
financial markets shaken to the foundations.

But the Japanese economic system is suffused with a distrust
of the market. Information and the control of credit ought, in
the view of Japan's administrators, to be concentrated in the

hands of those most capable of using them. To guard this concentration of power, credit decisions are kept informal and subjective. External oversight by accountants, investment analysts, financial journalists, or stock market participants is largely ceremonial.

The information needed to make good credit decisions is thus treated as a privileged commodity. To begin with, Japanese corporate reporting is, by American standards, largely a joke. Japanese companies were not, until very recently, required to report consolidated earnings, and they are granted extraordinary flexibility in their treatment of earnings and asset valuation. In seeking to halt the decline of the Tokyo stock market in the fall of 1992, for example, the Ministry of Finance simply told Japanese banks that they no longer had to report capital losses on their equity holdings.[2]

Indeed, the very idea that companies should be reviewed by independent professionals is suspect in the Japanese system. In an economy two thirds the size of America's, Japan has about 1 certified public accountant (CPA) for every 25 of them in the United States—9,000 against 250,000. Britain, less than half Japan's size, requires 65,000 chartered accountants. Even if Japanese corporations accepted rigorous audits, ten times as many accountants could not handle the work load. Just as the threat of litigation is nipped in the bud by ensuring that there are only a handful of lawyers, accounting standards that mean something are forestalled by limiting the number of accountants. True, large corporations (e.g., those with liabilities of ¥20 billion or more) and companies seeking listings must submit to outside audits, although even this formality is due to the Securities Exchange Law imposed by SCAP (Supreme Commander for the Allied Powers, the most widely used acronym for the occupation).* Outside auditors understand that they make waves at their peril.

Ratings might be another source of information on public

---

* Before 1948 outside audits were extremely rare; in almost all cases they were court-ordered and involved cases of criminal misconduct.[3]

companies, were they not controlled by the Ministry of Finance. Three of the Japanese agencies have official status—that is, a company seeking to issue bonds in the domestic market must use one of these agencies. They all have retired MOF officials in their senior management, and two of the three are owned by consortia of banks.[4] The only independent Japanese agency, Mikuni & Company, is denied official status for the purposes of Japan's stunted domestic bond market. Mikuni pays its way by selling credit information to foreign—and, increasingly, to Japanese—investors who have learned not to trust Japanese corporate reports or ratings by the official agencies.

As Japanese banks and companies began in the 1980s to raise money abroad, they were forced to seek ratings from international agencies, such as Standard and Poor's and Moody's. Otherwise their securities were not acceptable to many foreign investors. It was a rough road. It is common in Tokyo to hear complaints that S&P and Moody's are puppets of American business, rigging the system to give Japanese issuers lower ratings than they deserve in order to raise the cost of financing and thus weaken Japan's competitive edge.

Former Ministry of Finance bureaucrats are seeded elsewhere throughout the Japanese financial system in positions of authority. As of this writing, they include the recently retired chairman of the Sakura Bank, Japan's second largest; the chairman of the Bank of Tokyo, Japan's premier "international" bank; the president of the Bank of Yokohama* the governors of the Japan Development Bank, the Export-Import Bank of Japan, the Tokyo Stock Exchange, and the Bank of Japan. As of 1992, 114 retired MOF bureaucrats served in the senior management of Japanese commercial banks, while another 50 or so could be found in comparable positions of influence inside

*This bank has a key role in the Japanese financial system by virtue of its position as the largest and thus the acknowledged spokesman and leader of Japan's top-ranked local banks *(chihō ginkō)*—the sixty-four commercial banks that form the second tier of the banking system and are the principal financial institutions in Japan's prefectural capitals. The last four presidents of the Bank of Yokohama have been ex-MOF bureaucrats.

securities and insurance companies.[5] Important think tanks, such as the Sōgō Kenkyū Kaihatsu Kikō (National Institute for Research Advancement), the Kokusai Kinyū Kenkyūjo (Institute for International Finance), and the Seisaku Kagaku Kenkyūjo (Institute for Policy Sciences, Japan), are headed by ex-MOF bureaucrats. Prominent universities such as Keio grant professorial chairs to retired ministry officials.[6]

This network of retired MOF officials also controls information. In the words of Uchida Michio, editor of the influential independent financial journal *Tōyō Keizai,* "A major source of the power of the MOF is the accuracy and importance of the vast amount of information in its hands; it effectively enjoys a 'monopoly'. . . . The ministry can, at will, leak or retain portions of this information to politicians or newspapers; it can also force others to maintain silence."[7] During times of exchange rate and stock market instability, the ministry puts pressure on analysts and economists not to discuss their projections with the media.* The MOF's immense power and its network of retired officials make this a relatively simple task. The ministry can easily marginalize an economist, an analyst, or a financial journalist who chooses to go public. The noted Stanford economist Paul Krugman once expressed surprise at "finding Japanese economists from the *private sector* refuse to acknowledge that [Japan's] rice policy is costly [emphasis added]." What Krugman does not realize is that any so-called private-sector institution is likely to have former MOF bureaucrats in its senior management. Krugman supposed that such economists "did not feel it . . . their place to criticize their government to a foreigner."[9] More probably, they feared for their promotion prospects. "There exists no active freedom of speech on economic matters in Japan,"[10] said one of the few top Japanese analysts with the independence and courage to speak freely.

---

*This pressure got so crude in the weeks after the 1987 New York stock market crash that Tachibana Takashi, a journalist who helped topple the government of Tanaka Kakuei in 1974 with his revelations of Tanaka's financing methods, wondered in the press what sort of economy Japan had when MOF "guidance" to foreign exchange dealers in banks all over Japan not to discuss their projections with the media was taken as a matter of course.[8]

MOF control of financial information is noticeable in the pages of Japan's leading business-financial daily, the *Nihon Keizai Shimbun,* or *Nikkei,* to use the common Japanese abbreviation. The *Nikkei* does not have retired MOF bureaucrats in its senior management, and it puts on periodic displays of disapproval at the Ministry of Finance, criticizing, for example, the proliferation of ex-bureaucrats in the upper reaches of Japan's important financial institutions.[11] But the newspaper often reads uncomfortably like the house organ of the Finance Ministry. Uchihashi Katsuto, one of Japan's cheekier commentators, describes its editorials as "reading like MOF PR pronouncements."[12] *Nikkei* reporters have pride of place in the *kisha kurabu*—cartels of reporters with quasi-monopoly control on coverage[13]—assigned to the MOF and the institutions it oversees, such as the Tokyo Stock Exchange. The MOF uses the *Nikkei* regularly as a means of floating trial balloons. When it wanted to bring the securities firms to heel in the summer of 1990, for example, it leaked information on illegal compensation promises to *Nikkei* reporters.[14] When the *Nikkei* injudiciously reported on its front page in April of that year that major insurance companies were selling large quantities of their long-term stock holdings into the market, MOF arm-twisting resulted in an article the next day that weakened the tone of the previous reports.[15] The Finance Ministry used the *Nikkei* to put pressure on the American Stock Exchange in the fall of 1990. It blamed trading in derivatives linked to the *Nikkei* stock index for the Tokyo stock market's steep decline. Trading in these instruments accounted at the time for up to 35 percent of daily turnover on the exchange. The *Nikkei* controlled the copyright to the index, and had it rescinded its permission to use the index, trading would have had to halt.*

Of course, information on corporate financial health exists. It is doled out on a need-to-know basis. Management has the information it requires. A firm's "main bank" will know a lot. The relevant bureaucracies—MITI for an industrial company,

---

*The American Stock Exchange circumvented the threat by devising "a copycat index called the Japan Index, which could mimic the performance of the Nikkei."[16]

Health and Welfare for a pharmaceutical firm, the Transport Ministry for a private railroad, and the Ministry of Finance for just about everyone—will be clued in. Other companies in the same *keiretsu* will often be part of the loop. Ostensible competitors in the industrial associations will share information in a manner that would be illegal in the United States.

But an outsider will have a difficult time learning anything. And even if one could, it would be hard to judge the full extent of a firm's credit exposure. Companies that stand at the apex of vertical *keiretsu,* for example, are generally regarded as being ultimately responsible for the liabilities of their affiliates. Toyota may own only 10.9 percent of Hino, the truck and bus maker, but has an implicit obligation to bail Hino out should the latter ever get into trouble. Companies in the great horizontal *keiretsu* have what are essentially unlimited obligations to each other. It is inconceivable, for example, that a Sumitomo group company carrying the Sumitomo name would be allowed by other Sumitomo companies to default on its obligations, but exactly which company is responsible for how much is never defined.* Companies find themselves rescuing their erstwhile "competitors," usually at the behest of the industrial association or governing bureaucracy. At one point or another over the past thirty years, MITI has organized cartels in a number of distressed industries, such as textiles, rubber, steel, nonferrous metals, shipbuilding, and petrochemicals.[18] The MOF

* One defining test of *keiretsu* member obligations to one another did come in 1974 when storage tanks belonging to Mitsubishi Oil sprang leaks and despoiled huge swaths of Japan's Inland Sea. The restitution and repair costs were far beyond the company's ability to pay. Mitsubishi Oil was not a typical *keiretsu* firm. It was in the petroleum industry—one "strategic" industry that MITI had decided in the 1950s Japan should not try to control. Deals had been cut with the major foreign oil companies, giving them guaranteed access to the Japanese market and substantial equity stakes in the Japanese industry. Mitsubishi Oil was owned 48.7 percent by Getty Oil, and the initial reaction of other Mitsubishi group companies was that it was Getty's problem. As Rodney Clark writes, Mitsubishi Oil "was, in fact, Mitsubishi in name but not in nature."[17] Clark notes that other group companies referred to Mitsubishi Oil as *tozama,* the appellation for so-called outside lords, those unrelated to the Tokugawa family, during the Tokugawa Shogunate. Getty refused to become involved. Under great pressure, other Mitsubishi group companies eventually came around to providing sizable financing that rescued Mitsubishi Oil.

periodically engineers take-overs of weaker banks by their stronger brethren. The current restructuring of the securities industries has as its explicit purpose the bailing out of weaker firms.

With credit such a fuzzy concept in Japan, Japanese banks were naturally more interested in collateral and a borrower's place in the Japanese power structure than in such phantom numbers as cash flow projections and a firm's equity cushion. But when the banks ventured overseas in the 1970s and emerged as lead actors on the global financial stage of the 1980s, they brought with them the attitudes and ways of doing business of the domestic Japanese market. And they bought business by cutting prices.

Superficially this approach mimics that of the banks' industrial counterparts. An industrial company can, however, take advantage of so-called experience curve dynamics. Making no money or even losing money on the first batch of orders can make sense because the more you produce, the more you learn how to produce cheaply. If your business is lending money, however, learning to save a bit on the actual processing of loan applications is so trivial in the economies realized as to be meaningless in terms of the cost of the loan. A bank that lends more money doesn't get better; it just gets bigger. In fact, its cost of funds probably goes up as the market perceives it taking on more risks. Thus the truly classy names in American banking are not behemoths like Chase and Citibank but the slightly smaller, conservatively managed institutions such as J. P. Morgan and Brown Brothers Harriman.

Japanese banks didn't understand this. They could price loans the way they did and undercut their non-Japanese competitors at any time *because they could ignore the costs of maintaining the capital cushion*. All the lessons American bankers absorbed in their training about maintaining capital ratios were irrelevant for the Japanese. They did not have to raise equity; their equity was held mostly by industrial corporations in the same *keiretsu*, just as they held equity in these companies. They were not accountable to shareholders; if they were accountable to anyone, it was to the Ministry of Finance. They understood where they could safely lend on the basis of signals from the bureaucracy and the collateral a company could offer—primarily land. If a major customer ran into trouble, its banks need not declare loans nonperforming and take a hit in their quarterly results. Instead they could hide the problem by revaluing assets, a simple matter since asset value was determined largely by the collateral the banks held. Free of scrutiny from nosy accountants, they had the time to work with the relevant bureaucracy and other *keiretsu* members in straightening out the problem or restructuring the client. The banks thus put aside very little for loan losses. Not only did they find the practice unnecessary, but the tax bureau of the Ministry of Finance discouraged them from doing it. Setting aside reserves for loan losses reduced their taxable income, and banks as a group were the biggest taxpayers in Japan.

Industrial corporations could also ignore capital cushions and profitability, but they faced a crucial check that did not exist for banks. An industrial company not only had to make lots of products to be taken seriously but had to make lots of *high-quality* products. The quality of a bolt of cloth, a color television set, a sheet of steel, or a semiconductor chip is a matter of fact, not opinion. A Japanese bank has to make lots of loans to be taken seriously, but the concept of a high-quality loan cannot exist in the absence of objective credit standards.

If Japanese banks had applied conventional credit standards to their lending, the economic miracle of the 1950s and 1960s would never have happened. American banks are not supposed to lend to companies with thin, shaky capital bases. Most large Japanese manufacturing companies had, in those years, thin or nonexistent capital bases. American banks are not supposed to lend to companies that are not profitable. The chairman of Toshiba announces that he is prepared to lose money for ten years in order to establish the company's dominance in flat panel video displays. Toshiba has never had any problems with access to bank credit. Western banks are supposed to pay careful attention to the relationship between capacity and market within the industries they fund to ensure that they are not lending to create overcapacity. When the large Japanese electronic companies invested in giant semiconductor chip plants in the early 1980s, thereby saddling the industry with horrendous overcapacity, or the big auto companies built huge new plants later in the decade in the teeth of global manufacturing capacity estimated at some 130 percent of market demand, their bankers never quibbled.

Restraints on the banks came not from the results of poor credit judgments manifested as loans gone sour but rather from the Ministry of Finance and its operating arm, the Bank of Japan. The MOF and the BOJ controlled both the overall quantity of credit and could and did intervene at any time to tell the banks how and in what fashion to deploy it. Whether it was the so-called overloaning to strategic industries in the 1950s and 1960s, the piling into the jumbo syndicated cross-border lending of the late 1970s, or the frenzied lending for construction and real estate financing during the "bubble" years of the late 1980s, the banks went into and out of businesses not because of sober assessments of the profits to be made but on the basis of cues from the MOF. They left it to the MOF to call a halt to excess.

Understanding the way Japanese banks make credit decisions is the key to unraveling one of the enduring mysteries of Japanese business: the putative low cost of capital.[19] American businesses generally seek to make investment decisions in the most formal and transparent manner possible. This is not a matter of cultural preference or superior rationality; it stems from the fiduciary responsibilities that managements and directors have toward stockholders and creditors. Even where the justification may seem lame, as in the blizzard of acquisitions in the mid-1980s, management needs to provide some objective rationale for what it is doing—rationale in terms of profitability—or it opens itself up to the threat of litigation.

The most common procedure for evaluating at least the financial aspects of an investment decision is the discounted cash flow approach taught universally in American business schools. The objective is to attempt to determine as rigorously as possible whether the firm will be creating value by making the proposed investment, or, in finance jargon, to determine whether the return on the investment in question exceeds the firm's so-called weighted average cost of capital.*

For all its formulistic M.B.A. air, this exercise or something very like it is a necessary discipline for an American firm. The difficulty of ascertaining all the variables, particularly the cost of equity and the expected returns from a project, does not make the exercise any less important. In American capitalism, no firm can long ignore the cost of capital or the need to earn positive returns on investment.

American corporations faced with surges in capital spending from their Japanese competitors wonder how these surges are possible in what is supposed to be a capitalist economy. They conclude that Japanese industry faces a fantastically low cost of capital. This is the only conclusion that permits discounted cash flow formulas to work. The result is one of the most commonly proffered explanations for Japan's success: the low cost of capital. As we shall see in the next chapter, the Japanese bureaucracy did in fact deliberately create low capital costs for strategic industries.

But individual Japanese companies do not "do" cost of capital calculations, and investment decisions are not made on a discounted cash flow basis. Capital costs and borrowing costs

---

*The procedure starts by estimating the revenues and expenses the project will entail. The resulting cash flows are "discounted" by the firm's weighted average cost of capital—a number that itself depends on a series of assumptions—to determine whether the investment will create value. The pocket calculators carried by most business school students in the late 1970s were programmed to run the complex mathematics. The Hewlett Packard 12-C, the most popular model, is said to have wreaked more havoc on the American economy than any machine ever invented. It gave the illusion of hard numbers to chains of hazy assumptions—e.g., the cost of equity; cash flow five years out. Risk-averse managers could use these "numbers" to avoid investing in new plant and equipment; acquiring another firm was so much safer.

are thought to be the same. Japanese firms care about borrowing costs, and they can push their banks and brokers very hard to get the finest terms. They rushed, for example, to take advantage of the cheaper international markets during the 1980s. They are just as careful as Americans about investment decisions, but the criteria used to make these decisions and the parties that management must thereby satisfy are very different. Formal financial criteria are usually limited to a payback period; e.g., the investment must pay for itself within a certain number of years.

The lowering of capital costs to industry in Japan is a responsibility of the economic bureaucracy, not of the individual firm. This is in sharp contrast with the American experience, in which, with one glaring exception, the cost of capital to particular sectors of the American economy—as opposed to a generalized concern about the level of interest rates—is deemed the province of "market forces." The exception is the American housing industry, in which, from the 1930s to the early 1980s, an entire panoply of regulations, artificial interest rate controls, special classes of banks, and favorable tax treatment was employed to achieve the essentially political goal of bringing homeownership within reach of the American middle class.* Two generations after the American housing and Japanese industrial policies were initiated, one country had the finest housing on earth and run-down plants suffering from inadequate investment. Meanwhile the citizens of the other country lived in "rabbit hutches"—the term used in a notorious European Community study—and went to work in the world's most automated, well-equipped factories. That this should surprise anyone is itself puzzling.

---

* David Hale has suggested the U.S. pharmaceutical industry has also benefited from "strategic" favoritism. In writing of the industry, he notes, "It charges domestic consumers high prices in order to fund a robust level of investment which produces positive externalities for the economy, including a dynamic bio-tech sector, a trade surplus in pharmaceutical products and a large global market share for U.S. pharmaceutical companies. There are few other sectors in the U.S. which conform so closely to the Japanese model of a strategic trade sector. . . ."[20]

Large Japanese companies make investment decisions within an incentive structure more closely resembling that of American bureaucracies than that of American companies. Bureaucracies receive funding on the basis of their ability to curry favor with the right people, so Japanese firms obtain financing because of the quality of their connections. And in the manner of the familiar bureaucratic tactic of always using every penny of this year's allocation, lest one receive less next year, Japanese companies will generally use whatever financing is available to expand. The opportunity to grow is never turned down, even if growth is only minimally profitable.

The frenzied copycat behavior of Japanese companies is often regarded as some sort of peculiar Japanese cultural phenomenon. But it is not unique to Japan. Bureaucracies everywhere behave like this. One finds the same patterns in the interservice rivalry of the American military, the jostling among academic departments for support staff and graduate students, the wrangling in Congress to ensure that federal spending is spread out among the congressional districts. It is a phenomenon that can be observed anywhere that money is obtained on grounds other than the measurable ability for using it to make more money.

Given the incentives for expansion, the Japanese economy should have a built-in bias toward investment while the overall profitability of those investments should be poor. Analysis bears out these expectations. The bias of the Japanese economy toward investment is well understood. "On average between 1976 and 1983, investment as a share of nominal GNP was 31 percent in Japan compared with 18 percent in the United States, 20 percent in the United Kingdom, 22 percent in West Germany and 22 per cent in France."[21] At the same time, however, operating profits as a percentage of sales in the manufacturing sector have declined steadily from some 9 percent in the early 1970s to a current level of around 3 percent.[22] Indeed, one Japanese economist has argued that if "proper valuation adjustments are fully applied [to capital assets] . . . Japanese rates of return may have been negative."[23]

It is naïve to assume that bureaucracies are by nature incompetent. The word "bureaucrat" has become a derogatory epithet in the United States, but Americans forget that well-designed, well-managed bureaucracies can perform brilliantly. The American Navy won the Battle of the Coral Sea, and the American Army saved Europe from the Nazis. NASA put a man on the moon, while the Tennessee Valley Authority controlled floods and brought electricity to millions. That the American school system today is a mess does not mean it always was. The American school system of a hundred years ago performed the greatest job of assimilation and education ever accomplished. There are good bureaucracies and bad bureaucracies, just as there are good companies and bad companies.

But whether they are good or bad, bureaucracies, on the one hand, and private companies in market economies, on the other, measure themselves by different criteria and behave differently as institutions. One cares about profits and making money; the other, about status and influence. Profits come from making things or performing services that are worth more to consumers than the cost to the provider of making those things or performing those services. The status of the consumer is irrelevant as long as he or she can pay for the product or the service. Status and influence, however, come from fulfilling expectations—particularly the expectations of those in positions of greater power and authority—and thus in turn from acquiring the ability to demand that other groups live up to expectations. Large Japanese companies have not been very good at making money, but then they were not set up to do that. They performed exceptionally well at their primary tasks of providing stable employment and income for middle-class male heads of households and of building productive capacity in those industries deemed by the most powerful people in Japan to have strategic significance.

3. A Case of National Leverage

The Japanese Economic Miracle

THE YEAR IS 1979. We are going to meet a twenty-six-year old Japanese man who is, in fact, a composite of several people. But we'll give him a single name, Sato Eiji. Mr. Sato is entering his third year at—let's call it Mitsutomo Metals, a famous company, one of the biggest in Japan. He knows he is among the favored of his generation. If he works hard, plays by the rules, and avoids public scandal, he should rise in the company. While he might go all the way to the top, the odds are against it. But he expects at the very least to make it to the lower ranks of senior management. He does not fear that he will find himself on the street fifteen years from now "reorganized" or "downsized" out of the firm as his bosses frantically try to fend off hostile take-overs or mollify Kabuto-cho, Japan's Wall Street. Instead he anticipates a car and driver, eager subordinates ready to respond to his slightest whim, and a high degree of status and weight both in the company and in the wider world. He means to be a man of consequence. And when he does retire, the personnel department will find a suitable slot for a few additional years of work, income, and status—perhaps as an executive with an affiliate.

Mr. Sato will never get rich. He'll do well enough to own a small house an hour and a half from central Tokyo if he and his future wife are careful with money. He'll be able to send his children to prestigious schools, but he does not look forward to the spacious homes of his American counterparts, the annual two-week European or Hawaiian vacation, the dining out and couple-centered social whirl of the American business elite. Instead he will work and he will save.

But he doesn't feel deprived. Far from it. He thinks he is doing pretty well. He is paid ¥150,000 a month—about $750 at the mid-1979 exchange rate. When someone asks him—or any Japanese—how much he makes, this monthly figure is the one he quotes. His annual salary is considerably more than ¥150,000 × 12 because he gets two bonuses a year—usually three months' salary per bonus—so in a normal year he makes ¥150,000 × 18, or ¥2,700,000—$13,500. He knows better than to regard these bonuses as permanent fixtures, however. They have been cut back in the past, and they might be cut back again.[1]

Mr. Sato's equally bright twenty-four-year-old sister does not enjoy the same prospects, but by Japanese standards, she is also doing well. Like most girls from good families, she went to junior college. She had the brains to attend a four-year institution, but that would have compromised her chances of being hired by a large, well-established company. As late as the mid-1980s a majority of such firms refused to hire female graduates of four-year universities. While Mr. Sato is living in the company dormitory, his sister is at home with their parents. That is the only way she can hold her job; large companies will not employ young married women or women living alone. Thus, while her salary is less than two thirds of Mr. Sato's, her expenses are lower, and she actually has more money to spend on a day-to-day basis. Being a well-brought-up, attractive young woman and working for a major company, she will have no trouble getting married. But if she dawdles about doing so, the pressure on her to marry and leave the firm will become intolerable. The firm will replace her with a nineteen- or twenty-year-old girl—a malleable girl being greatly preferred to a mature, independent woman—starting at a monthly salary of ¥90,000.

Mr. Sato's salary of $750 a month doesn't sound like much in the world's most expensive city, but it's what every other third-year white-collar male employee at Mitsutomo makes. Furthermore, it's just about what is made by every salaried man his age, even those who work for smaller, less prestigious firms. Mr. Sato is doing better than men at such places, however, and expects to do even better in the future because he gets help with housing. A person who moves to Tokyo without housing provided by the company must find a place to live and the equivalent of six months' rent before moving in. Two months' rent goes to a deposit, two months to key money never seen again, a month to the agent, and then, of course, there is the first month's rent. A tiny studio with no bath and a squat toilet down the hall could go for as little as ¥35,000 a month, but a slightly bigger place with a closet-size bath and toilet of its own is going to run at least ¥50,000 and probably much more. When one is making ¥150,000, that's a lot of money.

Mr. Sato doesn't have to worry about housing because he is living in the company dormitory. The company docks his pay ¥12,000 a month, in return for which he gets not only half a dorm room but also dinner and breakfast. Finances are not the only reason he lives in the dormitory. It is not absolutely required, but no ambitious young man would forgo the opportunity. It is through dormitory living that men like our friend begin to build the all-important web of personal connections—*jinmyaku*—essential to moving up the corporate ladder. With his parents in the Osaka area, financial reality gives Mr. Sato no choice but dormitory living. His roommate, however, comes from a wealthy family with a comfortable house in central Tokyo and could avoid the forty-five-minute commute and the cramped, noisy dormitory, but he is much too ambitious.

In addition to the dorm fee, ¥22,000 is taken out of Mr. Sato's pay packet for national and local taxes, health insurance, union fees, and unemployment insurance. About the union fees, he has no choice. He must join this company union and participate in its annual May Day march, complete with fluttering red flags and empty, ritualistic militancy in favor of higher wages. He knows that being active in union affairs—negotiating with "management" on behalf of the "workers"—is one of the best things he can do to enhance his promotion prospects. As for "unemployment" insurance, it is actually a down payment on the lump sum he will receive when he retires from the firm. Meanwhile the company pays for his transportation to and from work by giving him a subway pass. He eats a cheap ¥250 lunch in the company cafeteria.

After these deductions Mr. Sato has about ¥110,000 left. Out of this he buys clothes, pays for his entertainment—limited mostly to going out with guys in his work group—gives himself a bit of pocket money, and saves the rest. He saves because he has to. If he doesn't save, he's not going to accumulate the down payment for a small house or the money to move into a decent apartment. And if he can't do that, he may have trouble getting married. Of course he wants to get married in a few years. He also knows he must if he expects to rise very far at Mitsutomo. So when Mr. Sato goes to buy a suit, for example, he listens carefully to the advice of the salesman at a good department store like Isetan or Takashimaya who tells him what other young salarymen are buying. Our friend doesn't want to waste money like a schoolmate of his now working for a bank who bought a suit with double vents. The man was sent home by his boss and told not to come back to work until he was dressed properly.

Frugality comes easily to men like Mr. Sato. He knows, when he stops to think about it, that unless his parents had scrimped and saved throughout his childhood, his prospects would be poor. In far more trying circumstances than he expects to face, Mr. Sato's parents had financed a small house and both his and his sister's educations. He was reasonably bright and had studied hard, but it was clear early on that he lacked that extra spark to assure him a place at the very top public high schools and universities where tuition was subsidized and low. Instead he had attended an expensive private high school with strong academic standing.[2] From his middle school days on, young Eiji had been tutored both individually and in special cram schools to enable him to pass first the high school and then the college entrance examinations. This latter test he failed the first time, so he had to spend an extra year in a special preparatory school—again an expensive proposition.

Eiji's parents did not begrudge the money—this was their son's only sure way to a decent future—but it required the most careful financial planning by the family. Eiji's father had a secure position in a good firm, and his mother had gone back to work after his sister was in school; money had nonetheless been tight. Family trips were limited to an annual visit to Eiji's grandparents while his grandfather was still alive. There was rarely much in the way of fancy food at home, except perhaps on holidays. Eiji's mother got up early every morning to prepare box lunches called *bento* for him and his sister and gave him money to buy subsidized milk at school. Eiji wore short pants until he was thirteen years old and got his middle school uniform. The only concession to winter weather was knee socks. Heating in the house was limited to kerosene space heaters and the heated table quilt known as *kotatsu* around which the family gathered for meals.[3]

Sato Eiji's parents got him through school and into a good job. His and his sister's weddings will be the final large sums they spend on their children.* But Eiji's parents are not out of the financial woods. His grandmother at eighty-five can no longer look after herself very well. She moved in with his parents when his grandfather died. While she is not much of a direct financial burden—national health insurance covers her frequent visits to the doctor—Eiji's mother had to quit her job to care for her. The bigger problem is Eiji's father. He will turn

---

*Weddings costs are most typically split in Japan between the families of the bride and groom.

fifty-five next year, and while he has risen to the rank of *buchō* (general manager), he has not been promoted beyond that and will have to retire. He will be getting a lump-sum payment equivalent to some three years of salary. The personnel department is already on the lookout for a job for him, but it will involve a substantial cut in pay and will be good for only five or six years. While Eiji's parents are probably secure until well into their seventies, he knows that at some point he may have to support one or both of them.

Sato Eiji and his family were atypical of postwar Japanese in one respect: They were better off than average. Both he and his father worked for well-established organizations where job security was taken for granted, as were regular and predictable increases in income. Men working for companies in the second tier—up to two thirds of the male work force—would not have enjoyed this level of either financial or job security.[4] As for women, smaller firms do not confine their female hiring to girls fresh out of junior college. They hire women of any age or marital status as temporary or part-time workers—and then let them go when business turns down.

Why 1979? I was twenty-six years old then myself, living in Tokyo, and Sato Eiji's life is a mosaic of people and incidents known to me. Being twenty-six in 1979 means birth in 1953—the date often labeled "Year One of the Japanese Economic Miracle."* And some of the more severe patterns began to break down after 1979. In the 1980s it became a lot easier to make money. Significant salary differentials opened up among various industries, and the air of prosperity as the decade wore on led to a more consumerist ethos. A younger man in the mid-1980s, for example, would probably have spent more money on "looking sharp." As renting apartments became more expensive, and buying them out of the question, many young men set their sights on fancy cars instead of down payments on houses in order to impress potential mates. A younger woman

---

*The conventional wisdom sees the U.S. procurement effort for the Korean War as ending the postwar doldrums and kicking off the high-growth years.

could possibly have aspired to the status of *kyariia ouman* (career woman), for with the passage under international pressure of the Equal Employment Opportunity Act in 1985, a number of large Japanese organizations began hiring a few women from four-year universities and treating them, formally at least, the same as managerial-track male hires.[5] A *kyariia ouman,* unlike other women in the company, for example, is usually not required to wear a uniform. That's how you know when you visit a large Japanese company whether you're dealing with a *kyariia ouman* or an *oeru* (OL, short for the Japanese-English term "office lady" or "female clerical employee").

If the eighties brought some changes, it is nonetheless striking how little those boom years affected basic Japanese household financial behavior or the key role of household savings in the Japanese economic system. The Japan of the late 1980s has been labeled one of the great speculative bubbles in history. But for all the hedonistic excess—the very smell of money—that characterized the period, planning for retirement, finding living quarters, and financing children's education still required sustained attention to family finances. And the great investment boom of those years was funded, like the economic miracle of the fifties and sixties that preceded it, by the systematic transfer of wealth from the household sector to industrial corporations.

One single statistic—held nearly constant from the early days of the economic miracle through the late 1970s, the eighties boom, and on into the recession that followed it—explains a great deal: the household savings rate, among the world's highest[6] and a rate that since 1960 has never dipped below 15 percent of household income. Indeed, with the passing of the hedonistic eighties, politicians, bureaucrats, and media pundits all outdid themselves in proclaiming their joy at seeing the return of traditional Japanese frugality—"holy poverty" *(seihin),* as it was called in an odd 1992 best seller.[7]

This traditional frugality is often cited in explanations of Japan's high savings rates. As with so many other aspects of Japanese economic life—from "lifetime employment" to *keire-*

tsu to harmonious labor relations—Japanese frugality is said to stem from innate cultural norms. But the cultural explanation simply does not hold water. In premodern Japan peasants had no choice but to be frugal, and some of the samurai made a fetish of it. Other segments of society, however, prided themselves on how quickly they went through money. The Tokugawa shogunate periodically enacted sumptuary laws aimed at suppressing lavish spending by merchants. It was said of the *Edokko,* or child of Edo (the pre-1868 name for Tokyo), that "he never slept overnight on his money." At the turn of the century "workers were notoriously poor savers."[8] Much as they might have extolled it, Japan's administrators could not rely on "innate" frugality to finance early-twentieth-century industrialization, the war effort, or the postwar recovery. Savings were deliberately and systematically mobilized.

In the late nineteenth century Japan's administrators had made two critical decisions that continued to govern policy making of every sort through a century of wars, depressions, catch-ups, occupations, recoveries, miracles, and "bubbles." The first of these decisions: Whatever it takes, Japan will be a powerful country that cannot be pushed around, a modern nation with a broad and sophisticated industrial base. The accumulation of production capacity, whether profitable or not, would be a primary political end. The second decision: The financing of industrialization will be carried out without relying on foreigners. The first of these decisions had to be redefined after the Second World War to mean "powerful" in narrow economic terms only. But the second decision remained intact.

An aversion to foreign capital was deeply ingrained in the institutional memory of Japan's administrators. Germany's Iron Chancellor, Otto von Bismarck, had warned a delegation from Japan in 1872 of the threat to national sovereignty posed by foreign capital.[9] The delegation had been headed by Iwakura Tomomi, later one of Meiji Japan's most prominent leaders. Citing Egypt and Turkey, whose failures to keep up with debt service payments gave the European powers an excuse to in-

vade, the great Meiji finance minister Matsukata Masayoshi had
assumed office in 1881 as a blistering critic of his predecessor's
heavy borrowing in the London markets. Matsukata vowed
there would be no repeat even at the cost of what came to be
known as the Matsukata deflation. An 1890 Japanese edition
of the German economist Friedrich List's *National System of
Political Economy,* with its arguments in favor of protectionism
and against foreign borrowing, had greatly impressed Japan's
elite. The translation came complete with an introduction cow-
ritten by the Bank of Japan governor Tomita Tetsunosuke, ap-
provingly summarizing List's arguments.[10]

The spiritual heirs of Tomita, Iwakura, and Matsukata did
not forget the lesson. "Bureaucrats at MOF . . . strongly opposed majority foreign ownership of major Japanese companies
and those domestic firms operating in important fields such as
heavy industry because they viewed such ownership as a threat
to national economic sovereignty," writes one scholar of postwar Japanese external economic policy.[11] He quotes an internal
1947 Ministry of Finance report that maintained that, "Japanese ownership of 'basic industries' is 'essential for the independence of the Japanese economy . . . we must be vigilant in order
to prevent foreign capital from gaining control of company
management' " and notes "Japanese business organizations
generally opposed with at least equal vigor free inflows of FDI
[foreign direct investment] because they feared increased foreign influence over their industries."[12]

In eschewing foreign capital, however, Japan's postwar administrators had set for themselves a formidable challenge if
they intended that their country ever again be something more
than a semiagrarian society dominated by handicrafts and light
industry. They met that challenge by mobilizing household savings to leverage the entire economy.

The concept of leverage is most often encountered in a
corporate context, cloaked with M.B.A. mystique and the jargon of eighties-style business journalism. But it can apply to

countries too. At heart it is a simple notion: Borrow a lot of money in order to grow as fast as possible and in turn rapid growth *must* occur in order to service the debt. When it works, leverage permits much higher growth rates than other financing methods—waiting to accumulate reserves, for example, or selling pieces of the enterprise (called welcoming foreign investment in a national context) to others. But it is also risky. Any slowdown can make it impossible to service the debt.

The linchpin of the strategy for Japan was the continuous transfer of wealth from households to industrial corporations. This was not simply a matter of the informal, but iron, norms among employers that suppressed salaries at all levels of corporate life from new hires to CEOs. Virtually every aspect of Japanese economic life is structured so as to boost savings and extract wealth from consumers. Take land. Vast tracts in the large cities are deliberately held off the market or designated for "agricultural" use. My apartment in southern Tokyo stands on a large, busy boulevard where rents for tiny quarters run at least a thousand dollars a month and the purchase prices for small condominiums start at several million. Down the street is a half acre of land sandwiched between a supermarket and an apartment building that is devoted to the growing of a few sickly cabbages. As long as the owner continues to grow cabbages, the lot is officially designated "agricultural" property and the owner pays virtually no property tax. If he were to sell his land, his huge tax bill would eat away most of the gains. So he continues to grow cabbages amid the roar of delivery trucks and the hordes of shoppers crowding into the diminutive supermarket next door where meager shelf space severely restricts choice.

Why do things this way? Why not induce my neighbor the cabbage farmer to become my neighbor the landlord of nice big apartments or my neighbor the supermarket owner with plenty of space for a broad range of imported products? You get a variety of explanations: Nōkyō (the national union of agricultural cooperatives)* and the Agriculture Ministry have a vested interest in urban cabbages and are too powerful to dislodge; banks don't want to see brought onto the market land that would reduce the collateral value of their existing holdings; Japan is a poor little island country that must maintain minimal food security. The first two reasons are of some help in understanding the situation. The last is pure propaganda (if Japan were cut off from the rest of the world, it could not possibly feed itself; food security for Japan comes only from reliable access to an open international trading system), which does not stop it from being used. But valid or not, these explanations miss a crucial financial implication. Housing is something everyone must have. If land for housing is kept deliberately scarce, if this scarcity is exacerbated by construction and taxation codes, people will be forced to save in order to secure this expensive but essential good.

Those savings are available for use by Japanese industry. For during those years that our young friend at Mitsutomo Metals was saving money, he was almost certainly putting it in a bank—surely the Mitsutomo Bank—and the bank was lending it out to Mitsutomo Metals, Mitsutomo Heavy Industries, Mitsutomo Paper, Mitsutomo Electronics, and Mitsutomo Steel so these companies could build state-of-the-art factories. And after our young friend gets married and his wife has their second child and they burst out of their tiny 2DK (Japanese real estate parlance for a two-room apartment with a kitchen), he makes the down payment on a small three-bedroom house an hour and a half from central Tokyo. He probably buys it from Mitsutomo Real Estate, a cash-rich company that painstakingly assembles the land for large housing estates on the edges of metropolitan Tokyo by purchasing lots from the families of farmers who have died off and have no one to carry on the family businesses. Mitsutomo Real Estate will promptly deposit the proceeds of the sale to our young friend in the Mitsutomo Bank.

*In a bizarre example of *imeji uppu* (image up), the acronym *Nōkyō* has been replaced with the Roman letters *JA,* thought to sound more up-to-date.

Education is another essential good that helps squeeze savings out of households. Japan's educational system is often praised for promoting high levels of achievement and a meritocratic base for the power structure; it is just as often condemned for making a *jigoku* (hell) out of the teenage years and stifling initiative and creativity. Whichever interpretation rings true, it certainly costs money. Public education may be free through twelfth grade and cheap thereafter, but beyond middle school there are far from enough slots for all those who wish them, forcing the majority of families to turn to expensive private schools. Meanwhile entrance to the best public secondary and tertiary institutions is virtually impossible without special tutoring from cram schools (*juku*). Thus, whether one goes the public or private route, securing a future for one's children means saving money.

Then there are Japan's notorious retail prices. Eight brussels sprouts cost ¥280 ($3.29) or better than 41 cents per sprout at my local store. Four grapefruit-type citrus called *hassaku* run for ¥480 ($5.65), a liter of milk for ¥188 ($2.21), a head of lettuce for ¥260 ($3.06), and two small cod fillets ¥600 ($7.06). I pay ¥3300 ($38.82) in tolls to go some sixty miles on the expressway. Fifteen liters (about four gallons) of gasoline for my car costs ¥1575 ($18.53), or almost $5 a gallon.

Last summer I tried my hand at gardening. A bag of fertilizer that in the States would go for $4 costs ¥3,000 ($35.29). When the external disc drive for my Apple Powerbook broke down, I took it to a repair shop and asked for a quote to get it fixed. I was told the quote would take a few days. I priced a new one on the way out of the shop at ¥33,000 ($344). I flew to New York the next day, and at J&R Computer World in lower Manhattan saw the identical disc drive for $129, which I promptly paid. A message on my answering machine was waiting for me when I got back to Tokyo. I could have my old disc drive repaired for ¥42,000 ($438). Both disc drives, incidentally, were "Assembled in Japan."

The famous $3 cup of coffee that crops up regularly in

newsmagazines is now well over $6. Japan's Economic Planning Agency claims Japan's cost of living is 60 percent higher than America's. Anyone who has lived in both countries finds this number suspect; prices in Japan appear many times higher.[13]

These prices represent a form of taxation. A retired senior Ministry of Finance official crowed to me in an interview about how lightly the Japanese household is taxed. He was explaining that lowering taxes in order to stimulate the Japanese economy, as the American government wished, was not possible because taxes were already so low. And if one examines the formal tax rates, he was right. But there is no economic difference between taxing away large chunks of income, on the one hand, and forcing consumers to pay prices many times the world market level for essential goods, on the other. The high tax country may choose to dole out generous sums to retirees while the high price country may subsidize a vast inefficient distribution system that "employs" tens of thousands of *obasan* and *ojisan* in the Japanese equivalents of mom-and-pop stores. The economic effects, however, are the same.

Not so the political effects. Japanese consumers do not experience their crushing tax burden as such. Instead of transparent tax rates debated in legislatures and the media and starkly visible every year when tax returns are prepared,* Japanese taxes are collected mostly in the form of the stupefying prices for household goods arrived at not in open political forums and only selectively in the open market. These prices are usually set in the endless, secretive informal negotiations that go on among companies in industrial associations, between companies and the various ministries, among the ministries, between banks and their *keiretsu* companies.

The high prices are justified with various, mostly fatuous, half-believed explanations in the Japanese media. Japanese con-

---

* Salaried workers in Japan do not typically prepare their own tax returns; these are done for them by their companies, and their pay packets automatically docked. The tax burden on the salaryman family is thus almost invisible.

sumers are unusually fastidious; they demand extraordinary levels of afterservice, insist on a wide selection of items, and so forth, as if prices for fertilizer and low-quality window glass at five times world levels could be attributed to fastidiousness. These retail "taxes" are siphoned off by the long chain of middlemen that separate the consumer from the producer and through manufacturers' control of distribution networks. They help stave off social unrest by providing some kind of work for people who in other countries might be unemployable. They buy off powerful groups like farmers and construction companies that might otherwise pose a formidable political challenge to the overriding goals of industrial policy. And most important, these "taxes" are available to subsidize companies in strategic industries. One category of products in Japan *is* cheap: industrial machines and components.

Until the 1980s Japanese households had effectively no option for financing major expenditures except for savings. Credit cards, installment plan financing for consumer durables, and other forms of consumer credit all were stymied in order to encourage savings at every point. A Japanese colleague in the late 1970s told me that when he resigned from a major Japanese bank to join Bank of America's Tokyo office, where we both were working, his credit card had promptly been revoked. This was a married man with plenty of money and a good job. His American counterpart would have had to throw away ten pounds of junk mail a month offering credit cards and other inducements to spend. But by changing jobs in Japan, this man had demonstrated instability.

It was common in 1970s Tokyo to see ads posted in telephone booths or flyers stuck in one's mailbox advertising household loans. Very seductive they were to the financially distressed, with soothing words and pictures of banklike offices staffed with pretty girls. But these ads were placed by *sarakin* (an acronym for "salary finance") firms usually controlled by gangsters, and the interest rates ran at least 50 percent per annum. In the papers one could read of housewives hounded into suicide by these outfits or, if they were unusually attractive, forced into prostitution to pay off the debts. Typically the poor women were several million yen behind in their payments. Gangsters would set up sound trucks in front of the homes of such people, denouncing them at all hours of the day and night. Such firms were, however, the only option available to someone in financial distress until very limited steps were taken in the 1980s to develop other forms of consumer credit. (My former colleague now has plenty of credit cards, although he is on his fourth job.) As far as consumer credit went, respectable banks gave mortgages, and that was it.

But surely Mr. Sato at Mitsutomo Metals earns a high return on his savings? No. He gets one big break: He pays no tax on his interest income.* But the only place he can safely put his money is low-interest–bearing deposits at the bank or the post office. Such deposits themselves will seem familiar to Americans over the age of thirty-five or so. Until the lifting of Regulation Q (not completely eliminated until 1986) and the introduction of money market funds, if Americans wanted to put money into a bank, low and fixed rates of return were all they could expect. There were, however, alternatives for American households: U.S. Treasuries, corporate bonds, the stock market.

Most of these alternatives did not exist for Japanese. There was no corporate bond market to speak of, no money market instrument. The stock market had the well-deserved reputation of a dangerous casino. No long-term fixed-income investment vehicle other than the debentures of the long-term banks were on offer until the early 1980s, and these were targeted at institutions, not households.[14] The Bank of Japan arbitrarily set interest rates on bank deposits. The longest-term deposit an ordinary commercial bank could offer was two years.

Extracting the highest possible savings out of households

---

* Until the late 1980s, interest from the first ¥3 million ($27,000 in 1989) in deposits was free of tax. Even this ceiling was easily circumvented by people opening up accounts at a variety of institutions or at the same institution in the names of various family members. Interest income is now taxed at 20 percent.

at the lowest possible cost was only the first step in financing the economic miracle. These funds had to be managed, particularly in the early years of postwar recovery, when Japan's administrators refused to allow "gambling" with scarce capital. This capital had been pried from households many of which were a paycheck away from destitution, and it could not be risked on enterprises that might go bankrupt or in industries in which Japan might not be competitive.

The need to manage credit in a leveraged economy can best be understood by looking at another M.B.A. concept, experience curve dynamics. The essence of this idea is that costs decline in an orderly fashion with every doubling of volume. If you can predict your volume, you can predict your costs. If you can be sure that next year you will sell twice as many textiles, steel plates, automobiles, or semiconductors as you did this year, you can price below today's costs because you have a pretty good idea what your costs are going to be with twice the volume.

American statisticians began to understand the experience curve during productivity studies conducted in the 1940s. The curve was applied to analysis of business strategy by the consultant Bruce Henderson in the 1960s and disseminated by the company he founded—the Boston Consulting Group—in the 1970s. But the Japanese used the idea at both the corporate and the national level to drive the economic miracle in the 1950s and 1960s. The trick was picking the right industries and then making sure volume grew rapidly so the industries came down that experience curve quickly.

The questions come immediately. How could Japan's administrators be sure they had picked the right industries? And how did they arrange for the necessary increases in volume? This was the core of Japan's industrial policy and the central role that credit allocation played in it. The first requirement was high-quality information—and lots of it. Anyone who has ever dealt with Japanese organizations knows they are gluttons for information; they wallow in facts. Then the information had to be widely disseminated among all relevant decision makers. Japan's great general trading companies—the so-called *sōgō shōsha*—had already in the 1950s restored much of their formidable prewar apparatus and by the 1960s boasted unrivaled business intelligence networks across the world. Together with the major banks, they sat at the center of the *keiretsu*, the famous prewar zaibatsu that had, by the early 1950s, been reformulated as the more loosely structured *keiretsu*. These *keiretsu* boasted companies in virtually every industry of actual or potential consequence. Leaders of the *sōgō shōsha*, the banks, and the major *keiretsu* industrials were in close daily contact with one another, as they were with their counterparts in the other major institutional pillars of the Japanese economy: government banks, such as the Export-Import Bank of Japan and the Japan Development Bank; nominally private banks with close government links, such as the Industrial Bank of Japan (IBJ), and the Bank of Tokyo; and the important economic bureaucracies—MITI, the MOF, the Keidanren (Federation of Economic Organizations, theoretically a private association of business federations, in fact a major bureaucracy in its own right), the Economic Planning Agency, and the Keizai Dōyūkai (the Committee for Economic Development, a sort of brain trust of industrialists and bureaucrats).

It was not a matter of picking "winners" and "losers," as it is so crudely described in the Anglo-American press. It was a matter of picking industries that met certain criteria at certain times over the past forty years. Did the industry have obvious growth potential on a global scale? Did the industry have "strategic" significance—i.e., was it an important upstream industry, like steel or semiconductors, for a cluster of other industries? Or, like automobiles or consumer electronics, did it sit at the nexus of a large number of related industries? Could Japan secure the necessary technology? ("We will take every measure possible to obstruct the success of your business," said a senior MITI official to IBM's representative, "unless you license IBM patents to Japanese firms and charge them no more than a 5 percent royalty."[15]) And most important, if the industry had access to the necessary financing, with capital costs cheap or nonexistent, could a Japanese industry price its products so as to ensure it could undercut Western competition and thus guarantee those vital increases in volume?

Reaching a consensus on the appropriate industries was not all that hard. Only once was there a really significant dispute—in the early 1950s, over automobiles. MITI, with the unsurprising support of Toyota and Nissan, wanted to foster a Japanese passenger car industry, arguing it would force domestic development of an array of related industries. But many in Japan's elite, led by the Bank of Japan governor Ichimada Naoto and the Ministry of Transportation, fought the idea, believing Japan's infrastructure was too primitive, its consumer purchasing power too small, and Detroit's technological lead too great.[16] The proponents prevailed, and the rest is history.[17]

Chalmers Johnson's description of MITI's role in nurturing new industries is worth quoting at length.

In its fully elaborated form, the late 1950's MITI system of nurturing (ikusei) a new industry . . . included the following types of measures: First, an investigation was made and a basic policy statement was drafted within the ministry on the need for the industry and on its prospects. . . . Second, foreign currency allocations were authorized by MITI and funding was provided for the industry by the Japan Development Bank. Third, licenses were granted for the import of foreign technology. Fourth, the nascent industry was designated as "strategic" in order to give it special and accelerated depreciation on its investments. Fifth, it was provided with improved land on which to build its installations, either free of charge or at nominal cost. . . . Sixth, the industry was given key tax breaks. . . . Seventh, MITI created an "administrative guidance cartel" to regulate competition and coordinate investment among the firms in the industry.[18]

Japan's was a forced march to ever-higher levels of technical sophistication, doing in 40 years what had taken the United States 150. The primary motive was undoubtedly the enhancement of Japan's national economic power. But there was also a compelling financial reason. For a leveraged entity—whether a single firm or an entire national economy—must continuously grow to survive. Otherwise the high levels of debt—and that is what leverage is—act as a trap.

Thus the critical importance of cheap capital at the right moments. MITI coordinated the process of industry selection and organized the competitive conditions within each industry, but it was the Ministry of Finance and its operating arm, the Bank of Japan, that had to ensure the right industries got funding when they needed it. Indeed, the entire financial system was designed to pour scarce capital into targeted industries. First came massive investments by large, well-connected companies in state-of-the-art facilities. Protectionist walls allowed companies to build momentum in the domestic market without worry over foreign competition while clear domestic champions emerged. Then, confident of their technological prowess, backed by limitless amounts of patient, low-cost capital, battle-hardened by the practice heats in the domestic market, supported by a vast global information network of affiliated companies, trading firms, banks, and the bureaucracy itself, the great names of Japanese industry strode forth from the walled-off home front for the assaults on global markets. Toray, Teijin, Hitachi Zosen, Nippon Steel, Honda, Matsushita, Komatsu, Nissan, Toyota, Sony, Toshiba: year after year, decade after decade came the "concentrated, torrential rain-type exports" to use a Japanese government term, driving foreigners from the field and establishing Japanese supremacy.

The industries differed, but the pattern was the same. Starting with textiles in the 1950s and then moving up the value-added chain through shipbuilding, steel, machine tools, motor-cycles, automobiles, construction equipment, consumer electronics, semiconductors, computer components, and so on, the waves of exports functioned as a signal to the rest of the world that no non-Japanese company could survive in hand-to-hand combat. The destruction of foreign competition was not the objective, although it was often the result. Japanese companies had no choice. The precious capital that had been poured into them could not be wasted. As the Japanese said in describing their own economy, the bicycle must be kept moving lest it tip over.*

The financial bureaucracy working through the Japanese banking system saw its central task as steering capital to the right industries at the right times. During the high-growth years Japanese companies had essentially one place to go for external financing: banks. There were no venture capitalists; seed money for new industries was an explicit purpose of the government-owned Japan Development Bank. Investment houses of the Wall Street sort did not exist; their functions of funding long-term capital projects were largely carried out by three specialized long-term banks with close ties to the Finance Ministry, IBJ the largest and most important of these. The bond market had not played a significant role since its 1927 collapse and functioned as an unimportant sideshow wholly under the thumb of the big banks. The stock market had served a useful purpose in the early 1950s as a means of putting the old zaibatsu back together as *keiretsu*. It proved itself useful again as a corporate finance tool in the mid-1980s. But in the intervening thirty-five years the stock market was a minor arena, at least for large, well-connected companies seeking financing. Japanese companies that needed money—and they all needed money— went to banks. Each year between 1947 and 1981 private banks met from 71 to 83 percent of *all* external financing requirements of Japanese industrial corporations, with government financial institutions providing an additional 8 to 14 percent.[20]

Is Japan's therefore a Continental financial system? Those familiar with the distinction between the so-called Anglo-Saxon systems with their heavy reliance on stock and bond

---

* Significantly, the one targeted industry in which Japan has failed to achieve clear success despite the use of all traditional tactics—limitless financing, cartels, government subsidies—has been computers and computer components. Japanese companies spent too much time copying IBM and were late in grasping the significance of the personal computer and networking revolution. But the lack of success became evident only in the early 1990s, when Japan could absorb the losses that thirty years earlier would have been catastrophic. And the failure has been only partial. Japanese firms dominate disc drives and commodity-type semiconductors, for example, and are the sole suppliers of display screens and laser printer engines.[19]

markets and the bank-centered systems of France and Germany may think so at first glance. But it is not so clear-cut. True, like these Europeans, Japanese firms relied on banks for most of their financing requirements. And close links exist in all three countries between specific banks and specific industrial companies, much closer than one would find in Britain or the United States. But the differences outweigh the similarities.

In Germany banks control large swaths of industry outright either through direct ownership of major blocks of shares or because they have the authority to vote the shares of customers they represent.[21] While Japanese banks hold equity in related industrial firms, the same firms own chunks of the banks, the essence of the system of cross shareholding known as *keiretsu*. The leverage that banks hold over their industrial customers comes not from their formal equity stakes—limited by law to 5 percent—but from their informal ties and their control of lending. This main bank system, as it is often called, sees large commercial banks acting as quasiowners of major companies despite the small nominal equity stake. Even after the early 1980s, when credit grew easier, banks were able to force many of "their" large corporations to take out borrowings no longer really needed.

Banks may have had a lot of control over their industrial customers, but in an ultimate sense they were servants, described often as "utilities" by bureaucrats defending them from foreigners seeking to crack open Japan's financial markets. Japanese industrial companies, not banks, manned the front lines of the leveraged economy. They made and sold the bolts of Toray polyester, the NKK steel tubing, the Panasonic televisions, the Nissan automobiles that would fuel growth. These companies had to use experience curve dynamics—flooding markets with products, pricing below their costs, relying upon rapid increases in volume—to drive costs down. The Japanese coined an English term for the waves of financing that industrial companies drew on at critical junctures: "overborrowing." They used the term because any failure to reach those volume targets would have fatally compromised a company's ability to pay back loans, because Western banks would never grant that kind of credit.

Japanese banks had assurances, however, that Western banks lacked. Both the bank that lent the money and the company that borrowed it knew that the risk of failure had been reduced by every means the bureaucracy could command. The ultimate guarantees on the viability of the loans came from the bureaucracy. It ensured the success of strategic industries and provided for bank access to low-cost funds. As Mikuni Akio put it, Japanese "banks enjoyed a guaranteed spread between costs arranged by the MOF and returns arranged by MITI."[22]

The financial authorities' responsibility for bank funding went beyond forcing households to save at low rates of interest. The postal savings system (despite its name, the world's largest bank) turned over many of its deposits to the likes of the Japan Development Bank and the Export-Import Bank of Japan. Meanwhile the three long-term banks enjoyed a government-decreed monopoly on long-term, fixed-rate funding. Both those rates and the rates on the capital loans they made—the so-called long-term prime rate—were set by negotiation among the banks, the MOF, and the BOJ. The Ministry of Finance arranged directly or indirectly for the three banks' funding.[23]

IBJ, the biggest and most important of the three long-term banks, played a key role in financing core strategic industries. It seems something of a fashion among younger academics today to highlight IBJ's role in allocating credit as if to suggest the financing of the economic miracle was more of a garden-variety, market-driven phenomenon than we had suspected.[24] But this misses the point. In fact, an institution such as IBJ illustrates the difficulty of separating the private from the public sectors in Japan. The government established IBJ in 1903 over the opposition of many zaibatsu bankers, and until the end of the Second World War the MOF appointed its senior management. SCAP temporarily abolished the distinctions among classes of banks that had given IBJ its special status. The occupation had scarcely ended, however, before IBJ was back in business as a designated long-term bank, ostensibly this time as a "private" institution. But with its funding, lending, and much of its management still overseen by the MOF, it cannot be regarded as a private-sector bank in the sense that, say, J. P. Morgan is a private-sector bank.[25]

But the most important credit allocation tool of all rested in the bureaucracy's control of ordinary commercial banking, the business of collecting deposits and lending money for day-to-day commercial activities. Japanese commercial banks may give the appearance of being a bit more independent of MOF control than an IBJ, but every one of them does business at the pleasure of the ministry and is subject at any time to any sort of intervention on any conceivable matter—personnel, branch locations, loan policies, interest rates, and indeed their continued existence as independent entities. The idea of merging the ancient and proud Mitsui Bank—a name once synonymous with Japanese finance, whose institutional forebears had bankrolled both the Tokugawa Shogunate and the Meiji Restoration—with that amalgamation of regional institutions known as Taiyo Kobe Bank to form the innocuously named Sakura (Cherry Blossom) Bank did not originate in the executive suite at Mitsui.[26]

Ultimately, bureaucratic control over the large commercial banks rested on one critical fact: The banks could not fund their "excessive" loans to corporations from their deposit bases. Nor, given their tiny capitalizations, could they afford to make any credit mistakes. One bankruptcy would have wiped out their capital. Like banks in most countries who found they had lent more than they could fund, they had to borrow money to make up the difference. But in Japan only one place had enough: the credit window at the Bank of Japan. And it was always the same banks that were short of funds, the great nationwide commercial banks that in turn controlled industrial Japan's access to credit. The phenomenon of overborrowing by corporations had its flip side in what came to be labeled with another Japanese-English term as "overloan" by the great banks.

Commercial banks everywhere borrow from one another

to keep their accounts in balance. In the United States this mechanism is called the federal funds market because the accounts are cleared through the Federal Reserve System. A bank with a surplus of deposits at the end of a business day lends funds through this market to banks that have made more loans than they have deposits. In the United States a bank will find itself one day a borrower and the next day a lender in the federal funds market. But in Japan's so-called call money market, one sort of bank was a perennial lender; another sort, always a borrower. The lenders: so-called local banks *(chihō ginkō)*, based in Japan's provinces, with more funds than they could lend to their upcountry customers. The borrowers: so-called city banks *(toshi ginkō),* the large nationwide institutions headquartered with a single exception in one of the country's three great metropolitan areas (Tokyo-Yokohama, Osaka-Kobe, and Nagoya).*

The city banks sit at the center of the *keiretsu.* The great names of Japanese business—Mitsubishi, Mitsui, Sumitomo, Yasuda—all were attached originally to banking houses, and indeed, the *keiretsu* are still sometimes called bank groups. Since the surplus funds of the local banks always fell far below the demands of the city banks, the latter needed the Bank of Japan to make up the shortfall. With its critical control over bank funding, the BOJ could thus intervene directly in the banks' affairs and in fact was consulted *daily* by the city banks as to the direction and quantity of credit extended.[27]

As main banks of the major corporations in the first tier of the Japanese economy the *toshi ginkō* were far more than simple arm's length lenders. They provided crucial input to all significant capital investment decisions, could be expected and relied upon to intervene at the earliest signs of financial distress, and acted generally more like partners or even owners with corporate management than banks would ever do in the United States.

---

*The exception is the Hokkaido Takushoku Bank, set up by the Meiji government to fund the development of Hokkaido in the late nineteenth century.

Overloan had its roots in measures taken late in 1943 to ensure that increasingly desperate war-related industries had priority access to funds. Prudential banking practices were suspended by law. Designated banks were permitted—indeed required—to lend to the munitions industry in excess of their deposit bases with the funding shortfalls made up by other banks and the Bank of Japan. The Ministry of Finance supervised the system, while MITI's institutional forebear, the Ministry of Munitions, determined credit allocation.[28] With the institutional arrangements already in place, transferring prioritized credit allocations from wartime munitions firms to postwar companies in strategic industries proved an easy task.

Overloan played a crucial macroeconomic role as well. It permitted higher levels of monetary creation than would otherwise have been possible without inviting inflation. Economists have long understood that rapid money supply growth can boost real output for a short period. But inflation usually sets in and dissipates the gains.

Indeed, an isolated look at money supply statistics during the 1955–72 period might lead one to conclude that the men running Japan were a bunch of irresponsible populists. The bare numbers suggest they had set about gunning the money supply to produce a short burst of "false" prosperity before the inevitable inflation set in. Hadn't Milton Friedman, the doyen of the monetarists, once recommended that monetary authorities aim at a predictable annual growth rate of 3 to 5 percent in the money supply?[29] The Japanese money supply expanded at a minimum of 15 percent a year.* Yet inflation as measured by the wholesale price index never even reached 4 percent until the economic miracle ended abruptly in 1973.

The Bank of Japan, however, steered this "excess" monetary growth directly into overloan, thus financing investments in production capacity. A panoply of industrial policy tools—cartels, export subsidies, rationalization, tariff and nontariff barri-

---

* As measured by M2 plus certificates of deposit.

ers—helped protect the value of the investments. The strategy involved a good deal of risk, particularly in the early days of Japan's high-growth period, when capital was so scarce. Unless the investment ended up paying for itself through the production and sales it generated, the money created out of nothing to finance it would have translated directly into inflation.

In essence, for the strategy to work, risk had to be socialized—another way of saying that in Japan's system, ultimate financing decisions, decisions on risk and leverage, were made at the national level rather than at the level of the individual enterprise. It could be argued that the Soviet-style states were attempting something similar. In many ways Japan's economic bureaucrats, mostly trained by Marxian professors at Tokyo University, are Marx's most successful disciples, if not his most faithful. The Soviet-type states, however, fell into the great trap inherent in risk socialization, the phenomenon economists term moral hazard. The perfect illustration of moral hazard is the bureaucratic sinecure. When someone knows the job is for life, that he or she can't be fired, the temptation is to slack off. Enterprises that cannot go bankrupt, that have access to unlimited amounts of cheap capital should be bloated, uncompetitive enterprises, and they were in countries that followed the Soviet model.

Japan avoided that trap owing in part to the discipline of leverage. Management could not slack off; the intense financial pressure alone saw to that. American partisans of eighties-style wild and woolly capitalism would sing the praises of leverage in waking up sluggish companies: Take on a lot of debt with a leveraged buyout, give managers the choice between riches and extinction, and you will get sharper, more zealous performance. The history of the Japanese economic miracle suggests that in the right circumstances it can work for countries also—in combination with what to laissez-faire cheerleaders are the deadly sins of protectionism, industrial policy, centralized credit allocation, and strict financial controls.

4. Closing the Circle

Exports, Exchange Rates, and the 1970s

EXPORTS WERE BOTH cause and effect in the leveraged economy. They bought for Japan the natural resources it lacked and paid for the capital goods Japan needed in the early stages of economic recovery. Exports allowed Japanese companies to keep production capacity humming after the country had learned to make most capital goods itself and enabled household earnings to flow into savings instead of consumption without depriving Japanese firms of markets in which to sell their products. Exports smoothed out the troughs in the business cycle. In short, exports closed the circle of the leveraged economy.

As Japan's postwar recovery of the 1950s turned into the Japanese economic miracle of the 1960s, Japan's administrators grew justly confident in the tools at their disposal. They controlled capital costs; they had the means to identify and grow strategic industries; they knew when and how to pour capital into such industries. They had crushed the Socialist-dominated labor movement. The administrators crowed about the so-called three treasures of Japanese management: lifetime employment, the seniority system, and single-enterprise unions. They could pick the right products at the right times and almost guarantee exports in the quantities necessary to keep the leveraged economy going full tilt, to keep the bicycle from turning over.

Almost. For one element of export success hovered out of the administrators' control: the exchange rate, the value of the yen against the dollar. And this number was to become an obsession, a variable so important that stable monetary and fiscal policies, macroeconomic fundamentals, and even Japan's foreign relations would be risked to support it.

For many years it was not so. During the first two decades of its high-growth period, Japan's currency was fixed to the dollar at the rate of ¥360 / $1. Tense negotiations over the appropriate rate in the late 1940s had pitted a Truman administration determined to wean Japan from American subsidies against a weak Japanese government supported by a sympathetic occupation. Washington wanted the yen fixed to the dollar, proposing a rate of first ¥300 and then ¥330. Japanese administrators thought these rates too strong to enable their goods to compete in global markets and lobbied, with the support of SCAP officials on the ground in Tokyo, for a far weaker yen. General Douglas MacArthur announced a compromise on April 23, 1949: The rate was to be ¥360.[1] Many businesses grumbled—they had gotten used to subsidies that made the effective rate much weaker—but it soon became clear that ¥360 in fact conferred a significant price advantage on Japanese exports.

That the rate had been settled mattered even more than the comfortable level at which it had been pegged. Fixing it was the ticket that gave Japan its seat back at the international economic table. The rate became a given, a part of the external framework that supported the leveraged economy. Other parts of that framework would include unlimited access to the U.S. market without reciprocal demands from the Americans, U.S. security guarantees that removed the burden of heavy defense spending, and the right to wall off Japan's financial markets from foreign capital.

So when the Japanese were pressured in the late 1960s to revalue the yen, to make the currency stronger against the dollar, they reacted with fear, bewilderment, and even a sense of betrayal. After all, Japan had kept its side of the postwar bargain. It had given the American military unrestricted access to a network of bases throughout Japan and had pretended not to notice American nuclear weapons in Japanese waters. Japanese officials had, with American urging, emasculated the Japanese left.* Japan had also paid lip service to American foreign policy goals, withholding recognition of the Beijing government and suppressing misgivings over U.S. policy in Vietnam.

But the very success of Japan's methods had begun to undermine the international monetary regime. This system had one fatal flaw: It lacked a means of forcing countries running trade and current account surpluses to recycle or bring their surpluses down quickly.† During the years that the United States was the world's premier surplus country, the flaw had been largely invisible. Scared by the early postwar successes of militant communism, the United States had recycled its surpluses with heavy military spending abroad and such foreign aid programs as the Marshall Plan. But when Germany and Japan replaced the United States as the world's preeminent surplus countries, the flaw in the system became blindingly clear. Unless these countries slashed their surpluses, the system's central pillar—the fixing of all the free world's currencies to the dollar with the dollar tied to gold—could not stand.

The system was known as Bretton Woods after the New Hampshire resort where in 1944 economists, government officials, and bankers from the Allied nations had gathered to design it. Its most important architect was the great British economist John Maynard Keynes, who had foreseen the flaw and tried to correct for it. Coming from an economically prostrate Britain, he did not want the adjustment burdens of trade and current account imbalances always to fall on deficit coun-

---

* Evidence is now coming to light that the CIA was intimately involved in helping to form and fund the Liberal Democratic party—in the beginning, essentially, an anti-Communist alliance.

† While the media tend to pay more attention to the trade balance, the so-called current account is actually the more important number. It measures trade plus other "current"—as opposed to capital—flows to and from the rest of the world and includes so-called invisibles (service payments such as consulting fees), interest, and dividend receipts.

tries. He tried to build a progrowth bias into the system by imposing limits on the size of either the surplus or the deficit a member country would be allowed to run. Under Keynes's original draft, surplus countries would be required to take proactive measures to increase their growth and import demand. Thus deficit countries could reduce their imbalances by increasing exports rather than just slowing imports.

Keynes tapped the United States to be the hegemon, the great power that sits at the center of the global economy. A hegemonic power supplies a universal currency or something close to it, it provides an open market in which foreign countries can earn that currency, and its central bank functions as a kind of global central bank, acting as lender of last resort and intervening to head off global banking and currency crises.[2] Britain had played this role in the Victorian era. Now the United States would assume the mantle of hegemony.

Americans approved most of Keynes's suggestions. Convinced that the twin disasters of isolationism and protectionism must never be repeated, the United States would commit itself to free trade, giving any non-Communist country access to American markets. The United States would maintain global monetary stability by fixing its currency to gold while other countries fixed their currencies to dollars. The United States would provide a full one third of the initial capitalization of the International Monetary Fund (IMF), to which countries in deficit could go for financing. But in one of history's ironies, the American delegation to Bretton Woods overruled Keynes's attempts to build in provisions that would force surplus countries into sharing adjustment burdens for payment imbalances. The Americans believed the United States would be a surplus country as far into the future as they could imagine, and they did not want it stuck with the bill for profligate policies in deficit countries. A quarter century later, however, the United States had itself become the leading deficit country, pleading helplessly with the world's other major economies that they reduce their surpluses.

While the United States could not have remained a surplus

country forever,* the Vietnam War greatly accelerated the switch from black to red ink in America's external accounts. For years Lyndon Johnson resisted raising taxes to pay for an already unpopular war. Nor did he wish to abandon his ambitious and costly social programs, seeing them as his principal legacy. The war was thus financed by deficit spending. In textbook style, the extra spending on the war effort without any increase in the fundamental production capacity of the country resulted in an overheated economy. Demand outstripped supply. Inflation and trade deficits followed closely behind.

On coming to power in 1969, Richard Nixon diddled, unwilling either to abandon the Democratic legacy of social programs and entitlement spending or to raise taxes further to pay for the war. Fundamentally uninterested in economic policy, which he saw as a distraction from his administration's central calling in foreign affairs, he allowed the resultant strains on the dollar to provoke a crisis. As Paul Volcker remarked, "Presidents—certainly Johnson and Nixon—did not want to hear that their options were limited by the weakness of the dollar."[4] With American trade deficits and inflation accelerating, foreign countries accumulated piles of unwanted dollars, the value of which they came to suspect. As early as 1965 French President Charles de Gaulle had warned of a limit to French willingness to accept dollars that might eventually be devalued.

The full-scale crisis broke out in August 1969, when the newly elected Pompidou government in France unilaterally devalued the franc (like the United States, France was running large external deficits). Would the other major deficit countries, Britain and the United States, have to follow and lower the

---

* Robert Triffin, a Belgian-born Yale economist, first spelled out the reasons why the United States could not remain a surplus country indefinitely under Bretton Woods. According to his analysis, the dollar's role as the universal currency meant that dollars were needed by other countries to fuel expansion. The only way dollars could end up outside the United States, however, was by American payments deficits, either through the current account or through deliberate recyclings. But if Americans ran persistent deficits, faith in their ability to maintain the dollar as a store of value would inevitably weaken. This problem came to be known as the Triffin dilemma.[3]

values of their currencies? Speculation against sterling was intense, and many doubted that the United States could withstand forever demands that it devalue the dollar by raising the price of gold from the official $35 an ounce. The Germans, conscious of their ballooning surpluses and afraid for the stability of a post–Bretton Woods world, voluntarily revalued the mark ("to revalue" means making a currency more expensive; "to devalue" is the opposite) in an effort to relieve some of the strains on the system. The major powers decided on a special increase of $9.5 billion in IMF reserves as a kind of war chest to stave off speculative attacks on member currencies. European governments began private discussions of a joint float of their currencies against the dollar, while secret memorandums arguing that the dollar was overvalued against gold by some 15 percent circulated in Washington.

Where was Japan? Economic fundamentals suggested that it could easily have followed Germany in revaluing its currency. Postwar recovery had long since been completed. Japan held world supremacy in a number of critical industries, such as textiles and shipbuilding. It stood on the threshold of dominance in steel and in many consumer electronic products— e.g., television. The country's economic strategy had paid off brilliantly. Proof lay in its burgeoning trade and current account surpluses. The rest of the world may have perceived these growing surpluses as threats to the international monetary system, as signs that the par value of 360 yen to the dollar needed to be reset to reflect economic reality. But to the Japanese bureaucracy—particularly the Ministry of Finance—they seemed just temporary respites from the harrowing days of the 1950s, when the country's ability to afford essential imports had always been in suspense.

More crucially the Japanese authorities could not see their own role in provoking the crisis. In a development even Keynes could not have predicted, Japan had become the surplus country he feared, unwilling to take any action to reduce its surpluses, thus forcing all the adjustment on the deficit countries.

This threatened not just global growth but the very system itself. For Japan's surplus had its deficit counterpart in the external accounts of the United States, the hegemonic power that propped the system up. A refusal by the Japanese even to consider revaluation of the yen against the dollar struck other countries as perverse. For who had benefited more than Japan from Bretton Woods?

But foreigners failed to grasp the mental universe of the Japanese bureaucracy. Men such as Kashiwagi Yusuke, who presided over the crisis as vice minister at the MOF for international monetary affairs, believed their job was the defense of the ¥360 rate, irrespective of the consequences. As the best account in English of the 1971 currency crisis notes, "MOF official policy from beginning to end . . . opposed any change in the fixed ¥360 = $1 parity of the yen. Expressions of doubt . . . were dismissed at first as empty academic 'theorizing,' then were banned absolutely within the MOF, and serious efforts even were made to prevent public discussion of the issue within the business community."[5]

To admit that the policy had outlived its usefulness would have meant thinking about other possible policies, the reasons the 360 rate had been adopted in the first place, how the world outside Japan had changed in the preceding twenty-two years, and what was really in Japan's long-term interest. But while they may have had these thoughts privately, men like Kashiwagi and his successor, Hosomi Takashi, were not paid to think these sorts of things. Their nominal political superiors—Finance Minister Mizuta Mikio and Prime Minister Sato Eisaku—were not expected to intervene and restrain the excessive zealotry of the MOF and its international monetary bureau. They were simply to act as public spokesmen with foreigners and the Japanese public for policies formulated by the "competent" officials.

Commentators such as Karel van Wolferen and Robert Angel have identified this lack of political input as the core of the problem faced by the Japanese bureaucracy in coping with the unexpected and the unpredictable.[6] Never having to explain or account for its actions, the MOF did not begin to grasp the depth of American and European antagonism to Japan's single-minded defense of the ¥360 rate.

The worst U.S.-Japan trade dispute since the 1930s amplified the currency crisis. In fulfillment of a campaign promise Richard Nixon had sought restraints on Japanese textile exports from Prime Minister Sato Eisaku. Nixon and Henry Kissinger, the president's assistant for national security affairs, believed they had cut a deal when the administration agreed to hand Okinawa back to Japan. They thought they were going to get the restraints.[7] Like administrations before and since, however, Nixon discovered that Japanese prime ministers lack the power to deliver on their commitments. With no progress on textiles, with Japan's dogged refusal even to consider a revaluation of the yen, Nixon decided to deliver, in the now-famous Japanese-English term, a *shokku* (shock).

Nixon's speech of August 15, 1971 (the anniversary of Japan's World War II surrender) was aimed squarely at that country. He announced an across-the-board 10 percent surcharge on all imports, a ninety-day wage and price freeze, and a closing of the gold window where the U.S. government was supposed to exchange gold for dollars whenever requested by foreign central banks. Nixon's underlying message: The United States would no longer support Bretton Woods in its current form; he blamed Japan for the system's collapse.

But the MOF chose not to hear what Nixon had said. It continued to live in a fantasy world, imagining its primary duty to be the defense of the 360 rate. For eleven days after Nixon's speech the Japanese authorities kept the Tokyo foreign exchange market open. America's other major trading partners, by contrast, closed their markets for a week and floated their currencies on reopening. But the ostrichlike Japanese accumulated the then-enormous sum of $4 billion, boosting Japan's international reserves by a full third, in order to keep the yen from strengthening.[8] These dollars were paid for at the old rate of 360 yen to the dollar when it was obvious to all that any day dollars would fetch less.* On August 27 the effort was abandoned in response to growing opposition from a business community fearful of the Nixon import surcharge and from the rest of the bureaucracy concerned over the burgeoning costs of suppressing the yen.

In the ensuing weeks the yen belatedly joined other major currencies in floating against the dollar. The currency may technically have been floating, its value from day to day theoretically established in the foreign exchange markets rather than fixed at a predetermined rate by the central bank, but in fact, Japanese financial authorities strove mightily to keep the yen down. And their power was immense. Aside from selling yen for dollars themselves in the market—the sort of tactic used by financial authorities in many countries when they wish to influence currency movements—the informal sway the MOF and the Bank of Japan enjoyed over the financial system meant that no Japanese bank could defy the authorities' wishes. Foreign bankers in Tokyo, who might ignore the bureaucrats' nods, grunts, and pregnant pauses, were subjected to narrow trading limits and meticulous daily inspections to ensure they did not circumvent MOF dictates. To prevent speculation, the ministry effectively banned all foreign exchange transactions except for those directly linked to trade in physical goods.

The financial authorities took these sorts of extreme measures because they believed that a system of fixed rates would be reestablished, albeit at slightly different levels. The idea of a permanent system of floating rates was so horrifying to them it scarcely entered their calculations. Instead they were jockeying to establish Japan's base position for the inevitable negotiations with the Americans and Europeans from as cheap a yen rate as possible.

The measures fooled nobody. While temporarily successful

---

*Although ministry officials denied it, many suspected one reason the MOF kept the market deliberately open at the old rate was to give Japanese banks time to unload onto the Bank of Japan and thus the Japanese taxpayer the billions of dollars they had accumulated at 360.

in suppressing the yen, the MOF's tactics proved immensely costly for Japan. They were costly in immediate financial terms, costly in the medium-term inflationary pressures released into the Japanese economy from the accumulation of so much unneeded foreign reserves, and most costly in the suspicion and fear of Japan and its motives sown among the American and European elites. In the parlance of the time, the Japanese authorities ran a dirty float—the practice of secret interventions by financial authorities to establish a predetermined level for a currency.

Dominating the developments that fall was Nixon's treasury secretary, former Texas Governor and Lyndon Johnson protégé, John Connally. Connally had been on the job only a few months and was something of a neophyte to the world of finance, but as his undersecretary Paul Volcker later wrote:

I still remember the sense of relief I had in my first substantive briefing. He quickly brushed aside my recital of where we stood on . . . [various] arcane details. I confessed that I was greatly concerned that sooner or later we would have to seek a substantial change in exchange rates, that the adjustment would be strongly resisted, and that there could be large political as well as economic ramifications. He plainly didn't need any instruction from me on those points. He had an instinctive grasp of what motivated men and governments and knew we would be in for tough negotiations.[9]

Connally's tactics were skillful: Bluster and then wait. The import surcharge and the closing of the gold window put pressure on both the Europeans and the Japanese. The reputation of the treasury secretary had preceded him when he arrived in Japan for a visit in early November, earning him the nickname Typhoon in the Japanese press. But Connally then switched poses on his arrival in Japan, playing the man of sweet reason. He had come, in his words, "as a gentle spring breeze."

Connally meant to convince Japanese officialdom that a substantial revaluation was inevitable. In this ploy he had help. Hoping to find allies in standing up to the United States, the Japanese had sent feelers out to the Europeans and Canadians. These feelers went nowhere. Whatever disputes other countries had with the Americans—and they were loud and nasty, particularly in the case of the French—the Japanese got little sympathy.

The fall's maneuvering culminated in a two-day conference at the Smithsonian Institution in Washington on December 17–18. The Japanese finance minister, Mizuta Mikio, had been given full negotiating authority by the Sato cabinet,[10] and he used it well. Connally had started off asking for 24 percent revaluation of the yen; the final number was 16.88 percent or a new yen / dollar rate of ¥308 / $1. Twenty years later his young interpreter at the conference, Gyohten Toyoo, who was to play a starring role himself in the currency crises of the 1980s, revealed that Mizuta actually had the authority to go as high as 20 percent. According to Gyohten's account, in the final one-on-one with Connally, Mizuta had insisted that the number must be below 17 percent.

We were in a very small room in the Smithsonian that seemed to be used for keeping the Institution's specimens; funny things were pickled in all manner of bottles and jars that were lined up on the shelves. Ignoring the background, Connally insisted that Japan revalue by 18.9 percent. Impossible, said Mizuta. He absolutely had to settle below 17 percent. Connally asked why.

Mizuta replied: "Because 17 percent is a very, very ominous number for Japan. Back in 1930 when Japan returned to the gold standard, the yen appreciated, and the magnitude was 17 percent. The economy was thrown into depression. The finance minister who decided upon this return to the gold standard was assassinated."[11]

The final figure did thus represent something of a victory for the negotiating skills of Mizuta and the MOF team. But it also established a dangerous pattern for the way in which Japanese bureaucrats handled major policy changes. After telling the Japanese public for years that the 360 rate was critical to the health of its economy, the bureaucrats had to justify their sudden policy switch by implying it was the result of angry and irrational foreigners punishing Japan for its success.

In addition to the yen revaluation, the Smithsonian conference agreed on a devaluation of the dollar against gold to $38 an ounce. The deutsche mark was revalued by 13.6 percent, and other European currencies by lesser amounts. The United States ended the import surcharge but did not reopen the gold window, leading wits to note that $38 was the new price at which the United States would not sell gold. President Nixon proclaimed the Smithsonian Accord "the greatest monetary agreement in the history of the world."[12]

The greatest monetary agreement in the history of the world began to crumble right away. Before it was six months old, the British, French, and Belgians had been forced to exit the system and float their currencies. In January 1973, when the Italians and the Swiss also abandoned the Smithsonian peg for the lira and the Swiss franc against the dollar, it was clear that the system could not survive.

The damage to Japan's reputation from the earlier crisis was fully evident during the buildup to the second and final floating of the yen. In the acrimonious secret negotiations of February 1973 that led to the creation of today's floating rate system, U.S. and European negotiators tried to forestall hidden interventions by forcing Japan formally to revalue the yen before floating it. The Japanese refused to revalue the yen but had to pledge publicly that they would not engage in a dirty float.[13]

The pledge was kept for two weeks. With the suspicious eyes of other central banks and finance ministries on Japan, the second yen float of late February 1973 was clean, and the yen promptly rose to ¥265 / $1. As is often the case when potential major policy shifts in Japan begin to assume an aura of inevitability, the business community and the wider public had been softened up for the float by a series of articles in major publications such as the *Nihon Keizai Shimbun* and the prestigious business-oriented weekly *Tōyō Keizai*. Gloomy speculation on the "severe blow to the economy"[14] in the latter publication was replaced by ruminations on the positive features of opting "voluntarily for a small revaluation" that would help "subdue Japan's economy."[15] Bank of Japan officials trumpeted the BOJ's policy of "letting the market determine the yen's rate."[16]

But bureaucratic obsession with controlling the exchange rate had not ended, irrespective of public pronouncements or press reports. Once the yen stabilized in the markets at 265, Japanese authorities resumed their interventions to ensure that the yen traded in a very narrow range around that level. While the rest of the industrialized world had more or less moved to a system of floating rates, the Japanese reinstituted a fixed-rate policy in all but name. If the currency rose above 263 or fell below 267, Bank of Japan intervention automatically occurred, just as 357 and 363 had been the parameters in the old days. Other countries tolerated Japan's dogged maintenance of the fixed-rate system because the yen was strong enough to reduce Japan's surpluses. The country's balance of payments indeed swung sharply into the red, with current account deficits during the second and third quarters of 1973 totaling $3.6 billion.

In a remarkable exercise through the next six months from March to September 1973, Japanese monetary authorities persisted in maintaining an *overvalued* currency—that is to say, intervening to keep the yen more, not less, expensive than it otherwise would have been. To a large extent they did so by selling for 265 yen many of the dollars bought eighteen months earlier at 360, at a horrendous cost to the Japanese taxpayer of 95 yen per dollar. The bureaucrats at the Finance Ministry and the Bank of Japan lost the battle to keep the yen fixed at 360 to the dollar. But they had not conceded their right to control the value of the currency, even if this meant a reversal of their historical policy of suppressing the value of the yen.

The stubborn and costly machinations in the foreign exchange markets formed part of a wider struggle that year against the most serious postwar challenge to Japanese bureaucratic power, the political ascendency of Prime Minister Tanaka Kakuei. A self-made politician from the *ura-Nihon* (backwater Japan) of Niigata Prefecture, Tanaka came to politics with none of the upper-class family background, the University of Tokyo education, or the network of elite connections that give most Japanese politicians a head start. He built from scratch a politi-

cal machine that dwarfed the fiefdoms of American counterparts such as Chicago Mayor Richard J. Daley, whom Tanaka in
many ways resembled. His mastery of the minutiae of Japanese
politics, his powerful electoral base, the vast network of *jinmyaku* (personal connections), his near-complete control of the
purse strings of campaign financing, and his lack of any obligation to the mandarins of the MOF or MITI enabled him to
bend the bureaucracy to his will in a manner not seen before or
since. Thanks to his energy, brilliance, and growing power base,
he captured a series of increasingly important appointments—
postal minister, finance minister, MITI minister—until in 1972
in the wake of the "Nixon shocks" (the secret trip to China as
well as the import surcharge), he took over as prime minister
from a shaken Sato Eisaku.

Under the rubric of "remodeling the Japanese archipelago,"
Tanaka set about gunning the engines of economic growth with
large-scale deficit financing and pork barrel spending. Grandiose schemes to build bullet train lines throughout Japan were
launched; never before in history did so much pork rain on so
few. Great tunnels were blasted through mountains so that
children in hamlets could get to school a few minutes more
quickly; anyone fortunate enough to marry or die in Tanaka's
district was the recipient of lavish wedding or funeral gifts.
Tanaka forced a cowed MOF into loose monetary policies and
postoccupation Japan's first substantial government deficits. Already high growth reached towering levels in 1972 and 1973;
the lax monetary policies swelled the large pools of liquidity
still existing from the vain attempts back in 1971 to forestall
the yen's revaluation.

Finance Ministry bureaucrats found a strong yen useful in
containing the inflationary effects of Tanaka's schemes. But the
tools they used to keep it strong were suddenly needed for far
more urgent reasons, for beginning in October 1973, the major
Arab oil-exporting countries suspended oil shipments for six
weeks and then quadrupled oil prices. Japan was absolutely
dependent on imported petroleum, its domestic energy sources

hardly worth mentioning. This oil shock caught by surprise a country dangerously overheated by excess liquidity and Tanaka's runaway fiscal policies. Conventional wisdom, shared to a large extent in Japan and abroad, was that the country was finished. The clearest signal of this was a full-scale run on the yen.

Runs on currencies happen when market players believe that for whatever reason governments cannot sustain currencies at particular values. Speculators attempt to sell as much of a currency as they can because they think the price will fall and later they can buy back the currency, pocketing a profit. Speculators win these sorts of battles when governments give up trying to defend particular rates and lower the prices of the currencies. Governments win when they can meet all demands without having to lower the price and the speculators retire from the field, licking their wounds, convinced that no near-term chance exists for a cheaper currency.

Two years earlier the authorities would have been happy to see the yen taken back beyond 300 to the dollar. But late in 1973 Japan suddenly faced crippling oil import bills, and the authorities were desperate to keep the yen from weakening. Nonetheless the speculators at first carried the day.[17] On October 29, 30, and 31 anyone could walk into a bank in Tokyo and buy a dollar for 266 yen, which the bank could then reexchange at the Bank of Japan. But on November 1, after spending $450 million of Japan's foreign exchange reserves on those three days to support the yen, the authorities lowered the intervention point to 270. That is to say, the authorities went from selling a dollar to any buyer in return for 266 yen to selling a dollar for 270. The price of a dollar had gone up; the yen had weakened, the speculators had won the first round. The market still viewed the yen as "too high," however, and speculators smelled further profits. Between November 2 and 12 the Bank of Japan had to raise the price of the dollar to 275. On November 13, authorities hoping to put an end to the run raised the dollar price by 5 yen to 280. For seven harrowing weeks the government tried to support the yen at 280, spending more than $4 billion in the effort. But the market believed the yen had farther to fall.

When six Persian Gulf countries announced a more than doubling of the price of their export crude on December 22, the selling pressure on the yen grew even more intense, forcing the government to spend hundreds of millions from a rapidly dwindling pile of dollars to support an increasingly unrealistic rate. Finally, on January 7, 1974, the Bank of Japan reset the intervention point to 300, and it was determined to make it stick. In a mirror image of the tactics used in the fall of 1971 to keep the yen from becoming too expensive, the authorities brought out the whole panoply of informal control instruments, this time to keep the yen from cheapening. Suddenly any Japanese bank seen buying large quantities of dollars and thus speculating in the market was forced on the spot to repay all overloans from the Bank of Japan. The amounts of dollars Japanese residents could hold were restricted, and on January 22 the Ministry of Finance and the Bank of Japan summoned executives of Japan's major financial institutions and demanded they suspend all "speculative" dollar selling to customers. Just to ensure that institutions got the message, inspectors from the ministry and the BOJ were put on standby to conduct spot investigations of anyone seen to be uncooperative.

The arm-twisting worked. The 300 rate held, and by early February 1974 speculative dollar buying / yen selling had all but ceased. Yet the conviction that Japan was in trouble was hardly limited to players in the Tokyo foreign exchange market. Indeed, the statistics emerging at the end of 1973 form a numerical portrait of an economy in crisis. Inflation was rising at more than 20 percent, with the few interest rates set by market forces (e.g., the *gensaki,* or forward bond repurchase rate) rather than by administrative fiat climbing nearly that high. The current account plummeted deeply into the red, and between September 1973 and January 1974 the country lost more than a quarter of its accumulated foreign reserves, reserves needed to pay for oil. Industrial production fell by more than a fifth as Japan entered its first real postwar recession.

The pessimism over Japan's future was most visible in the international banking arena, where Japanese banks found themselves paying a full two percentage point premium for funds in the London market. This premium was a very significant indicator, perhaps the most important, of what the world thought of Japan's future in the wake of the oil shock. London is the preeminent international financial marketplace, a market where, unlike New York or Tokyo, transactions among nondomestic parties form the majority of business. Banks there borrow and lend to one another at rates that track so closely that to all intents and purposes they are single rates. The rate is known as LIBOR, or London Interbank Offered Rate, the most important rate in cross-border transactions. If a bank has to pay above LIBOR, even by a few basis points, or hundredths of a percent, it indicates concern by the financial community about the creditworthiness of the bank. The Ministry of Finance viewed this "Japan rate" as a major humiliation; the overriding goal of MOF guidance of the international activities of Japanese banks during the mid to late seventies was to wipe it out and ensure it was never reimposed.

Meanwhile, back home, a Japanese public was hoarding such items as toilet paper in anticipation of a return of wartime scarcity. The government went so far as to arrange a secret billion-dollar loan from Saudi Arabia in the summer of 1974, when it appeared that Japanese banks might be frozen out of international markets altogether.[18] But contrary to all expectations—from panicked housewives and frightened bureaucrats, from wary creditors and quick-kill–seeking speculators—Japan survived the oil crisis relatively unscathed and recovered more quickly and more strongly than any other industrialized country. Inflation in 1975 fell in less than one year from over 20 percent to an astoundingly low 3 percent. By the latter half of

1975 GNP growth was up again and Japan's current account had returned to equilibrium. In 1976 it moved into the black, setting the stage for the record surpluses of 1977 and 1978. Meanwhile in the United States inflation was not tamed until 1982. In the years from 1975 to 1978, while Japan accumulated an overall balance of payments surplus of more than $21 billion, the U.S. deficit totaled $85 billion. And two incumbent presidents lost elections because the "misery index" (inflation plus unemployment) was too high.

In the view of Japan's administrators, bureaucratic control mechanisms had made the quick recovery possible. Chalmers Johnson noted that the oil shock "once again reminded the Japanese people that they needed their official bureaucracy."[19] There were rumors of actual cheering at MITI on the news of the oil embargo because of the restoration of bureaucratic control it implied.

Ruthless monetary controls stamped out inflation, but what pulled Japan out of recession was exports. In the face of sluggish global recovery from the worst recession since the 1930s, Japan in 1976 increased its exports of manufactured goods by more than 20 percent, almost double the average for the industrialized world. Nearly one quarter of the *total* increase in global manufactured exports came that year from Japan. Its government's reckoned that exports contributed some *60 percent* of GNP growth in the critical recovery period of fourth-quarter 1975 and first-quarter 1976.[20]

While Japan's administrators may have confirmed their faith in bureaucratic control mechanisms and the importance of exports and exchange rates, the rest of the world suspected that Japan's economic success arose at the expense of jobs and industries in other countries. Japan's rapid recovery excited bewildered alarm abroad. The policy elite in Washington knew little of Japan's economic methods. The attention-getting economics debates of the mid-1970s saw the ascending monetarists, led by Milton Friedman, attacking the defensive neo-Keynesians, who retreated into ever-higher levels of abstraction through quantification—e.g., efforts by people like Lawrence Klein at the University of Pennsylvania to simulate the entire economy in vast computerized models, thus supposedly enabling governments to fine-tune their monetary and fiscal policies. Both monetarists and neo-Keynesians were attempting to explain the puzzling new phenomenon of stagflation—simultaneous high unemployment and high inflation rates. They may have differed sharply over policy responses. Monetarists wanted predictable and steady slow growth in the money supply while the neo-Keynesians promoted activist fine-tuning. But both schools assumed that macro-level policy levers were the ones that mattered. Whatever their ideological stripe, orthodox economists took it for granted that the behavior of individuals and firms was a profit- (or utility-) maximizing given. When they thought about Japan's post-1974 recovery, they thus focused on macroeconomic instruments of exchange rate and demand management. They had scarcely any awareness of compensation practices, financing methods such as overloan, company unions, interlocking corporate ownership, MITI's blueprints for Japan's industrial structure—the so-called visions, or the subordination of political and economic life in Japan to constant increases in production capacity. Part of it was simple ignorance; part, a kind of willful denial. Governments were supposedly no good at this sort of microeconomic structural intervention, so Japan must not be doing it.

The neo-Keynesians temporarily triumphed over the monetarists with the victory of Jimmy Carter in the 1976 election. The new administration wasted little time in taking direct aim at Japan under the rubric of locomotive theorizing, the supposed need in the post–oil shock world for economically powerful countries to act as locomotives. The locomotives by their own fast growth would create demand for the products of oil-poor developing countries, enabling them to grow out of recession and pay their oil import bills. The United States could no longer act alone as the global locomotive, particularly because the other two strongest powers, Germany and Japan, were, by growing slowly and running external surpluses, acting as further drags on the global economy.

The locomotive theorists wanted two things out of Japan: an end to micromanagement of the exchange rate—dirty floating—and measures to stimulate the domestic economy. Carter administration officials strong-armed the Japanese in 1977 into publicly pledging a domestic growth target of 6.7 percent. Similar demands, at least with respect to domestic growth, were made of the Germans. Thus the two countries were to join the United States at the front of the global economic train, pulling it out of the valley of the OPEC-caused recession.

But the Germans would have none of it. Led by their premier, Helmut Schmidt, they retorted that American failure to lift price controls on energy—thereby encouraging wasteful consumption—was at least as big a problem for the world as was ostensibly slow growth in Germany. Schmidt went so far as to tell American economists urging German stimulus to "please shut their mouths."[21] Forcing countries to grow at rates beyond those that their economies could reasonably sustain simply invited inflation.

Why did the Japanese cave into American pressure while the Germans stood up to it? Germany resembles Japan in a number of obvious ways that include modern economic history and relationship vis-à-vis the United States. But the German elite had engaged in deep soul-searching on the question of what had led to the disaster of the 1930s. One answer lay with the hyperinflation of the 1920s, which had so undermined social stability that extremists had found fertile ground in which to sow their vile ideas. German leaders, accountable to themselves and to their electorate for policy decisions, able to articulate why certain policies were superior to others, could resist American pressure with passionately held, logically convincing arguments.

By contrast, the Japanese administrative elite thought, in the words of one Japanese analyst, they had been pulled into the war by a sort of "natural disaster, a convulsion of nature, eclipsing all human powers,"[22] and they were convinced Japan had lost, in the words of another, because of inadequate production capacity.[23] The unlimited expansion of production capacity that drives Japan's political economy had thus become a sort of given, engraved in the nation's institutional memory by the late-nineteenth-century race to catch up with the West and reinforced by the war and the devastation that followed. It was much less a product of conscious analysis and choice than the deliberate policies that lay behind the *Wirtschaftswunder*.* But then "political aims need not be fully conscious to be realized."[24]

They do, however, have to be conscious to be defended with arguments that others can accept or at least understand. The Japanese had no arguments with which to stand up to American pressure. They promised the 6.7 percent growth target, even upping it to 7 percent in order to have an *omiyage* (souvenir) to give U.S. Trade Representative Robert Strauss when he visited Japan in January 1978.† And in March the Japanese authorities finally gave up dirty floating and allowed the yen to seek its own level. The currency peaked in October, when it took only 176 yen to buy a dollar. A mere twenty-one months earlier it had cost 300.

The Carter administration expected Japan's growth priming and a clean yen float to reduce the bilateral trade deficit, Japan's overall current account surplus, and the U.S. trade deficit. But instead of an improvement in the trade numbers, the Carter people found they had a first-order currency crisis on their hands that helped drive them from office after one term.

---

*Both the German and the Japanese postwar recoveries had started only after the inflation of the immediate postwar years had been ruthlessly stamped out. Ludwig Erhard, a German publicly defying the Allied occupation, had put Germany through the anti-inflationary wringer; significantly, in Japan's case the administrators gave the impression the policies had been forced on them by the Detroit banker Joseph Dodge, sent from Washington.

†Strauss's comments at his Tokyo press conference make amusing reading sixteen years and innumerable trade crises later. "We have really redefined the economic relations between our two great nations," he remarked.[25]

Americans, alas, believed what their textbooks told them: If GNP grew faster in Japan, consumer demand would also rise. Greater consumer demand should mean higher demand for imports, while a rising currency would make Japan's exports more expensive in global markets. But Keynesian pump priming in Japan did not lead to an upsurge in domestic demand; it simply resulted in higher levels of capital formation. Imports in Japan had never been allowed to compete on price. Instead the soaring yen lowered energy costs (in yen terms) to Japanese industry back to where they had been before the oil shock. And competing for market share rather than for profits, Japanese corporations were loath to raise export prices. Rather, they launched waves of cost cutting and rationalization.

By talking down the dollar, Carter administration officials found they had created the decade's third full-scale currency crisis. After badgering the Japanese to abandon dirty floating, they had to go back to Japan in November 1978 and ask for its resumption in the form of help in mounting, together with Germany and Switzerland, a four-country rescue of the dollar. Soaring inflation, the product of a loose monetary policy and the trashing of the dollar in the foreign exchange markets, helped destroy the Carter presidency.

Events in the Middle East again made moot the decade's second experiment with *endaka* (high yen). The dollar rescue package was scarcely a month old when the shah of Iran fell from power and oil prices tripled. Having learned what to do the first time around, Japan's administrators easily handled the crisis. Both current account surpluses and international reserves fell, but without the panicked reactions of 1974. The Bank of Japan moved quickly to tighten money; MITI busily set about organizing energy conservation measures with the enthusiastic support of industry. Meanwhile monetary authorities viewed foreign exchange markets with equanimity as the yen slid back from its high in the 170s in the fall of 1978 to some 240 by the end of 1979.

It was a sharp contrast with the bewilderment and fear of

ten years earlier. Japan's administrators had begun the decade of the 1970s frightened for their future. The crumbling of Bretton Woods had threatened to destroy what they regarded as one of the key pillars of the leveraged economy, a stable, undervalued yen. But Japan survived, prospered, and triumphed over not just currency instability but a whole series of shocks—inflation, commodity shortages, recession—which devastated the morale and economies of such countries as the United States, Britain, and France that Japan had theretofore looked to as models and teachers. The shocks led to profound political upheaval in those countries, but they confirmed to Japan's administrators the rightness of their course. A note of pride, even boastfulness, began to creep into Japan's public profile. The Japanese version of Harvard Professor Ezra Vogel's *Japan as Number One* became the best selling nonfiction translation ever in Japan. Vogel had subtitled it *Lessons for America* and had written it as a wake-up call to Americans, but it was in self-congratulatory Japan that the book had its widest audience.

Much of the self-congratulation was well deserved. It is difficult not to admire the way Japan came storming out of the OPEC-induced recession of 1974 or the diligence and foresight of its managers and workers as they pulled ahead of Westerners in most basic industries. But the waves of change from the outside world that crashed over Japan in the 1970s and the growing competence with which these challenges were met served to obscure some fundamental shifts in the Japanese economy.

The most important of these was probably deleveraging—the weaning of industrial Japan from its dependence on debt financing. Household savings patterns had remained unchanged right through the seventies. But Japan's economy was no longer growing so fast. The nation was never again to see the 10 percent plus growth rates of the late 1960s, despite the robust recovery from the 1974–75 recession. With growth slowing while savings and indirect taxes continued as high as ever, the Japanese economy began to experience a surplus of capital. In other words, it began deleveraging.

On a macroeconomic level, Japan's burgeoning current account surplus provided the strongest evidence of this. While a country saving "too little"—e.g., the United States in the past two decades—runs a current account deficit, a country saving "too much" runs a current account surplus. Japan has run a surplus every single year since 1976 with the sole exceptions of 1979 and 1980, when the effects of the second oil shock temporarily drove its current account back into the red.

At the micro level of the individual corporation, the clearest sign of deleveraging lay in the buildup of cash reserves with Japanese companies.* The use of excess cash had never been a problem before; collective memory thus offered little guidance. Companies in most countries would use excess cash to pay down debt, but Japanese firms that had been dependent on their banks for decades were not about to terminate relationships. Banks pressured them into continuing their borrowing, even when they had no direct use for the money.

An American company that finds itself with a lot of excess cash on hand has a number of alternatives. It can raise everybody's pay, from multimillion-dollar packages in the executive suite to handsome deals for the work force hammered out with unions like the United Auto Workers. Management can boost dividends, pleasing shareholders, raising the company's share price and making raiders think twice about going after the firm, or for extra "antiraid" insurance, a company can buy back its own stock. Also, a management with predictable returns in a staid industry can liven things up by launching its own raids on others. About the only thing an American company with a lot of cash on hand will not do is let it sit there, where it does nothing but attract take-over artists.

Japan in 1981 had few of the vast array of instruments

---

* In financial terms, cash flow from depreciation accounted for the buildup of cash reserves.[26]

available to American corporate treasurers for the management of surplus cash. There was no commercial paper market, no free market in short-term government securities, and only a very stunted repo market (the so-called *gensaki* market). But beyond the relative dearth of cash management techniques, however, lay unwritten rules of Japanese corporate life that made such things as raising salaries or launching acquisitions difficult or impossible. Given the strength of the informal agreements on compensation practices and the weight of such institutions as the Nikkeiren (Employers' Association) in backing them up, no Japanese company or industry could contemplate paying its people wages that were far out of line with the national average. There were to be no twenty-eight-year-old investment bankers or software engineers earning several hundred thousand dollars a year.

Nor would any major Japanese company break ranks and start paying dividend rates three and four times the average, not to mention conduct stock buybacks. Aside from the irrationality of the practice in an economy where stock ownership's most important role is the cementing of long-term business relationships, no company could afford to antagonize its all-important network by doing something so clearly out of the mainstream as to pay high dividend rates. And if dramatically higher dividends and compensation were out of the question, how much more so would be American-style high-stake, big-ticket acquisitions. In Japan acquisitions happened to companies in distressed industries at the behest of the bureaucracy. Greenmail and hostile raids were strictly the province of gangsters and con artists. The management of a self-respecting Japanese firm in a successful industry would no more launch a hostile raid on another establishment firm than it would conduct its annual shareholders' meeting in the nude.

But something had to be done with the cash. Like the relentlessly climbing yen, the growing piles might have served as a signal that the system described in this and the previous three chapters had outlived its usefulness. Japan had pulled ahead of most other countries by any measure of brute economic power one cared to use. It would become dangerous to rely so heavily on exports to close the circle: politically dangerous because other governments would be forced by their voters to resist the loss of jobs and industries at the hands of the Japanese; economically dangerous because as Japan's share of the global economy increased, the rest of the world would become progressively less able to pay for Japanese exports, particularly so since foreigners usually wanted to buy those exports with a means of payment that Japan's political economy had been designed to reject from outside: manufactured products.

The cash buildup implied that a financial system designed to scrounge for each spare yen had become out-of-date. More money needed to be spent improving the livelihood of Japan's people and less on investments of dubious merit. Japan's corporate governance needed an overhaul so its managers would think in terms of profitability, not just sheer size. The banks and insurance companies needed to change a culture that idolized the buildup of deposits and policies. Certainly Japanese households, after a generation of hard work, deserved to keep more of what they earned.

But if banks began to extend credit on the basis of a demonstrated capacity to generate profits, they would discover that sometimes even the biggest and best-connected of companies could not pass muster. Some such companies, unable to obtain credit, might then fail, or banks rash enough to finance them would themselves be forced to close their doors. Improving living standards would require substituting market forces for bureaucratically rigged prices in broad areas of Japanese life. Allowing large gaps in compensation to open up between different industries could foster a genuine labor market and the potential instability of a politically awakened middle class, heretofore stymied by the salaryman culture of the large corporations. Companies that began to pay big dividends or use their cash hoards to make acquisitions would threaten the status quo of Japanese business that saw firms acting as checks on each other. The Tokyo Stock Exchange could become a genuine market in corporate control, undermining the *keiretsu* system.

Such potential developments seemed nightmarish to Japan's administrators in the economic bureaucracies, large companies, and business federations. For their legitimacy was based on a track record of sustaining employment and institutional survival in the areas of Japanese life under their purview. A Ministry of Finance that let banks fail, a MITI that permitted large manufacturing firms to go under taking thousands of "lifetime" jobs with them, an Agriculture Ministry unable to sustain farmers' livelihood with high prices could find their own mandates questioned and undermined.

But it turned out the administrators didn't have to do anything yet—about either the climbing yen or the growing cash hoard. The Reagan Revolution, a development neither expected nor understood in Japan, would reverse for a while the relentless rise of the yen and would provide a safe channel for Japan's excess cash that need not undermine the existing hierarchy and indeed would help perpetuate it. The threat of change could be postponed for another decade. Postponing a reckoning, however, made it easier for Japan's administrators to avoid considering the possibility that the methods they had used so brilliantly might one day no longer work.

I I

Lending

5. Weak Claims

Japanese Finance and the American Deficit

I am 56 years old. If I were a Japanese nearing retirement, and enjoyed a life expectancy which in that longevitous country, I am told, would be about 85, I would not look with equanimity on my generation's converting, year after year, $50 billion of current output into financial claims on a foreign nation on which my government seems to exert relatively little influence. I would rather see some of that output sold at home in a way that enabled me to accumulate financial claims on my neighbors. Our social bond and my vote will enable me to collect these claims even in times of stress. Americans are and show every sign of remaining, in contrast with Japan, a short-term oriented, mercurial, polyglot, multiethnic, mobile, and heavily armed people. Claims on such a people need to be accumulated and exercised with care.

ALBERT M. WOJNILOWER [1]

O N DECEMBER 18, 1980, David Stockman flew to New York for a day on Wall Street. Stockman had not yet started his new job, but he was already famous. Two weeks earlier he had been plucked from the relative obscurity of junior congressman from Michigan and nominated to be Ronald Reagan's director of the Office of Management of the Budget (OMB), point man of the Reagan Revolution.

On the same day Saito Satoru of Sumitomo Life Insurance

went to his forty-first-floor office in Tokyo's Sumitomo San-kaku Biru (Sumitomo Triangle Building). Like David Stock-man, Mr. Saito would soon have a new job. His new responsibilities would make him a figure of some interest to Wall Street's Tokyo representatives; I was one of the foreign bankers who came to know and enjoy working with him. Sumi-tomo planned to set up a new international investment depart-ment to manage its growing cash pile, and Mr. Saito was to be in the thick of it. Thus, on a typical day like December 18, 1980, investment bankers were likely to give Mr. Saito a call or perhaps drop by to offer their services. These men worked for many of the same firms David Stockman visited later that day in New York.

Stockman had a problem. Wall Street didn't believe what it was hearing out of the Reagan transition team. Bankers and brokers may have voted Republican. They may have read the glowing notices for the coming revolution in the *Wall Street Journal*. But the numbers they were seeing didn't add up. Cut taxes, raise defense spending, and cure the deficit all at once? While the Fed was putting the U.S. economy through a defla-tionary wringer? They were shaking their heads in utter disbe-lief. And their disbelief was reflected in the financial markets, described by Stockman as "in a total rout."[2] Interest rates were scraping all-time highs with the benchmark prime rate—the rates banks charge their best corporate customers—at an eye-popping 21.5 percent.

For David Stockman and the rest of the Reagan Revolution general staff, this was *the* problem. As long as the markets con-tinued to believe deficits were going up rather than down, long-term interest rates would stay high. After all, if a greedy federal government demanded more and more of a dwindling savings pool, interest rates would inevitably go up, reflecting this higher demand. Higher interest payments would swell the deficit yet further and burden the economy. Tax revenues would fall, leading to yet higher deficits, yet higher interest rates, and so forth in a classic vicious cycle.

Mr. Saito's problem was of a happier kind: how to invest an ever-increasing flood of cash. The Japanese economy was only just emerging from the setback of the second oil shock. Growth by historical standards was sluggish, and few expected that Japan would ever again attain the torrid double-digit growth rates of the late 1960s and early 1970s. As a result, Japanese companies were not investing so heavily. So they weren't borrowing as much. But savings rates stayed very high. There had been little change in the financial facts of life for Japanese households. Getting the kids through school, owning a home, financing retirement still took the most careful discipline and planning.

Mr. Saito and his colleagues at Sumitomo Life couldn't allow other life companies or the banks to muscle them aside in the struggle for Japan's savings pool. If they let up competing for policyholders on the ground that investment opportunities were just too few, Sumitomo's cherished status as Japan's third-largest life insurance company would be at risk. So the company's salesgirls continued to knock on doors and visit offices, soliciting clients. Other Sumitomo group companies automatically steered their employees toward Sumitomo Life for insurance needs, and advertising campaigns continued unabated. But in the meantime what were the overworked investment officers like Mr. Saito to do? Where were the profitable investment opportunities that would pay off policyholders?

Back on Wall Street, David Stockman was having a rough day. As he trekked from Bear Stearns to Morgan Stanley, Salomon Brothers, and other leading firms, he repeated the same message: The tax cuts were going to be paid for—"earned," in the words he used in these meetings, "through the sweat of the politicians."[3] The Reagan Revolution was different. No longer would the federal budget be a Christmas tree laden with ornaments for every special interest group able to buy a proper K Street lobbyist. Sure, welfare spending would be cut, and the Great Society rolled back. But also to disappear were farm support programs that went to enrich wealthy growers, Social Security benefits for teenagers in college, energy price controls, subsidized credits to airlines, Export-Import Bank funding, the synfuels plant program, and the innumerable other subsidies, pork barrel boondoggles, and middle-class entitlements that larded the federal budget. "We are going to attack weak claims, not weak clients," Stockman had told *Washington Post* editor William Greider.

The Street was not convinced. Gurus like Henry Kaufman of Salomon Brothers, dubbed Dr. Doom for his gloomy forecasts of the U.S. economy, looked askance at the wilder predictions of the supply-side crowd—in particular, the idea that tax cuts were going to pay for themselves in higher revenues. They were glad to hear that Reagan's nominee for OMB director intended to take a machete to much of the budget. But they suspected the unchecked jungle growth of entitlements, programs, pork barrels, and bureaucracy would prove too much for one young budget director, irrespective of how bright he was, how zealously he swung his machete, or how much support he had from the administration.

That evening at a dinner at New York's Century Club Stockman discovered he might be overestimating this support. In attendance was much of the brain trust of the Reagan Revolution, and Stockman found himself the subject of a public dressing-down from Jude Wanniski, the former *Wall Street Journal* associate editor whose 1978 book *The Way the World Works* had been the supply-siders' Bible. Wanniski accused Stockman of selling "root canal" therapy and told everyone Stockman had spent the day "threatening to heave widows and orphans into the snow."[4] Wanniski and Lew Lehrman, another supply-side luminary present at the dinner, insisted that tax cuts and a return to the gold standard would make worries about the welfare state moot; growth would be so great the programs could easily be paid for. They warned Stockman he was risking the Reagan Revolution by wasting its political capital on a battle for budget cuts.

In retrospect, everyone that day in New York turned out to be mistaken. David Stockman was wrong, as he later admitted in his remarkable mea culpa, *The Triumph of Politics*. The shrinkage of the federal government did not happen, and defense spending swelled. A handful of visible domestic programs were cut, but core middle-class entitlements spending and the vast pork barrel projects that lay at the heart of the federal budget remained untouched; indeed, they expanded during the Reagan years.

The supply-side intellectuals who gave Stockman a drubbing that night at dinner were also wrong. The Reaganites delivered on the tax cuts. Depending on the measurements used, the cuts may even have boosted tax revenues a bit. But they did not close the deficit and did not lead to great investments in plant and equipment. They did stimulate the economy, but the mechanism was a classic Keynesian tool: huge deficits. Deficits soared, consumption soared, and America's *rentiers,* "executives," and "professionals" poured their money not into factories and new companies but into tax-driven real estate deals and lavish residences. The vaunted Laffer curve* was not so much wrong as irrelevant. It left out too much—most important, the Fed's tight money policies—and it led, in Stockman's words, "to a free lunch message and a mindless political addiction to tax-cutting without regard to the fiscal consequences" by people who would "rather bring on calamity than admit that they were wrong."[5]

The men who ran Wall Street were just as wrong as the supply-side intellectuals. The gargantuan deficits turned out to be pretty easy to finance after all. It took a year or so, but interest rates began to come down. Not only did the shrinking savings pool prove no obstacle, but much of corporate America

---

*The economist and supply-side theoretician Arthur Laffer had suggested that there were two tax rates—a high one and a low one—that could generate the same tax revenues. It was an article of faith among Laffer and his followers that the United States in the late 1970s was on the upper end of his curve—i.e., that lowering tax rates would increase tax revenues.

followed in lockstep the pattern set by the government: going deeply into debt. The 1980s were to be the best decade for Wall Street since the 1920s, but unlike the twenties, when the money had been made in equities, the 1980s saw the real riches made in the packaging, trading, and selling of various debt instruments—junk bonds, mortgage-backed securities, securitized loans, and futures and options.

The solution to Stockman's dilemma—allaying Wall Street's fears so that interest rates would start coming down—lay halfway around the world in the way the obscure Mr. Saito would solve *his* problems.

The powerful bankers, gurus, and bond traders that Stockman met on December 18 knew little of Sumitomo Life. Back in those days, the Street had no more than a token presence in Japan. Men like Bill Brown, the jovial ex-priest and former accountant who had set up Goldman, Sachs's operation in Tokyo in the mid-1970s, or the patrician George Hutchinson of Salomon Brothers headed up tiny representative offices and did little more than trudge back and forth from the Japan Development Bank to Tokyo Electric Power, soliciting Yankee bond business.* These men were almost invisible to the senior managers of their firms; only a few spotted the early-warning signs of a hurricane that would transform global financial markets and extract the Reagan Revolution from the mess it deliberately created for itself.

At the eye of this hurricane was the Japanese life insurance industry. It is highly concentrated; there are only 25 life insurance companies in Japan versus 1,440 in the United States. Just 3 firms control some 50 percent of all life insurance assets. As with its counterparts in banking and manufacturing, the goal of growth was the only one that really mattered. For life insurance companies, that meant selling policies, and the biggest companies boast armies of saleswomen who blanket the country seek-

---

* Dollar bonds floated by foreign issuers in the New York markets.

ing new policyholders. Many in this sales force are middle-aged housewives who have gone back to work after their children are in school. They bang on doors, soliciting policies from other housewives. The rest of the sales force is mostly younger women who roam offices during the lunch hour, selling the same policies to younger salarymen. Almost any firm in Japan from giant manufacturer to tiny four-person publisher will be visited by a life insurance saleslady who, day after day, week after week, brings little candies, packs of tissue, or memo pads to the desks of harried office workers until in desperation one breaks down and buys a policy.

But the policy premiums had to be invested. The more successful the salesladies, the more pressure on men like Mr. Saito. Indeed, the search for adequate returns by the life insurance companies became a key ingredient in the explosive and bizarre Tokyo financial markets of the 1980s. Until the early 1980s the investment decision had not been much of a challenge. It was mostly a matter of choosing among a small number of safe outlets delineated by the Finance Ministry—this much for Japanese government bonds, that much for blue-chip equity—and as a result, the life companies were very thinly staffed on the asset side. Their international investment departments tended to consist of six or seven men with experience ranging from a few months to a decade or so, assisted by two or three "office ladies" in their early twenties. But with the deleveraging of the Japanese economy and the relative shrinkage of domestic investment opportunities, by the early 1980s this handful of people were to find themselves responsible for the deployment of billions of dollars' worth of assets.

Stepping in to help were creative investment bankers. To give life companies a crack at the lucrative loan business to Australian states, for example, packages on offer combined below interest rate bonds and higher interest rate loans. Foreign banks set up dummy holding companies in the Cayman Islands and Hong Kong to "season" securities, thus qualifying them technically for purchase by Japanese insurance firms. Odd bond issues were structured to meet the quirks of Japanese insurance accounting.*

But in all the blizzards of financial paper that blew through Tokyo during the 1980s—the Canadian and Australian dollar twofers, the reverse dual currency bonds, the Samurai bonds, the Sushi bonds, the instantly repackaged perpetuals, the zero-coupon bonds, the square trips and double-dip leveraged leases—U.S. Treasury notes, bills, and bonds held pride of place. These securities—Treasuries, as they are collectively called—were backed by the full faith and credit of the U.S. government. They formed a liquid market of great depth; the securities were traded around the world, and buyers and sellers were thus available twenty-four hours a day. Most other dollar debt securities were priced off Treasuries. The yields in nondollar markets were systematically compared with Treasuries, and with the development of interest and currency swaps,† nondollar markets would be linked directly to Treasuries. The Federal Reserve managed the American money supply by the buying and selling of Treasury securities. With the dollar still functioning as a universal currency, the U.S. Treasury market served as the linchpin of the global financial order.

---

*The most important of these quirks allowed insurance companies to pay policyholders only out of dividend and interest income; capital gains could not be used. Engineering artificially high coupons (often with capital losses) thus became the most widely used technique in making deals attractive to the life insurance companies.

†An interest rate swap involves two borrowers who trade each other's interest obligations (usually fixed obligations for floating obligations) with borrower A paying borrower B the funds needed for borrower B to pay off debt it has incurred while borrower B pays borrower A the funds *it* needs. In a currency swap the two borrowers trade obligations in different currencies. From small beginnings in the late 1970s, the interest and currency swap markets are now trillions of dollars in size as measured by the so-called notional principal amounts. Virtually all major banks and securities houses worldwide have swap teams that do nothing but trade obligations for their own books and for their customers. The greatest impact of swaps has been to break down barriers separating the various national markets. A borrower who needed, for example, fixed-rate dollars but could borrow floating-rate sterling more cheaply would swap the obligations with a borrower who wanted to pay floating-rate sterling but could borrow fixed-rate dollars more cheaply. One side of a swap quotation is usually a spread over U.S. Treasuries.

Japanese institutional investors early in the 1980s found U.S. Treasuries irresistible. An institutional investor such as an insurance company has two principal concerns: safety and income. Usually a trade-off is involved. A triple A corporate or government bond offers a high degree of safety but relatively low income, while speculative securities, such as junk bonds, promise high return but possible default. For Japanese investors, however, U.S. Treasuries in the early 1980s seemed to offer both safety and high income. Interest rates on Treasuries were more than five full percentage points higher than on Japanese government bond issues of equivalent maturities, yet they were just as secure—maybe even more so—as the highest-grade Japanese investment. Who could believe that the United States, the greatest and most powerful country in the world, would ever default on its own securities? And certain U.S. Treasuries had the added bonus, at least for life companies, of maturities much longer than any Japanese debt security. Life insurance companies anywhere like long-term, fixed-rate investments. It gives them a way to use actuarial tables in matching income with payout decades down the road.

One small cloud lay on the horizon. Insurance companies such as Sumitomo Life ultimately had to pay off their policyholders in Japanese yen, while U.S. Treasuries paid interest and principal in dollars. During the years Sumitomo held a Treasury bond, the yen might strengthen against the dollar, thus reducing the ultimate return available in yen. While people like Mr. Saito knew of this risk, they tended to think it fairly minor. The interest rate differentials between U.S. Treasury securities and comparable Japanese investments were so large that the yen would have to strengthen far beyond the rate of 203.60 yen to the dollar at which the foreign exchange markets closed at the end of 1980. By historical standards this was already a high yen rate—not as high as the 177 to the dollar that had briefly prevailed during the currency crisis of summer 1978 but much higher than the 240 that had closed the previous year. Even if the yen strengthened again to around 180 to the dollar, however, analysis showed that a yen-based investor was still better off buying U.S. Treasuries than an equivalent yen security; dollar interest rates were so much higher. And no one seriously entertained the possibility that the yen could strengthen beyond 180.*

Suppose the Japanese government did lose control and the yen strengthened beyond 180? There was one final escape hatch. The U.S. Treasury market was so huge that a seller could always get out. There could not be a panic. Panics occur in financial markets from time to time when buyers cannot be found at any reasonable price and everyone wants to sell. According to the conventional reasoning, this could never happen with Treasuries. The market was too enormous and liquid, a virtual universal financial market; the U.S. government itself could create and reduce supply in the market at will.

All these assumptions turned out to be wrong. The dollar ultimately ended up far weaker than 180 yen, and Japanese institutional investors found themselves trapped: unable to move out of Treasuries lest they destroy the global financial system and in any case prevented from doing so by their bureaucratic overseers. But these mistakes were not visible for a number of years; indeed, the experience of the early 1980s seemed comforting. Instead of strengthening, the yen began to weaken fairly dramatically. By September 1981 it had fallen to 220 to the dollar; a year later it stood at 270, making those among the Japanese who got on the bandwagon early look even smarter. For in yen terms, a $10,000 Treasury bond bought for 203,000 yen when the yen was at 203 to the dollar was worth 270,000 yen with the yen at 270. And the Treasury market ballooned. As the federal deficit soared, Treasury securities outstanding were to double from the $900 billion where they stood when Ronald Reagan took office to $1.8 trillion a mere five years

---

*The widespread view in Japan in the early 1980s that 180 was the highest the yen could ever go was not just talk. In 1985 Japan Air Lines, a company ultimately run by the Ministry of Transportation, bought some $3 billion of foreign exchange contracts for eleven years' duration at that rate. The subsequent strengthening of the yen way beyond 180 has cost the airline more than $1 billion in cumulative losses.[6]

later. But there was no problem in finding buyers for these securities; indeed, Treasury yields began to fall after 1982, suggesting no shortage of investors.

Japanese money came pouring into the market. Japanese life insurance companies would more than double their holdings of foreign securities in 1981 alone, double them again by 1983 and triple this figure by 1987 so that life companies in that watershed year were to own some $67 billion worth of foreign securities. Meanwhile the foreign share of their total securities holdings went from 8 to 28 percent.[7] Similar trends followed at other Japanese institutions—trust banks, property and casualty companies, the regional banks. Overnight, Wall Street houses transformed their Tokyo branches from small information-gathering offices to vast trading floors filled with young bond salesmen. Market gurus around the world focused on Tokyo, where Japanese appetite became the key determinant of the bonds' prices. Japanese institutions tended to move as a group, often buying as much as 30 percent of a given issue, and they were particularly heavy buyers at the long end of the market. Indeed, Japanese appetite for the long bond—the thirty-year Treasury security—was to keep long-term dollar interest rates much lower than they otherwise would have been.*

Mr. Saito's investment decisions, writ large, transformed Japan's external accounts. In 1980 Japanese institutions lent or invested some $11 billion overseas in long-term funds while borrowing $13 billion. In 1981 the amount borrowed stayed roughly the same, but the capital sent out of the country more than doubled to $23 billion. By 1986 Japanese borrowing had almost disappeared while the long-term capital exports in that year totaled over $130 billion—more than half the $220 billion 1986 U.S. federal deficit. Most of these capital exports bought U.S. dollar instruments.[8]

Twelve years later David Stockman admitted that no one in Reagan's inner circle had anticipated that the Japanese would

---

*In bankerspeak, the yield curve was unusually flat, reflecting high Japanese demand at the long end.

appear out of nowhere to finance the deficit.* Washington's savviest moneyman, Federal Reserve Chairman Paul Volcker, writes about the financing of the deficit: "[T]he shortage of domestic savings was compensated in substantial part by an enormous inflow of mainly borrowed capital from abroad. That inflow was at one point running at a greater rate than all the personal savings in the United States and *turned out to be far larger than I had thought possible* [emphasis added]."[9]

By the fall of 1981 the cut-spending side of the Reagan Revolution had collapsed while the government's revenue base had been gutted by that summer's tax bill. In Stockman's words, "What had been required [to pass the tax bill] guaranteed that the massive tax cut enacted on July 29, 1981 never stood a chance of being paid for by a commensurate shrinkage of the welfare state."[10] People like Stockman feared disaster—"catastrophe" is the word he used in *The Triumph of Politics*—as the financial markets digested the news that the American government had locked itself into annual deficits of $150 billion plus as far as the eye could see. Fuzzy-thinking supply-siders complained that the tax cuts weren't fully in effect until late 1982. And they began to sing that old cheap liberal whine: The Fed was "too tight." From the mouths of people who had been urging a return to the gold standard, this line sounded as if the Amadeus Quartet had switched to hip-hop. The California Mafia around Reagan—Ed Meese, Mike Deaver, Lyn Nofziger—cared about appearances more than policy. They would not expose the president to the political heat of taking on the middle-class entitlements. Instead they stage-managed the day's sound bite and finessed the annual $150 billion deficits. The president himself had an intuitive grasp of where he wanted to take the country and the knack of translating his vision into plain language. He lacked, however, the intellectual stamina to go further into the hard world of numbers and bruising political

---

* Stockman even told me that a delegation of senior Japanese officials had visited the White House in late February 1981 seeking advice on how to reduce the *Japanese* deficit!

battles necessary to cope with the contradictions in his platform.

If you wanted to, you could describe what happened in the dry tautology of macroeconomics. The United States legislated huge deficits, which stimulated the demand side of the economy beyond what the supply side could provide. The difference was filled by imports, mostly from Japan. The dollars to pay for the imports went to Japan and were reexported back to the United States as financing for the deficit, enabling the cycle to continue.

Or you could let a little passion seep into your analysis. The Republicans had captured the White House with a simplistic platform and a simplistic leader. They pretended to the American people that they were solving the country's problems when what they were doing was borrowing money. Borrowing money made it possible for Americans to spend more than they had earned, and they spent it on Toyotas and Panasonic VCRs. The Japanese could then lend the money back to the Americans so that the party could keep going. Political elites in both countries pretended that the party could last forever, and neither elite was honest about the price that would eventually be exacted.

But paying the price was in the future. For the time being, the flood of money was dissolving the contradictions in the Reagan platform, and nowhere was it more welcome than at the Treasury Department. It was up to the Treasury actually to raise the money to finance the deficit. Treasury Secretary Donald T. Regan had been the chief executive of Merrill Lynch, Wall Street's biggest firm, until coming to Washington. Like many self-made businessmen and successful Wall Street tycoons, he was impatient with theoretical hairsplitting.[11] He cared about actual market conditions and the results he could get out of those conditions. As far as he was concerned, the gradual decline in interest rates that set in after 1982, the flood of foreign money into the United States, and the strong post-1982 recovery proved the administration's policies fundamentally sound. He would undiplomatically lose his temper in meetings with his foreign counterparts when they started to complain about American deficits. The judgments he listened to as treasury secretary, just as he had at Merrill Lynch, were those of the markets. The markets told him everything was fine: The dollar was strong, and bonds were buoyant.

Regan himself may not have been much of an ideologue, but many of his subordinates at Treasury, including Beryl Sprinkel, who held the key undersecretary for monetary affairs slot, were ardent monetarists. Sprinkel's job gave him control over the international side of the Treasury's operations, and his ideological disposition reinforced Regan's perceptions. Sprinkel was contemptuous of the moaning from supply-siders in early 1982 that excessively tight money was forcing the economy into a direction opposite from that which they had so brashly predicted. In fact, he had gone to the other extreme, "taking shots at Volcker for being too loose."[12] To a monetarist like Sprinkel, many of America's problems could be laid at the feet of a decade of loose and erratic monetary policy. The prime goal of a government's economic policies ought to be a steady and predictable growth in the money supply that tracked the underlying real growth potential of the economy. If it took a recession to crush inflationary expectations and restore monetary health, then so be it. Postponing the cure simply made it harder.

The burgeoning foreign—mostly Japanese—claims on the United States were, however, bothering some people, notably Paul Volcker. He was concerned that it was all too good to be true, that eventually foreigners would lose their enthusiasm for Treasury securities and dump them in the market in a frantic flight from the dollar. "Sooner or later," he wrote, "there would all too likely be a sickening fall in the dollar, undermining confidence, as had happened so often in the 1970's. Yet there was an administration that simply didn't seem to care."[13]

Volcker was right; it didn't care. To White House ideologues, his fears seemed misplaced. The news on the deficit front was as bleak as ever, but this did not faze the markets. As 1982 turned into 1983, foreigners poured ever-vaster sums into Treasuries. As long as this continued to happen, the demand for dollars would soar and the dollar would gain in value against other currencies, particularly the yen. With Japan converting so much of its wealth into dollars, demand for dollars was driving up the price of the currency. A dollar worth 205 yen when Ronald Reagan took office would buy 220 yen at the end of 1981. By September 1982 it would buy 270 yen.

The strong dollar began to cause trouble for the White House, however, from an unexpected quarter, the boardrooms of American industry: CEOs, straight-as-die businessmen, chambers of commerce presidents, big Republican contributors, personal friends of the likes of Bush, Baker, and Regan. And they were getting slammed. They had to face closed or restricted markets in much of the world and could not rely on a slow and often unsympathetic federal bureaucracy in dealing with dumping and other violations of U.S. trade laws. They were often outmaneuvered by the slick lobbyists and lawyers hired by their foreign competitors. But fundamentally they believed they were being killed by the high dollar. From Detroit to Silicon Valley, from big Rust Belt steel companies to the high tech firms of Massachusetts's Route 128, the same cries were heard: The soaring dollar made it impossible for American industry to sell in Japan, to compete in third markets, and, most important, to hang on at home. American industry was being overwhelmed by waves of imports against which, with a high-cost position stemming from the superdollar, it could not fight.

The administration had to listen. Yet it found itself boxed in by its ideology and its policies. The several obvious ways to deal with the complaints were all unacceptable to one or another of its factions. The idea of protectionist quotas and tariffs horrified the supply-siders and free market ideologues in the White House. They were also dangerous. Draconian protectionist measures would cut off the supply of dollars going overseas to pay for the foreign goods. Without the dollars being sent overseas first, they could not come back as the proceeds of bond and Treasury note issues.

The administration could cut the deficit. But halfhearted

attempts to make real spending cuts had been soundly defeated back in the fall of 1981. No one in the White House had the courage to take on Social Security or other middle-class entitlements; they had been burned too badly. Meanwhile Defense Secretary Caspar Weinberger and the Pentagon had effectively been given veto power over serious cuts in defense spending, and a renewed, beefed-up defense was a central Reagan commitment. But if defense was a central commitment, so were tax reductions. Ronald Reagan simply would not hear about increased taxes. The administration would do or say nothing about the deficit.

That left the foreign exchange markets themselves. Expert opinion was mixed on how effective market intervention by governments could be if it stood against the prevailing market forces. The experience of the 1970s—particularly the joint interventions of 1978 to halt the dollar rout—suggested to some that properly conducted policies could reverse market psychology, and calls went up for direct intervention in the markets to push down the dollar.

Treasury rejected this course. The administration's monetarists were gathered there, and the sanctity of the foreign exchange markets topped the list of monetarist doctrines. The floating-rate system constructed with such trial and error in the 1970s was one of monetarism's greatest triumphs. A good monetarist like Sprinkel would not easily violate one of the central tenets of monetarist orthodoxy by intervening in the foreign exchange markets.

Sprinkel had made this clear during hearings before the Joint Economic Committee back in March 1981. At the time the full scale of the Reagan deficits had not yet become obvious, and Sprinkel brushed off deficit-snowballing fears. Representative Henry Reuss, Democrat from Wisconsin and chairman of the committee, asked Sprinkel how he would handle a scenario that in fact turned out pretty much as Reuss predicted. "Suppose," Reuss asked, "that you are not right [about the deficit's not being a problem], and suppose that that deficit gets to work. It will raise interest rates, and those interest rates will make the dollar extra strong. Will that fact . . . be sufficient to cause our intervention?"

"It is very doubtful that we would intervene in a circumstance similar to that," Sprinkel had responded.[14] Indeed, no major intervention in the foreign exchange markets occurred on the Regan-Sprinkel watch. Still, something had to be done. In a reversal of the usual metaphor, it ended up with Peoria composing the tune and finding it would play in Washington. Peoria's biggest employer was Caterpillar, the world's premier maker of construction and earth-moving equipment. Until the 1980s Caterpillar had dominated markets around the world except, of course, for Japan, where the usual mixture of "guidance" from MITI and the Construction Ministry and the closed construction industry kept Komatsu the market leader. But buoyed by the cheap yen, Komatsu launched a global offensive under the internal slogan *maru C* (encircle C—Caterpillar), undercutting Caterpillar's prices in third-country markets and pushing the company to the wall in the United States.

Its executives begged Washington for relief. In congressional hearings Caterpillar Vice-President Donald Fites pleaded for action on the dollar, telling members of Congress and administration officials that the company needed a rate of ¥200 to the dollar in order to compete. His arguments fell on deaf ears, at least at the Treasury, where Sprinkel reiterated his policy of nonintervention. But rather than simply retire from the field, licking its wounds, Caterpillar set about giving the administration an ideological excuse to take action. The company commissioned a study by Professor Ezra Solomon of Stanford. The study, entitled "The Misalignment of the United States Dollar and the Japanese Yen: The Problem and its Solution," argued ingeniously that the problem was not that the dollar was "too high" but that the yen was "too low."[15]

This seems a meaningless semantic distinction, but in fact, it was important. For Professor Solomon contended in the paper that it was not *American* policy that was keeping the dollar high; rather it was *Japanese* policy that was keeping the yen too low. In the words of Caterpillar Chairman Lee Morgan lecturing congressional committees, the "present exchange rate imbalance should be corrected by measures which would decrease world demand for dollar assets and increase demand for yen assets."[16] In other words, the Japanese financial authorities had discouraged the use of the yen worldwide as a reserve currency, thus artificially depressing demand for yen. This was not news to students of Japanese finance. But to the monetarist ideologues at the Treasury, it carried the force of an ex cathedra papal bull. The Japanese were depressing the value of the yen by interfering in markets! So one was theologically justified in taking countermeasures!

Suddenly the call went up from Washington for reform of the Japanese financial system: to internationalize the yen, to liberalize the Japanese markets. Regan and Sprinkel—the "greatest bond salesmen in history," as one commentary labeled them[17]—thought they might be able to sell even more Treasuries to the Japanese if the markets there were opened up further. Surprised by this unexpected development, the Ministry of Finance agreed to a shared effort with the U.S. Treasury to study "liberalization" and yen / dollar issues. A joint announcement made on November 10, 1983, provided for the establishment of a working group staffed equally by Treasury and MOF officials. The Americans made it clear they would not accept meaningless face-saving gestures. At a press conference in Tokyo on February 24, 1984, Regan visibly lost his temper, pounding the table and demanding an end to Japanese recalcitrance.

The MOF was a trifle bewildered by this display and ultimately contemptuous of the Americans.[18] They understood the contradiction in what Regan and Sprinkel were calling for: that the Americans were trying to run a heater and an air conditioner simultaneously, to quote the *Nihon Keizai Shimbun*.[19] If Regan and Sprinkel had really gotten their way and sparked a wholesale liberalization of the Japanese financial system—complete with market-determined domestic interest rates, unrestricted movement of capital into and out of Japan, a deep and liquid Tokyo yen bond market, and a real Japanese money market where commercial paper, bankers acceptances, and government bills freely traded—the result most probably would have been a wholesale move by investors worldwide out of dollar securities and into yen. That would certainly have deflated the dollar quickly. It would also have ended the ability of the U.S. Treasury to finance the federal deficit without economy-crushing interest rates.

Such thoughts were, of course, academic. Regan's bluster aside, the Ministry of Finance had no intention of permitting the financial system to slip out of its control, implied in a true internationalization of the yen. In the process it would save Regan and Sprinkel from themselves, even if these impractical Americans lacked the sense to see it. As usual when the Japanese succumbed to irrational American pressure, something would have to be conceded that would mollify Washington without undermining MOF control. This was a delicate problem because various groups in Japan were always eager to make a "concession" that would benefit themselves. Banks would delight in greater flexibility in issuing domestic certificates of deposit, and securities firms would jump at a freeing up of foreign markets for yen bonds, the so-called Euroyen market. But banks were loath to see the Euroyen market opened up lest they lose some of their traditional lending business, while tax authorities opposed any easing of withholding tax. Thus, in order to prevent any single group from using the opportunity to give itself a boost at the expense of all the others, the real negotiations had to be conducted among the Japanese themselves. When that horse trading had been concluded, something could be offered to the Americans.

The Yen/Dollar Committee, commissioned in November 1983, issued its report the following May. This document on the surface is a bland exercise in symmetry.[20] Both sides are committed to open, liberal capital markets. The MOF will seek to liberalize the Japanese financial system; the United States will work to bring down the deficit. Each side will treat the other's institutions as it treats its own. The Treasury will try to head off unitary taxation by the individual states, while the MOF will try to persuade the Tokyo Stock Exchange to admit foreign brokerage houses. All very unexceptional, reasonable-sounding, and dull. But to those with the taste for it, a thoughtful, slow chew on this cud of bureaucratic prose can extract a fair amount of unexpected nourishment.

From its title page on, this document is loaded with clues pointing to the yawning gap that separates the reality of Japanese from American policy making. The page describes the document as a "report" by the committee's "working group" to Finance Minister Takeshita Noboru and Treasury Secretary Regan. All very standard. Except that Takeshita has no real power over this group, while Regan has a great deal of it. The American side is actually reporting to Regan, but it would be more accurate to describe Takeshita as reporting to this group rather than the reverse. Takeshita is off doing his real job: cutting deals with construction companies to ensure an adequate flow of funds to his faction in the Diet. When needed, the group will tell him exactly what to say and to whom about yen / dollar issues. But Regan needs to worry about what the group is doing because he in turn is accountable to the president, and if that uninvolved man is unlikely to stir himself enough to be interested, the treasury secretary will surely be hauled before congressional committees to testify on the committee's work. Takeshita will never have to answer to anyone for what the committee does. He will read the script the Japanese group prepares for him.

The next page lists the committee's members: thirteen each from the Ministry of Finance and the Treasury, cochaired by Sprinkel and Vice Minister Oba Tomomitsu. On the U.S. side there is a clear chain of command. Sprinkel is on top. Reporting to him are David Mulford, the assistant secretary for international affairs. Mulford has his two direct reports, and they in turn have their reports. The people on the team are all involved in the international side of the Treasury's business.

But the Japanese side does not consist of Oba's direct reports. Instead there are the number one and number two men from most of the MOF's important bureaus—banking, tax, securities, financial, international finance. These are in fact quasi-independent fiefdoms. They both determine and execute policy, and they act as advocates for their constituencies—banks, securities companies, tax agents. A committee with roughly comparable reach for the United States would need to consist of representatives not only from the Treasury but from the Fed, the SEC, the IRS, and the Office of the Comptroller of the Currency. And you would need the chairs of key congressional committees with jurisdiction over tax matters and the banking system and securities markets. To round it off, you would have to add a couple of heavyweight lobbyists from the banking industry and from Wall Street.

Reading on, one discovers American "commitments." But these are beyond the scope of the Treasury and thus largely meaningless: things such as cutting the deficit, ending unitary taxation, allowing interstate banking. The Treasury may oppose unitary taxation, but it is state legislatures that are enacting these taxes in an effort to extract income from foreign companies operating inside their states. Similarly, the Treasury may support interstate banking, but it is something Congress must decide and approve.

The Japanese side of the report—and this is the real report; the American side is ultimately cosmetics—has hard information in it. Some things will happen; others will not. Banks will get some additional funding powers. Foreign banks in Japan will be given the right to trade Japanese securities, and banks, both Japanese and foreign, will be allowed to convert any amount of foreign currency they wish into yen. Foreign banks will be permitted into the trust banking business in 1985, and Euroyen issues by non-Japanese will be allowed late in 1984.

On the other hand, the Americans can complain all they want, but the MOF is not going to lift the withholding tax on interest and dividend payments to foreigners. The document is unusually blunt, "[T]he removal of the withholding tax would impair the basic principles of Japan's tax system and . . . there is no willingness to consider removal." Nor can Japanese residents hold securities accounts abroad (where they could more easily elude MOF oversight). And "a too rapid establishment of a free Euroyen market may have adverse effects on Japanese fiscal and monetary policies, exchange rates, and Japan's domestic financial system." (Translation: Too free a Euroyen market might undermine MOF control of the financial system.)

Taken together, the report's clues point to what happened: Unfortunately for Caterpillar, but fortunately for the continued ability of the U.S. Treasury to finance the deficit, the effort to browbeat the Japanese into liberalizing their financial markets and internationalize the yen was largely unsuccessful. The few important, although limited, concessions extracted* had no effect on exchange rates. After hitting a low of 272 in November 1982, the yen had strengthened to some 230 by early 1983. But it had stayed stubbornly in the 225–245 range since that time. The report issued in May 1984 and the implementation of its measures did nothing noticeable to bring down either the dollar or Japan's trade and current account surpluses. In fact, beginning in the summer of 1984, the yen started weakening again, going from the 231 it had been in May to 245 by July. By early in 1985 it stood at 259. And the trade surplus that had been $31 billion in 1983 was $44 billion in 1984 and $56 billion in 1985. Meanwhile the capital kept right on flowing;

---

*The most important of these were probably the end of limits on the amounts of swap transactions and the permission freely to attach swaps to Eurobonds. The development of the Tokyo swap market was to have two very significant effects the MOF may not have anticipated: It eroded the distinction among classes of commercial banks in Japan by permitting the city banks for the first time to match-fund their longer-term fixed-rate yen assets by raising floating-rate dollars and swapping them into yen, and it encouraged disintermediation as Japanese corporates could issue bonds overseas in whatever was the most suitable currency and then swap the proceeds into yen.

Japan exported $18 billion of long-term capital in 1983, $50 billion in 1984, and $65 billion in 1985.

People knew this could not last forever, irrespective of bureaucratic tinkering. The high dollar was laying waste to swaths of American industry. The accompanying high interest rates, still extremely high, even if down somewhat from the stratospheric levels of a year or two earlier, were the proximate cause of the Third World debt crisis. Latin American and other countries found themselves facing debt service payments far higher than they had ever imagined possible. As country after country went into rescheduling, worries mounted over the health of the U.S. banking system. The nonperforming loans to countries in rescheduling exceeded the capital base of many large U.S. banks. Meanwhile the mix of a cheap yen, a high-consumption U.S. economy, and high U.S. interest rates was indeed helping Japanese exporters beyond their wildest dreams, while institutional investors like Sumitomo Life were earning more money on their dollar investments than they ever imagined. But thoughtful Japanese officials were worried. "We started to feel very nervous," noted a senior MOF bureaucrat in discussing the time.[21] A correction must come. Markets would force a correction, protectionist measures would be enacted, or perhaps new leaders would come to power in Washington.

At the London summit of the industrialized countries in June 1984, Ronald Reagan had blocked any mention of the U.S. budget deficit in the final communiqué, arguing no evidence linked budget deficits to high interest rates and an "overvalued" dollar. His Democratic opponent that year, however, drew an explicit connection. "Here is the truth about the future," Walter Mondale thundered at the Democratic National Convention. "We are living on borrowed money and borrowed time. These deficits hike interest rates, clobber exports, stunt investment, kill jobs, undermine growth, cheat our kids, and shrink our future."[22] Mondale's frankness cost him the election—he promised to raise taxes to deal with the problem—but despite the Democrats' defeat, Reagan's second term did in fact offer new leaders and radically different approaches on at least exchange rates and the trade deficit. The era of the high dollar would end abruptly, and the high dollar / cheap yen / high interest rate environment of Reagan's first term would be replaced by an entirely new set of macroeconomic conditions.

We shall look at what happened in the next chapter. But in the meantime a fundamental question still remains, the question raised in the quotation at the beginning of this one. Why would the Japanese put so much of their wealth into a currency that at some point they all expected to cheapen, into the government securities of a country they viewed as a somewhat dangerous, unpredictable power in decline? The simple fact that it happened obscures its strangeness from an historical perspective. Clearly by the early 1980s the economic balance of power in the world was moving away from the United States and toward Japan. Japan had not simply established supremacy in a growing number of core strategic industries; it had demonstrated that as a society it could mobilize human and physical resources in the service of national power and sustain that mobilization over the course of many decades, while the United States with its babel of self-serving interest groups and pandering politicians had seemingly lost that capacity. Japan was becoming the world's largest creditor country; the United States, the world's biggest debtor.

This unsettling power shift was hardly a new story in the annals of history. The city-states of Italy that had dominated trade and finance in the late Middle Ages had seen their wealth and power shift first to the Iberian Peninsula and then to the Low Countries. Amsterdam had in turn yielded to London as the hub of global capital. Britain's manufacturing prowess and commercial supremacy was overtaken first by Germany and then by the United States. But in all these previous power shifts, no rising nation had poured its growing wealth into the fiat paper securities of the declining power. Seen from Tokyo, the U.S. government was destroying its own revenue base, borrowing an enormous amount of money from its fiercest

economic competitor, and indulging in a long orgy of consumption while its infrastructure and industrial sinews were
deliberately allowed to rot. Why would anyone exchange goods
of real value—VCRs, machine tools, automobiles, semiconductors, specialty steel—for paper backed by nothing but empty
promises from such an entity?

Several answers suggest themselves. First is the dollar's role
as a universal currency. It had only been a little more than a
decade since the collapse of Bretton Woods. No real substitute
had evolved for the dollar. If anything, it was becoming even
more entrenched as rapidly evolving financial technology—particularly the booming swap markets—linked financial instruments around the world to it. Second, there was an attitude of
what you might call residual respect for the United States. It
had defeated Japan in war and then provided Japan with the
wherewithal to rebuild. Even more important, the postwar political setup in Japan was predicated on continuing U.S. power,
with the United States guaranteeing Japan's security and assuming worldwide burdens of both military and financial sorts
in maintaining the liberal capitalist world order. Facing up to
declining U.S. power meant facing up to the erosion of a key
prop in Japan's carefully calibrated domestic power balances,
an understandably distasteful exercise to be avoided unless absolutely necessary. Then there was the continuing need to export. For all the many changes that had occurred since the end
of the high-growth period in the early 1970s, exports were
still needed to keep the bicycle of the Japanese economy from
tipping over. By buying such high quantities of Treasuries, the
Japanese were ultimately financing their own exports, leading
to the famous quip about Americans buying VCRs on thirty-
year installment plans, referring to heavy Japanese purchases of
thirty-year Treasury securities. The terms were very favorable
to the Americans because ultimately they did not have to earn
the dollars to pay back the financing; they could just print more
of them. Dangerous it might be, but it permitted the Japan
export machine to continue roaring along.

Finally, where would other courses of action have led? If Japan had acted on a pure calculus of economic rationality, it might have insisted that the United States finance its purchases of Japanese exports in yen, that if the United States wanted to be so profligate, it would need to borrow in a currency the Japanese could control. Or if the returns on exports were becoming so dicey that one could sell them only by virtually giving them away, then the economy needed another engine of growth, such as domestic demand. The transformation of the Japanese economy over three decades from one of abundant labor and scarce capital to one of abundant capital and expensive labor should have induced a wholesale restructuring of the financial system, one in which a Sumitomo Life would not have felt the need to hunt about for foreign investment vehicles. Indeed, one of Japan's most astute observers of its financial system has written:

There were two motives behind [the Japanese] system. The first was to expand Japan's productive capacity as quickly as possible. The second was to keep control of Japan's productive assets out of the hands of foreigners. The strains in this system first started appearing in the late 1960's, when Japan began running chronic trade surpluses. The result has been constant upward pressure on exchange rates. The increasing value of the yen should have served as a signal to Japan's policy elite that it needed to shift the driving force of the economy from exports to domestic demand. But Japan, alas, has lacked the political infrastructure capable of carrying out such a wide-ranging policy shift.[23]

Here is the heart of the matter. Had the Japanese forced the United States to finance and pay for its Japanese imports and its government deficit in yen, the internationalization of the yen would have greatly accelerated. The wide use of the yen as a settlements and reserve currency, however, is incompatible with continued informal Ministry of Finance control over the financial system and monetary policy. The shift to a consumer economy is likewise incompatible with informal bureaucratic control over credit allocation. As the decade proceeded, the system came under greater and greater strain, and after the collapse of the so-called bubble economy, genuine alternatives began at least to seem possible. But in the early 1980s the only real alternative Japan had to propping up the existing order with its massive purchases of U.S. Treasuries was a fundamental shift in the direction and structure of its economy.

Such fundamental shifts cannot be undertaken by bureaucrats, no matter how talented they may be. They require political direction. And this political direction Japan lacked, never more conspicuously than in the early 1980s. The prime minister was Suzuki Zenko, a complete nonentity who owed his position to his predecessor's untimely death and the machinations of Tanaka Kakuei, still the "shadow shogun" of Japanese politics despite his nominal disgrace in the wake of the 1974 Lockheed scandal. As one account notes, "The bureaucrats despised Suzuki. His ministers ignored him to an extent previously unknown in post-war Japan. . . . One of the nicknames that Suzuki earned as prime minister was 'tape-recorder' because for meetings that could not be avoided the bureaucrats had to train him to recite the answers by heart."[24] Suzuki could not even perform his basic international duties of "explaining" Japan's position and seeking foreign "understanding." The situation was so embarrassing that Tanaka joined hands with his longtime rival and the other great éminence grise of Japanese politics Kishi Nobosuke to arrange for Suzuki's ouster and replacement by Nakasone Yasuhiro in late 1982.

Nakasone was to prove himself a very different kind of prime minister, with a genuine passion for leadership and some understanding of the consequences to Japan of its lack of a political center that could take decisions and act on them. Nakasone helped engineer the important change in course of September 1985 and even asked Ronald Reagan to his face to do something about the American deficit, something none of his predecessors would have considered.

But in the meantime the lack of political direction and a structural inability to make hard political choices ensured that Japan would drift into a closer embrace with the United States than it had ever contemplated. Yoshida Shigeru had sought to soothe his humiliated countrymen in 1945 with the widely quoted and prophetic remark that history had many examples of nations that had lost wars but won the subsequent peace. It was he more than anyone else who had created the structure of postwar U.S.-Japan relations, trading an end to the occupation, American security guarantees, and tacit American aid in getting the economy restarted in return for unrestricted U.S. military access to Japan and at least passive, rhetorical support for U.S. Cold War objectives.[25] But surely he never dreamed that winning the peace meant that Japan would actually be propping up an American economic recovery. And his legions of critics across the Japanese political spectrum, who accused him of settling for "subordinate independence," never imagined that Japan's independence would be compromised in quite this way. By the end of Reagan's first term the Japanese had accumulated claims on the U.S. government totaling hundreds of billions of dollars. Keynes's nostrum that "If you owe the bank a thousand dollars, the bank owns you; owe the bank a million dollars, and you own the bank" was never more apt.

But it cut both ways. Americans were unaccustomed to seeing their economic fate in the hands of strangers, people whose politics, language, history, and ways of doing business they had never taken the trouble to understand. For the disjointed fiscal lunacy of the Reagan Revolution had, in combination with the rudderless Japanese political economy, made both countries hostages to each other in ways that neither country had ever experienced or could even begin to understand. Neither one could pull away from the other without doing incalculable damage, yet the embrace itself was dangerous and unstable. Extrication was going to prove tough.

6. Units of Account

The Plaza Accord

THE TYPICAL undergraduate economics course touches at some point on the doctrine of mercantilism, the discredited notion that a nation's economic goals ought to be the accumulation of trade surpluses and piles of gold. Mercantilists are said to confuse wealth with its unit of account. Real wealth consists of a nation's productive capacity—its natural resources, its factories and fields, its bridges and roads, the skills and motivations of its citizenry, the ethics and vision of its leaders and managers. When mercantilist countries like the Spain of Philip II or Louis XIV's France went to war, plundered the New World, and restricted trade in order to accumulate and preserve gold hoards, they were confusing gold with what it could buy. At great cost in bloodshed and toil, Philip II brought to Madrid shiploads of gold seized from the Incas. He thought he had increased the wealth and power of Spain. All he had really done, however, was foster inflation. The gold did not increase Spain's genuine wealth, its capacity to create the goods and services Philip's subjects could use and enjoy. Nominally poor England proved the point, demonstrating with its superior shipbuilding, design, and navigational skills the illusory nature of a gold hoard as a substitute for real national power.

This confusion is not confined to European monarchs of the baroque era. Their modern successors are obsessed with the

amount of gold in Fort Knox or the level of international reserves (gold plus freely convertible currencies like the dollar
and the mark) on the books of central banks. Of course, a
country needs a certain minimum level of reserves in order to
finance trade smoothly. But what really counts is a country's
access to credit, and that in turn is a function of the real wealth
of its economy and the country's reputation for prudent economic management.

It is easy to laugh at seventeenth-century European monarchs and contemporary East Asian central bankers with their
Midas-like gloating over big gold and international reserve
hoards. But if condescending ridicule is the appropriate response to mercantilism, what is the appropriate response to a
country that practices a sort of reverse mercantilism, a country
that goes out of its way to reduce the value of its accumulated
reserves? Imagine a seventeenth-century king who started giving gold away to his enemies or perhaps a Taiwanese central
banker who arranged for half his country's international reserves to be transferred to the accounts of its economic competitors in Beijing, Seoul, and Kuala Lumpur. The idea is so
preposterous no rejoinder has ever been thought necessary by
any school of economists.

Yet between September 1985 and February 1987 this is
precisely what the United States did. The highest officials of
the U.S. government set about halving the country's buying
power in world markets, in the process slashing the prices of
American companies, farmland, golf courses, office buildings,
and factories by 50 percent. Nor were their actions particularly
controversial. They were cheered on by much of the economics
profession. The business community generally welcomed what
was happening. Mainstream journals hailed the actions as a
newfound pragmatic approach. Political opponents had little
to say and never tried to make an issue of it.

No other country had ever acted in quite this way. Of course
there had been the so-called competitive devaluations of the
1930s and developing countries—often at the urging of the

IMF—from time to time do reduce the value of their currencies in order to improve trade performance. But there is a crucial difference between these common devaluations and the politically engineered halving of the dollar's value in the mid-eighties. Ordinary countries devalue in hopes of *increasing* their holdings of the world's reserve currency of the day—be it gold, sterling, or dollars. Because their own currencies are "too expensive," their exports are likewise "too expensive." They reduce the price of their exports in an effort to sell more and thus capture more of the universal reserve currency. But when an American company exports, it is rarely paid in yen, deutsche marks, or gold. It is usually paid in dollars. The individual exporter might chalk up more foreign sales, but for the country as a whole the notion of cutting the dollar's price in order to capture more dollars seems ludicrous; the United States controls the supply of dollars anyway. But that is what happened.

The story begins with a man tired of his job and another seeking to safeguard a major investment of time and energy. The tired man was James A. Baker III, chief of staff in the Reagan White House; the other, Treasury Secretary Donald T. Regan.

What happened is well known. In the wake of Ronald Reagan's reelection in November 1984, Baker felt underappreciated and taken for granted.[1] Meanwhile Regan had spent much of the previous year working on a voluminous plan to overhaul the U.S. tax code. He had put a great deal of energy and thought into the plan and, wanting to leave his mark, was very concerned that it be enacted into law in something close to its original form. He knew this would require the support of the White House, and he was increasingly critical of its managerial sloppiness and the primacy of image there at the expense of policy. His anger boiled over when remarks he made at a cabinet meeting on November 15 were leaked to the press. He telephoned Baker, cursed him out roundly, accused him of planting the leaks, and sent a resignation letter to the president. The letter was not accepted. Baker went over to Treasury to patch

things up, and after they had apologized to each other, Regan
suggested that the two of them switch jobs.[2]

According to Regan, Baker was so surprised he nearly swal-
lowed the pen he was holding between his lips, but he came
around to agreeing this would be a good move for him. It
would get him out of the White House and provide him with
some crucial foreign policy experience. While State or Defense
might have provided more, those jobs were unavailable. And
the Treasury Department is directly responsible for international economic policy. It has primary authority over such crucial cross-border matters as exchange rates. It might not seem
so to the general public, but the job of treasury secretary is
thus one of Washington's four or five most important "foreign
policy" posts in addition to its obvious role as the premier
"economic policy"-making position.

Accounts of the Regan-Baker job switch have usually focused on Don Regan's unsuitability as chief of staff.[3] He is said
to have substituted a hierarchical environment in the White
House for the more collegial atmosphere under Baker. His
relations with the First Lady were bitter. His poorly developed
political instincts are blamed for public relations disasters like
Reagan's speech at the Bitburg cemetery for the German war
dead and for the failure to foresee and contain the Iran-contra
scandal. But in the long run Baker's tenure at Treasury may
have left the more important legacy, for Baker, perhaps the
supreme pragmatist of late-twentieth-century American politics, completely reversed the policies of his predecessor in the
international arena.

Don Regan had spent his working life listening to the financial markets. But Jim Baker was the consummate political
operator. What mattered to him were the Texas business community, the White House, the Congress, the mainstream of the
Republican party. Don Regan was reinforced in his predilec-
tions by the ideological monetarism of his key subordinate,
Beryl Sprinkel. Sprinkel left Treasury with Regan, however, to
become chairman of the Council of Economic Advisers. In

Sprinkel's place, Baker installed his own right-hand man, the brilliant and acerbic Richard Darman. If anyone had political instincts equal to those of Jim Baker, it was Richard Darman. Hedrick Smith, who writes of Baker as "smart, cautious, patient, and decisive . . . he sees the interrelationships of issues, people, money and votes,"[4] portrays Darman as having "an intellectual's fascination with power and process, with puzzling out the conundrums of government, with plotting, planning, drafting, scheming, making the pieces fall into place."[5]

When Baker and Darman took over their new jobs at Treasury, they instantly recognized a political crisis in the making and set about creating the groundwork for a political solution. The crisis had its roots in the continued deterioration of the U.S. trade position, particularly vis-à-vis Japan. Bad trade numbers coincided with a rebounding dollar, climbing again after a temporary retreat in late 1984, and received opinion was that the one explained the other. The only dissenters were a handful of monetarist ideologues in the White House, where Sprinkel, now holding court at the Council of Economic Advisers, continued to maintain that the markets determined the proper value of the dollar, and a scattering of Japan specialists—Clyde Prestowitz at Commerce, Joseph Massey and Glen Fukushima in the Office of the U.S. Trade Representative—who thought exchange rates an insufficient explanation for the bilateral trade deficit. But the Japan specialists were a tiny group of mid-level government officials, while the ideologues at the White House were finally being overwhelmed by the forces arrayed against them. As one Washington pundit is reputed to have said, "There's nothing wrong with the U.S.-Japan trade deficit that a rate of one hundred eighty yen to the dollar won't solve."[6]

The pressure on Congress and the administration to do something about the high dollar grew intense. Lee Morgan of Caterpillar, whose efforts to persuade the administration to take action on the high dollar are noted in the previous chapter, received explicit support in his campaign from the prestigious Business Roundtable.[7] He was joined by a host of America's most prominent CEOs—Philip Caldwell at Ford, Roger Smith at General Motors, Colby Chandler of Kodak, David Roderick of U.S. Steel, Robert Galvin of Motorola, Ruben Mettler of TRW, and, as one might expect, Lee Iacocca of Chrysler. The board of directors of the National Association of Manufacturers came out against the strong dollar, as did the AFL-CIO Executive Council. Members of Congress and cabinet officials were besieged by requests to do something.

Meanwhile congressional leaders, feeling the heat from their constituencies, began muttering that if the administration did nothing, they would take matters into their own hands. By the spring of 1985 the administration's relations with Congress were in bad shape, despite Reagan's landslide reelection and a Senate nominally in the hands of Republicans. The administration's unyielding opposition to anything that smacked of higher taxes wrecked an elaborately crafted attempt by the Republican congressional leadership to deal with the deficit. The administration appeared particularly insensitive on trade issues. In February the White House had signaled Tokyo that Japan's "voluntary" restraint on Japanese cars and auto part exports could be lifted without any counterbalancing concession. The president had moved Bill Brock, the U.S. trade representative, over to become secretary of labor and then left the trade office without a leader for more than three months. A petition to protect the besieged footwear industry was rejected. These sorts of incidents compounded the impression that the White House didn't care about trade or what the high dollar was doing to American industry. A seething Congress openly threatened protectionist legislation.

The pressure on Baker to do something was not limited to Congress, the business community, and the policy hustlers of K Street and Dupont Circle. At their regular private weekly breakfasts Paul Volcker repeatedly warned Baker of the potential for a sudden market adjustment in the value of the dollar, with earthquakelike effects on the stock exchange and bond prices. Trade hawks in the administration, such as Commerce

Secretary Malcolm Baldrige or Agriculture Secretary John Block, conveyed the panic from their respective constituencies.

It was a classic political dilemma of the sort Baker had confronted often in his public life. A seasoned politician caught in such a squeeze looks around at the various tools at his disposal, picks up one to see if it works, and, when it doesn't, tries something else. One tool that had clearly failed was the Yen / Dollar Committee from the Regan / Sprinkel regime. Japanese concessions extracted by this committee had lowered the walls marking off Japan's financial institutions and increased the financing options for its corporate treasurers. They had provided nimble foreign investment bankers in Tokyo with ways of making money, but they had done nothing to bring down the dollar.

If "liberalizing" the Japanese financial markets wasn't bringing down the dollar, what else might? Serious deficit cutting would help, but the president refused to consider either raising taxes or running down his political capital by tackling the middle-class entitlements spending that formed the core of the deficit problem. Without presidential leadership, Congress would not act. If progress on the deficit was thus out of the question, how much more so was a fundamental overhaul of the structure of global trade and economic relations, an overhaul that would replace the United States as the supplier of a universal currency and every other country's market of last resort. While this would indeed bring down the dollar, such a course was fraught with peril—among other things, the United States would no longer have been able to finance its huge deficits with impunity—and in any case doing anything along such lines went way beyond Baker's mandate.

But Baker did have the power to intervene in foreign exchange markets. With their ideological constraints, his immediate predecessors had not used it, and such power in any case had limits. Foreign countries could undermine it. Monetary policy could contradict it. For intervention to be effective, the Fed had to be on board as well, although as Volcker himself later acknowledged, the Treasury has "a certain pride of place in exchange rate and intervention policy."[8] For all the constraints on its use, however, the Treasury had the final say on foreign exchange market intervention, and Baker seized it.

The Treasury's clout derived from its position as the ultimate force in the foreign exchange market. Until the early 1980s exchange rates were thought to be driven by trade. A Japanese exporter receives dollars in return for the goods he has sold to Americans. He takes the dollars to the bank and gets yen in return. The bank in turn sells the dollars for yen. If more banks are seeking to sell dollars for yen than to sell yen for dollars, the price of dollars in yen terms should fall, reflecting the higher demand for yen.

But it turned out not to be this simple. Capital flows—investments seeking high returns—began to dwarf trade flows. Investors all over the world saw dollar interest rates soar in the early 1980s and poured their money into dollar securities, driving up the price of the currency in terms of other currencies. In turn investors invited speculation. The speculators were not the shadowy moneymen of popular imagination, lurking the back streets of Geneva and Zurich, but mostly the foreign exchange departments of banks and securities companies. These departments had originally been set up as service centers to handle the needs of customers involved in international trade. But as the demand for foreign currencies grew with investors seeking ever-higher returns, the banks realized the potential profits to be made from speculation and began to trade for their own account. When foreign exchange traders sensed the dollar would be rising, for example, whether because of interest rates, U.S. government financing needs, trade flows, or loose remarks from central bankers, a quick in and out from an institution able to commit hundreds of millions to the market could result in profits of tens of thousands of dollars from a morning's trade. Monetarist economists had confidently predicted long-term currency stability from the floating-rate system instituted in 1973. Instead the tens of millions of potential trading profits in currency movements led at times to speculative frenzies that exaggerated swings in foreign exchange prices, sucking billions of dollars into the market. The daily turnover could reach as high as a trillion dollars. But financial authorities could, if they chose, lean against the market. Currencies in the post–Bretton Woods era were ultimately the fiat creations of finance ministries and central banks. Their ability to create money at will, to influence the price (in interest rates) and quantity of money meant that they were the ultimate powers in the foreign exchange markets. As noted, their power had limits. Market intervention not backed by appropriate monetary policy (so-called sterilized intervention—e.g., selling dollars while keeping money tight or vice versa) was ultimately unconvincing. Then power over money was shared in most countries between finance ministries and central banks, with nervous politicians always hovering in the background. One institution could not easily work at cross-purposes with the other, particularly in the United States, where the power of the two was roughly equal. (It was a different story in Japan, where the Finance Ministry clearly had the upper hand over the Bank of Japan, or in Germany, where the Bundesbank was much more powerful than the Finance Ministry.) And of course it mattered very much what foreign authorities were doing. If, for example, the United States wanted a cheaper mark while Germany favored a more expensive one, an attempt by the authorities in one country to achieve its ends might be canceled out by the authorities in the other.

But most of these constraints on Baker's ability to act were absent in early 1985. While tight money policies at the Fed were one of the key reasons behind the soaring dollar, Paul Volcker had been concerned for years at the possibility of a sudden reversal in market psychology and a catastrophic hard landing for the dollar. He was prepared to be helpful in any measured attempts to let some steam out of the currency. Further, money had been eased significantly late in 1984, with two cuts in the discount rate, so monetary policy would not be working against attempts to reduce the value of the dollar.

Perhaps even more important, finance ministers and central bankers in other countries were largely united in their belief that the soaring dollar posed a threat to the global system. As one of Japan's most eminent journalists writes, "US trading partners were utterly exasperated by the hands-off approach of the Reagan administration. They had pleaded for three years for a reduction of the budget deficit and a decrease in the value of the dollar, but their requests had fallen on deaf ears. Currency relationships oscillated wildly, straining the world trading system. Trade wars, both between the United States and Japan and between the United States and Western Europe, seemed ready to erupt. Something needed to be done."[9] Karl Otto Pohl, the president of the Bundesbank, had repeatedly expressed his frustration with the cavalier American attitude toward the high dollar and had authorized several massive interventions by the German central bank in late 1984 and early 1985 in vain attempts to halt the dollar's inexorable rise against the deutsche mark. When, in early 1985, the British pound slipped so low that it neared a humiliating one-to-one with the dollar, Margaret Thatcher took leave of her orthodox, intervention-eschewing monetarism and telephoned Ronald Reagan urging action to support the pound and stem the dollar's rise. Facing elections that same year, French President François Mitterrand's Socialist government was terrified at the prospect of having to raise interest rates to support the franc, which stood early in 1985 at a post-1960 low against the dollar.

But nowhere was there more concern than in Japan. Exchange rate control had long dominated external economic policy making in Japan. Certainly the early 1980s had been a kind of golden age for Japan's export industries. Spurred on by the tremendous cost advantage derived from the strong dollar / weak yen, Japanese companies had achieved dizzying successes across a range of products. Automobiles, consumer electronics, construction equipment, machine tools, semiconductors, steel. But it had become all too easy. Japan's elite officials feared the growing protectionist clamor in Congress. More fundamentally the prospect of a hollowed-out, deindustrialized America genuinely dismayed them. They were profoundly disturbed by what the United States was doing to itself. Japan's administrators regarded manufacturing as the sine qua non of national wealth. They were obsessively concerned with international competitiveness. They viewed deficits and loose fiscal policies as cancers that sapped vitality from a country and destroyed economic discipline. From their perspective, the United States had embarked on slow-motion suicide.

That the destruction of the American industrial base was happening largely at the hands of Japanese companies only worsened their apprehensions. The administrators recoiled from direct restraints on industry in its pursuit of new markets and more capacity; the likes of the "voluntary" restraints imposed on Japanese auto exports in 1981 to forestall congressionally imposed quotas were invariably extremely unpleasant exercises.* But they did come around to believing they could do something about the yen. In the words of Nakasone Yasuhiro, prime minister during the period:

In the first half of 1985, we tried very hard to solve Japan's surplus problem. We initiated MOSS [Market Oriented Sector Specific] talks with the U.S. administration to open Japan's markets. And we decided on action programs to liberalize further. We were thinking of another liberalization plan some time for September. But by June it became more evident that those specific trade liberalization negotiations simply were not enough to cope with the imbalance problem. Therefore, I made up my mind to launch a comprehensive scheme to tackle the issue with US support. It, of course, included yen-dollar currency realignment. I told my idea to [then Finance Minister] Takeshita and [then Finance Vice Minister for International Affairs] Oba. They both agreed.[11]

Nakasone had long believed there could be advantages for Japan in a strong yen. Years earlier, during a time when most of Japan's administrators operated under a kind of "weak yen

---

*The great MITI veteran Amaya Naohiro, often identified as one the architects of the economic miracle, found himself labeled a "running dog" of the Americans by industry figures for his implementation of the voluntary restraints. He retired from MITI shortly afterward to "take responsibility."[10]

good, strong yen bad" mantra, Nakasone had pointed out how inappropriate it was for a strong, self-confident Japan to hide behind a weak currency. His views had been dismissed as naïve. By the mid-1980s, however, Nakasone was prime minister of the country, popular with the voters, and ambitious to wrest some power away from the bureaucracies and lodge it where he believed it properly belonged, with Japan's elected politicians.

Nakasone was particularly skillful in the use of so-called *shingikai* (councils of experts formed to study a problem). He convened a *shingikai* to look into currency and capital market liberalization matters and commissioned a private study from one of its members, the great éminence grise of Japanese finance Hosomi Takashi. Hosomi had been vice minister for international affairs at the Ministry of Finance during the second great postwar currency crisis, the floating of the yen in 1973. He had participated directly in the Smithsonian negotiations that led to floating rates. He recommended to Nakasone that the yen be gradually revalued to the range of 170–180. He also encouraged Nakasone to consider the possibility of a new international monetary order that would replace what he viewed as the instability and chaos of freely floating exchange rates with a so-called snake arrangement—bands within which currencies could float, with limits to be enforced by the joint intervention of the world's major central banks. Nakasone wholeheartedly endorsed Hosomi's conclusions. The prime minister "instructed" the MOF to begin a comprehensive study of how such a system might be implemented. Even more important, he told Jim Baker what he was thinking when the latter was in Tokyo in June 1985.

Baker was receptive. The new treasury secretary had wasted no time in reversing his predecessor's hands-off policy toward the foreign exchange markets. The dollar had started to rise again in February, a few weeks after Baker took his new post. He immediately ordered market interventions, assuming, perhaps a bit naïvely, that the mere signal of policy reversal would be sufficient to effect a change of course. But the efforts were to no avail; the markets shrugged them off. Bundesbank interventions were similarly useless. The dollar stayed stubbornly high—above the ¥250 rate—right through the spring. Thus, when Nakasone clued Baker in on his ideas, Baker seized the opportunity to begin exploring coordinated intervention.

He instructed his assistant treasury secretary David Mulford to sound out the Japanese bureaucracy. On June 19, 1985, Mulford met Oba Tomomitsu, vice minister of finance for international affairs. Mulford wanted Oba's reaction to the idea that Baker propose formally to then Finance Minister Takeshita Noboru joint action to bring down the dollar, with, as one account of their meeting notes, "the Europeans [being] asked to assists."[12] Oba's reaction was favorable, and on June 21 Takeshita and Baker met to give the idea of joint intervention a formal seal of approval.

Mulford and Oba negotiated through the summer. Both sides needed political cover. Baker had to contend with the monetarist ideologues in the White House; much of the Japanese media and indeed many of the administrators were still conditioned to thinking automatically that a strong yen was dangerous for Japan. Predictably the Japanese side pushed for measures to reduce the American deficit, which Baker knew to be politically impossible. The Americans wanted to see fiscal stimulus and tax cuts out of the Japanese; the MOF viscerally opposed anything that smacked of fiscal indiscipline. But sufficient common ground was found to give the two sides what they needed for cover purposes: The Americans would commit themselves to tax reform (Baker was in fact pushing Don Regan's tax reform legislation), and the Japanese would continue financial market "liberalization."

Mulford went to Europe to ensure that Germany, France, and Britain were on board. The Europeans believed that responsibility for the problems lay with Japan and the United States. U.S. fiscal indiscipline combined with Japan's closed markets and structural trade surpluses had brought about the situation. Why should they risk political capital? Why should

Germany be designated as a mischief-making "surplus country" when in Bonn's view, it was all Japan's and the United States' doing? But the potential danger to the liberal world trading order convinced the Germans they had to go along. Japanese negotiators couldn't politically accept sole responsibility for system-straining surpluses. So the Germans grudgingly agreed to a designation as a "lesser" surplus country.[13]

Meanwhile, back in the States, Baker needed to secure his domestic base. Paul Volcker could easily destroy Baker's plans and credibility with any hint that the Fed was planning to tighten. Volcker had, after all, let the Jimmy Carter who had appointed him go down to defeat rather than ease up on monetary policy. He had been vilified as a latter-day Scrooge from the length and breadth of the American political spectrum for his ultimately successful efforts to purge inflation out of the economy. A man with this sort of track record was not going to reveal to a neophyte treasury secretary his plans for monetary policy. But Baker got the signal he needed. In Volcker's own words:

Baker explained to me his idea of a G-5* meeting to coordinate intervention to reduce the value of the dollar. He also said he was aware the whole thing would be undercut if monetary policy were tightened, and he did not want to proceed against that possibility. I replied, as any Fed chairman should, that I was not in a position to give anyone commitments about monetary policy over any substantial period of time. Nonetheless, I was personally convinced that, quite independent of any policy he might adopt toward the dollar, there was not a serious risk that monetary policy would need to be tightened during the next few weeks or months. I pointed out that the economy was slowing and inflation was declining to the lowest level in years. That seemed to satisfy him.[14]

Then there was the problem of the diehard monetarists in the White House. Again, to quote Volcker: "I recall asking how he [Baker] was going to get all this past Regan and Sprinkel in

* "G-5" refers to the periodic informal meetings, begun in 1973, of the finance ministers of the world's five leading industrial powers: the United States, Japan, Germany, France, and Britain. Later the group was expanded to G-7, bringing in Italy and Canada.

the White House, and ultimately President Reagan. He quite properly told me that was his problem, not mine. I was later told he did not notify the White House until a day or two before the Plaza meeting, and he did it by using his close relationship with the president to inform him directly and in the most general terms."[15]

Baker had thus prepared the groundwork for a momentous financial conference, comparable in its effects to the Versailles Conference of 1919, the Bretton Woods Conference of 1944, and the Smithsonian Conference of 1973. The participants were the G-5 finance ministers and the heads of their respective central banks. The place was the Plaza Hotel in New York. The result was the Plaza Accord.

The accord was, in essence, two things.* First, it was a signal of the dangers to any speculator or investor continuing to bet on the dollar's going up. The world's important finance ministries and central banks were all agreed that the dollar had gone up too much. No longer, they hoped, could the market play off the Bundesbank against the Bank of Japan, the Treasury against the Fed, and people who tried it were going to get burned. The famous photograph taken at the press conference announcing the accord reveals a lot. It shows the five finance ministers (Baker, Takeshita, Nigel Lawson of the UK, Gerhard Stoltenberg of Germany, and Pierre Bérégovoy of France) with Jim Baker pushing a sheepish-looking Paul Volcker out in front of them. Now Jim Baker may not have had graduate degrees in monetary economics, but he certainly understood photo ops. The photograph said, unmistakably, "We're all on board here, including the Fed."

Second, the accord represented an actual agreement to do what it took to bring down the dollar. The agreement was

---

*This account of the of the Plaza Accord and its immediate aftermath is largely drawn from Funabashi Yoichi's *Managing the Dollar: From the Plaza to the Louvre.* Funabashi is with the *Asahi Shimbun,* Japan's most important general newspaper, and is one of Japan's leading correspondents. Funabashi wrote the book in English, not his native language, and it reads somewhat haltingly as a result. But as a piece of reporting it is brilliant.

secret with respect to how far the signatories wanted to see
the dollar fall. Part of this secrecy was deliberate—keep the
speculators guessing—but part of it reflected genuine disagreement among the parties. The Germans, continuing to view the
problem as a yen / dollar misalignment, sought only a modest
decline in the dollar vis-à-vis the mark. The Americans wanted
to see much more. Takeshita surprised the meeting by voluntarily announcing Japan was prepared to see the yen rise to
¥200 to the dollar from the ¥239 where it then stood. While
the Europeans, used to Japanese recalcitrance, were delighted,
some Treasury officials privately wanted the yen to rise much
farther. But all the Plaza participants could agree on the desir-
ability of a 10 to 12 percent weakening of the dollar against the
other major currencies, and they determined to set aside $18
billion among them as a war chest to finance the interventions
needed to bring this about. The United States and Japan were
to contribute 30 percent each, the countries of the European
Monetary System (EMS), led by Germany, would contribute
35 percent, and Britain—not yet a member of EMS—would
kick in the remaining 5 percent.

On a short-term basis the tactics agreed on at the Plaza
worked brilliantly. To understand what happened, one needs to
keep in mind that the world's financial markets operate on a
twenty-four-hour cycle, opening in Tokyo, moving to London
(during the summer 5:00 P.M. in Tokyo is 9:00 A.M. in London), finishing the day in New York, and then returning to
Tokyo for the new day. The only break in the circuit occurs over
the weekend, between the New York close on Friday and the
Tokyo opening on Monday. Governments usually announce
developments likely to shake the financial markets during this
break, and so it was with the Plaza Accord. The news conference announcing the accord started about 4:00 P.M. Sunday
in New York. Ordinarily this would have given the finance
ministries and central banks (the latter are actually responsible
for the mechanics of intervention) fewer than four hours to

get ready, for 4:00 P.M. in New York was already 5:00 A.M., September 23, in Tokyo.

But September 23 is a holiday in Japan. So the governments waited for Europe to open, with a full eleven hours to marshal their troops. Meanwhile action shifted from New York to the world's only open financial market in a small city nestled around a bay—Wellington, New Zealand. On Wellington's modest trading floors, pandemonium broke loose as news of the accord flashed over the wire services. The greatest symbolic reversal of wealth and economic power in the history of the world was under way. The previous Friday the yen had closed at 239 to the dollar. By Monday evening, when Wellington handed the baton to an awakening Europe, the yen was trading at 234— and the $18 billion war chest was untouched. The photograph of Volcker and the Gang of Five had done a lot.

During the morning in Europe the dollar fell another 4 yen to 230. When it rose in the early afternoon to 231, the first intervention occurred. The Bundesbank started to sell dollars in Frankfurt. It was the first time since the previous spring that the Bundesbank had intervened. Early afternoon in Europe coincides with morning in New York, and the New York Fed joined the fray, driving the dollar down to 225. Post–Plaza Day One had seen the dollar drop from 239 to 225.

Tuesday morning in Tokyo saw the first real test. Speculators entered the market in droves, seeing cheap dollars and doubting the resolve of the Bank of Japan and its overseers at the Ministry of Finance. The BOJ poured money into the market, spending nearly $1 billion in one breathtaking morning— much of it between ten-thirty and eleven—to halt the dollar rise. That day marked the largest turnover in history to date in the Tokyo foreign exchange market. The speculators were beaten back, but only temporarily. In the following two weeks the Americans would sell nearly $500 million against the yen and the deutsche mark. But it still wasn't enough. Heavy upward pressure on the dollar came in the days after the October

7 meetings of the World Bank and the IMF in Seoul. The meetings produced no new statement of resolve, and many believed that the dollar depreciation had run its course.

To counteract this impression, the Fed made its first-ever sale of dollars in the Tokyo market, a tactic deliberately leaked to the press. The Fed sold another $800 million in New York, driving the dollar down to 205. When, in early November, the dollar threatened to rise again, a final double whammy from the Fed and the Bank of Japan on November 7 kept it to that level. The back of the strong dollar had been broken. By the end of the year the dollar had sunk below 200, a level not reached since. More than $10 billion of the war chest had been spent. In six weeks the Plaza Accord signatories had mounted the most impressive coordinated multinational attack on currency markets by governments in history.

The objective of bringing down the dollar had been achieved. Economists and historians will argue for decades whether the dollar would have fallen anyway. Those who maintain this note that the dollar was already on a downward trend, having dropped from 259 earlier in the year to the 239 where it stood on the eve of the accord. They also point to the "unsustainable" U.S. current account deficits at those levels. But the 1980s made a mockery of such talk. Many "unsustainable" imbalances are, nearly a decade later, still being sustained—among them the U.S. trade deficit, the U.S. federal deficit, and the Japanese current account surplus.*

Others argue that the Plaza Accord permanently changed market psychology, pointing to the waves of speculative attacks that had to be beaten back by the central banks. Only after speculators had lost tens of millions of dollars did the markets become convinced the G-5 governments had an agreement with teeth, that they would do whatever it took to drive the

---

*C. Fred Bergsten said in 1986 that he "sharply disagreed" with the view that "the world will sustain external surpluses on the part of Japan on the order of $50 billion or so for the rest of the decade."[16] Five years into yet another decade, the Japanese are still sustaining annual surpluses of $50 billion on their trade and current accounts, except that these surpluses are now closer to $150 billion.

dollar down. Had there been no Plaza Accord, might the dollar have stayed in the 210–250 range for a few more years? The question will never be answered.

Jim Baker had again proved himself America's most adept political operator. He had done something about the high dollar blamed for crippling American industry, he had secured the cooperation of the other major economic powers, and most important, he had dragged in the Japanese. After all, their companies were now supposed to lose market shares and see their profits fall. Their insurance companies and trust banks had to suffer losses on the dollar securities in which they had invested so heavily.

The work of diplomacy done, the exhausted traders of the G-5 central banks could sit back and let the magic of macroeconomics take over. First, it would be necessary to wait out the so-called J-curve effect. Orders had already been placed for Japanese goods. With the falling dollar, these goods would end up being more expensive in dollar terms. Thus a temporary, short-term effect of the dollar's devaluation would be, as good economists pointed out, to increase the Japanese surplus. But this wouldn't last long because Japanese companies might be expected to raise their prices in dollar terms and orders for Japanese goods might be expected to fall. Perhaps Japanese companies, as they saw their profits dwindle and disappear, would retreat from markets where they had established beachheads. And of course Japanese consumers, seeing cheap American goods on their store shelves, would snap them up, leading to massive increases of U.S. sales in Japan.

But it didn't happen that way. Against the market economies of Western Europe, U.S. trade numbers showed a marked improvement. But if you looked at the U.S.-Japan trade statistics without knowing the timing of the Plaza Accord, if you did not know that between the spring of 1985 and the summer of 1987 the dollar had lost half its value against the yen, the statistics would yield no hint that this had happened. In fact, the trade deficit with Japan expanded each year between 1984 and

1987. While it finally, after 1987, dropped back a bit, the deficit never fell to the level it had been in 1984, and by the early 1990s it was rising again. The greatest short-term shift in "hard" currency values in history led to *no discernible impact* on trade numbers. The entire exercise, the doubtless permanent and irrevocable diminution of American economic power, had been done *for nothing*.

How was Jim Baker to know this? His advice came from the upper levels of the economic policy–making apparatus in the American government—the Treasury, the Council of Economic Advisers, the Office of Management and Budget. These bureaus were staffed by the finest products of Harvard, Yale, MIT, and the University of Chicago, where they had been taught to think of corporations as profit- and utility-maximizing black boxes, responding rationally to a rational world of price signals. For these men and women, successful economies were prima facie organized along market lines, and the extent of government interference in an economy defined the extent of less than optimal economic performance. That there were corporations somewhere in the world for whom profit making was an unimportant, if not positively unworthy, goal did not enter their considerations. They had never thought about the possibility that economic entities could be free of the fear of bankruptcy and still be competitive or that there were successful economic systems where credit was allocated on a basis that had nothing to do with the capacity to generate profits.

So no one stood close enough to Jim Baker to tell him how Japanese corporations would react when the yen was forced up against the dollar, to let him know that they would not surrender markets recently conquered, to point out that with infinitely patient financial backing, they could afford to see their profit margins on exports disappear and still hang on. There was no one to remind him that the prices of imported goods were not going to fall in Japan, irrespective of the external value of the yen, or to talk to him about the actual choices Japanese consumers were permitted to make or just where the balance of power lay in Japan among manufacturers, importers, distributors, and consumers.

None of Baker's advisers had studied the way business and government interact in Japan. None of them grasped that although Prime Minister Nakasone and Finance Minister Takeshita were genuinely concerned about the trade imbalance and hoped currency realignment might help bring it down, they lacked the power to dictate policy. There was no one to warn him that the Ministry of Finance would compensate Japanese industry for the damage of the Plaza Accord and, no matter what it took, ensure that Japanese industry got the financing it needed to remain competitive.

Instead, as the fall of 1985 turned into the winter of 1986 and the trade numbers didn't improve, Baker and his people began to worry. They had pushed the dollar down, endangering the ability of the United States to continue to finance its federal deficit, and had little to show for it in the trade numbers. If an economy isn't responding to the price signals that a change in currency values implies, then, if you've been properly trained by Keynesian economists, you recognize the problem as a lack of aggregate demand. And the textbook solution to that is low interest rates and government pump priming.

So Baker began to arm-twist his counterparts in Bonn and Tokyo to stimulate their economies. If aggregate demand rose, consumers would have more money to spend and would buy more imports, or at least that was the theory. The Japanese were willing to consider half the package—they might lower their interest rates, although this had little to do with putting more money in consumers' pockets; it was rather a way to help industry cope with the higher yen—but they were not going to buy off on fiscal stimulus. The Ministry of Finance detested deficits. Orthodox Keynesian economics may tell you that deficit spending increases aggregate demand by putting into consumers' pockets money that is then spent on goods. But the MOF knew that with rigid labor and distribution markets, deficit spending in Japan did not translate into pay raises and extra hiring, not to mention more spending on imports. Instead it weakened the ministry's key weapon over the other ministries, particularly the Construction Ministry: its control of the budget.[17]

Deficit spending in Japan played the economic equivalent of the continuous warfare in George Orwell's *1984*. In *1984*'s Oceania the idea was to keep people working without increasing purchasing power. In Japan it had much the same effect. Deficit spending allowed the Construction Ministry to boost its political power at the expense of the MOF. If you visit the Japanese countryside, you will see roads cut through mountains—magnificent feats of engineering—that go from nowhere to nowhere. You will see, winding their way through the paddies, tiny creeks encased in huge concrete embankments sufficient to contain the high-water surges of major rivers. At the seashore you will see immense harbors cut from rock with no ships, vast breakwalls protecting a few huts. These are the results of Japanese deficits, "concrete" manifestations of the world's most formidable "iron triangle"—the bureaucrats in the Construction Ministry, the construction *zoku* or (tribe) in the Japanese Diet, and the Japanese construction industry, riddled with graft and underworld connections.

So the MOF was not about to agree to any new round of deficit spending. In describing the first post-Plaza G-5 meeting, held in early 1986 in London, Funabashi Yoichi notes, ". . . the Japanese Ministry of Finance revealed its priority in a strategy it would use again and again. [Finance Minister] Takeshita sought to maintain autonomy in his own domain, fiscal policy, by evading international coordination. He therefore directed attention on monetary policy and, specifically, on coordinated discount-rate cuts to relieve the pressure on him to stimulate the economy with fiscal tools."[18]

The Germans weren't even willing to go that far. While a Bank of Japan show of independence in October 1985—the BOJ had raised interest rates on its own—had been quickly slapped down by the Ministry of Finance, the Bundesbank was no BOJ. The strongest and most independent of the world's major central banks, the Bundesbank had as its constitutionally charged mission the ensuring of the deutsche mark's integrity. No one would dictate interest rates or monetary policy to this proud breed of central bankers, irrespective of the pressure their finance ministry might be getting from an American treasury secretary.

With neither Japan nor Germany willing to stimulate its economy to make up for the loss of American purchasing power in the wake of the Plaza Accord, Baker turned to "dollar terrorism." The dollar still functioned as the central pole supporting the world's financial and trading systems. Baker's tactics in essence amounted to shaking this pole and threatening to bring down the entire tent unless the other occupants did what he wanted. Of course the tent would have fallen on him as well—the United States was absolutely dependent on foreign funding for the deficit—but Baker had a well-honed sense of how far he could push his counterparts.

The perennial wrangling among factions of Japan's "ruling" Liberal Democratic party (LDP) played into Baker's hands. Japanese elections were scheduled for July 1986, and Nakasone desperately wanted a third term as prime minister. For this to happen, the LDP would have to do exceptionally well at the polls. Nakasone had been a popular prime minister with the voters, arguably the most popular in the postwar period until Hosokawa Morihiro ended the LDP hegemony in 1993. In Japan, however, voters do not choose their leaders. Between 1955 and 1993 these leaders were chosen for them by party elders in careful rotation to preserve the balance of power among the factions that constitute the LDP. For Nakasone to disrupt the careful rotations, he would have to lead the LDP to a great victory. And Nakasone's Achilles' heel was the yen / dollar rate.

The Japanese public had long been conditioned to equate a high yen with trouble for Japan. With the yen soaring in the wake of the Plaza Accord, the newspapers were filled with the woes of small exporters and the crisis atmosphere at large companies. Takeshita Noboru, who as finance minister had directly negotiated the accord, acquired the nickname *Endaka Daijin* (Minister High Yen); fellow LDP Dietmen didn't even want to be seen on the same campaign platforms with him. Nakasone's rivals in the LDP were particularly scathing, chief among them Miyazawa Kiichi.

The yen continued its inexorable rise. It had ended 1985 at just over 200 to the dollar. Three months later the dollar had fallen to 179 with no bottom in sight—real political trouble for Nakasone, as the yen closed in on its previous postwar high of 177, set during the 1978 currency crisis. On April 8 Baker and Takeshita met in Washington, while Volcker and Bank of Japan Governor Sumida Satoshi met on April 10. The Americans arm-twisted the Japanese into agreeing to coordinated interest rate cuts. Had the Americans acted alone, the unilateral move would have set the dollar back sharply, as investors fled to currencies with higher interest rates.

The coordination in interest rate cuts was not enough. The dollar continued to sink. The annual summit of the world's industrialized powers was held that year in Tokyo in the first week of May. Nakasone acquitted himself brilliantly, acting as a deft and forceful chairman, erasing the image of the obsequious, timid, unreliable Japanese politician. But the summit did nothing to halt the dollar's rise. The yen broke ¥160 / $1 the week after the summit, and Nakasone, for all the kudos he had received for his summit performance, was in serious trouble. The *Asahi Shimbun* described the situation as a "rebellion by the market" symbolizing a major miscalculation by Nakasone,[19] while the *Nikkei* noted that despite Nakasone's confident words, "we hear no applause from the audience."[20]

Baker came to the rescue. For the first time since he had taken office as treasury secretary, he hinted that the dollar had fallen fast enough, letting his remarks come in testimony to the Senate Finance Committee on May 13. The markets interpreted Baker's statements as a vote for Nakasone, as he had intended them to do, and upward pressure on the yen abated temporarily.

Baker's support, however, came at a high price. Over the next eight months the Americans would continually remind Nakasone and his ministers of their support and use it to extract more cooperation in lowering interest rates and perhaps even getting some fiscal stimulus. After a stunning LDP victory in the July elections, Nakasone got his third term and then proceeded to make a typically very astute move. He gave the Finance Ministry portfolio to the leading internal party critic of the soaring yen, Miyazawa Kiichi. Now Miyazawa would be forced himself to contend with the tremendous pressure Baker was applying.

Miyazawa was a headache to career MOF officials. He had risen through the ranks at the ministry before launching his political career and was thus less susceptible than usual to manipulation by his nominal subordinates. Miyazawa is a brilliant, headstrong man with a thorough command of the intricacies of exchange rate and monetary policy, a skilled negotiator completely fluent in both English and French.* He was perfectly capable of conducting complex negotiations with the Jim Bakers of the world and, unlike most of his predecessors or successors, had no need for a small army of MOF bureaucrats at his side to choreograph his every move. Miyazawa also had his own opinions on fiscal stimulus. Far from having the usual MOF allergy to deficit spending, Miyazawa could see the uses of extra discretionary funds to politicians. And whatever his background, he had become a politician.

But the most skilled and astute politician cannot ultimately control a Japanese bureaucracy bent on sabotaging a policy or a leader not to its liking. First the permanent bureaucracy

---

*Miyazawa is respected for his brilliance but not terribly well liked by his colleagues, particularly because he tends to advertise his intelligence. Laid out on the coffee table in his office anteroom are current issues not only of the *International Herald Tribune* but of *Le Monde* as well. Such ostentatious displays of erudition do not go over well in Japan's political world.

disrupted a private meeting that Baker had sought with Miyazawa on September 1, when he was in Tokyo.[21] Miyazawa did give the press and the bureaucracy the slip for a secret meeting with Baker in San Francisco a few days later. Baker pushed for lower interest rates and fiscal stimulus, explicitly reminding Miyazawa of the support he had given Nakasone. Miyazawa insisted that America stop "talking down the dollar" and help to stabilize the yen / dollar rate. At a second meeting on September 26, in Washington, Baker pointed out that in the intervening three weeks the yen / dollar rate had stabilized around ¥153 / $1, hinting that the United States was now in agreement on the need to stabilize the dollar. He extracted a commitment from Miyazawa to a supplementary budget stimulus of some $23 billion as well as a Bank of Japan discount rate cut of another 50 basis points. News of the Baker-Miyazawa agreements was greeted with apprehension in Europe. With the Germans unwilling to consider any sort of stimulus to their economy, it appeared as if Baker had begun playing a "Japan card." Commentators spoke openly of the replacement of G-5 with G-2.

Baker and Miyazawa agreed to issue a communiqué on October 31 containing their agreement. But as the day approached, the yen began to weaken, heading toward ¥170. It looked as if either Miyazawa were double-crossing Baker or, more likely, MOF bureaucrats were deliberately sabotaging Miyazawa by destroying his credibility with the Americans. Tense telephone conversations ensured. The communiqué was rescued, but only at the cost of a significant dilution of the announced American commitment to stabilize the dollar.

As the year closed, the situation continued to deteriorate. The much-vaunted fiscal stimulus turned out to be little more than moving some numbers around from the following year's budget. A senior MOF bureaucrat later admitted that "Miyazawa was being undercut by the central bank and his own bureaucracy."[22] The favorable impression he had initially made with Baker and Darman was crumbling as they finally realized, like so many of their predecessors and successors, that Japanese politicians cannot deliver commitments.

Not that the Americans were trustworthy either. Repeated "commitments" to reduce the budget deficit against the background of the Gramm-Rudman Act that "mandated" budget cuts were gradually seen as just so much noise. Republicans lost control of the Senate in the November 1986 elections, meaning that the administration could no longer argue convincingly it was in a position to forestall protectionist legislation. And with the growing brouhaha of the Iran-contra scandal, the political capital of what had once seemed the strongest administration in a generation was almost depleted.

At the end of the year the November trade figures were announced. The United States recorded the worst monthly deficit ever. Panic hit the foreign exchange markets. The dollar dropped through the psychologically key ¥150 level to ¥149. A desperate Miyazawa, his political future in the balance, rushed to Washington on January 21 to try to induce American help to hold the dollar at ¥150.

Baker seems to have been finally convinced that a weakening dollar could pose a real threat to his entire economic strategy by provoking a bond market panic. Private foreign investors were fleeing the market for U.S. government securities. Virtually all the foreign buying was being done by central banks, led by the Bank of Japan. Paul Volcker was warning of renewed inflation and a dollar free fall. The Germans, who had maintained a haughty distance, were jousting with upheavals inside the European Monetary System, and the French were joining the Americans in pressing Germany to consider some stimulus.

The Americans signaled that they would not oppose a massive Bank of Japan effort to halt the fall of the dollar. They themselves even intervened to support the dollar for the first time since the 1978 dollar crisis. And the Germans, Japanese,

Americans, British, and French all agreed to the urgency of a new Plaza Accord type of meeting. Nigel Lawson, the British chancellor of the exchequer, called it Plaza II.

The meeting was held on February 22, 1987, at an even more famous site than the Plaza Hotel, the Louvre in Paris, a wing of which was occupied by the French Finance Ministry instead of by the art museum. The site may have been more famous, but the results were not. The Plaza meetings were convened for the specific purpose of driving down the dollar; they succeeded. The Louvre meetings were convened for the specific purpose of supporting the dollar; they failed.

The failure was due to the contradictions laid bare by the success of the Plaza Accord. For the signatories to the Plaza Accord, backed by armies of economists, commentators, and policy hustlers, had fallen into the old mercantilist trap: confusing wealth and power with their units of account. The signatories knew the growing external imbalances of the G-5 were dangerous. They knew that in particular, the American trade and current account deficits together with their mirror images, the Japanese trade and current account surpluses, were threatening to wreck the liberal capitalist global order and that such wreckage would bring unmanageable political and economic dislocations in its wake. But to deal with the underlying imbalances, the Plaza Accord signatories thought it was enough to change the way wealth was measured.

The real causes of the imbalances were twofold: first, the U.S. federal deficit, which the Reagan Revolution had structurally embedded into the U.S. body politic, and secondly, the Japanese "developmental state" system of national leverage, centralized credit allocation, and credit risk socialization analyzed in Part I, which required exports to close the economic circle. Changing the units of account had not the slightest chance of dealing with these fundamentals. But they made for a more unstable world. They increased both the economic and political costs of hegemonic power burdens on the United States. And the soaring yen spurred paroxysms of activity in

Japan aimed at preserving the core of its economic system. In the four years after the Plaza Accord the Japanese economy was to embark on the greatest wave of plant and equipment investment ever undertaken by a country in peacetime.

The Louvre Accord set up a $4 billion war chest to finance interventions "stabilizing" the principal currencies within agreed-to bands. Except that the participants couldn't agree to the bands. Miyazawa insisted that the yen must have a ceiling of ¥150; anything higher would be political suicide. Baker and Darman talked of ¥140. Eventually the participants agreed on a midpoint of ¥153.50 / $1 and DM1.825 / $1. The agreements muddily called for a 2.5 percent deviation from the midpoint to trigger a "voluntary" intervention; a 5 percent deviation would require "consultation."

It was a fudge. Massive Bank of Japan intervention plus some halfhearted intervention from the American authorities was unable to keep the dollar from falling past the 5 percent floor to ¥147. An April G-7 follow-up meeting required the participants to reset the yen midpoint at ¥146. Miyazawa again promised fiscal stimulus, but this turned out to be nothing more than an LDP proposal that had not even been put before the Diet and was easily torpedoed by MOF bureaucrats. The Germans said they could do no more. The Americans went through the motions of pretending to do something about the budget deficit. Two days later the market gave its verdict: The dollar slumped to a new ¥144 low.

Efforts at international cooperation stalled. The dollar continued to drop. Baker for the first time tried "talking up the dollar," but it was too late. The Japanese "stimulus" package for fiscal year 1987 amounted to a grand total of $77 million, a percentage increase of 0.02 percent over the previous year. Richard Darman resigned in April, taking with him what was probably the brightest mind in the administration's economic policy–making apparatus. In August the White House shook the financial markets by refusing to reappoint Paul Volcker chairman of the Federal Reserve. Instead Reagan installed the

untested Alan Greenspan. Greenspan felt he had to demonstrate he was no White House puppy, and one of his first acts
was to raise interest rates. Baker pleaded with the Japanese and
Germans not to follow suit, but his pleas fell on deaf ears. A G-
7 communiqué in September failed to mention interest rates
and monetary policy. The markets correctly took this to mean
disagreement among the participants. The Bank of Japan made
a one-time hike in the discount rate; the Bundesbank embarked
on another round of monetary tightening, repeatedly raising
rates. An angry Baker publicly said that he while his goal was
not a cheaper dollar, if foreign central banks persisted in raising
rates, he was not going to follow suit in order to support the
dollar.

On October 14 the August trade figures were announced.
They were far worse than anyone had anticipated. The yen was
testing the ¥140 / $1 barrier. It had nearly doubled in value in
two years, but the trade numbers were as bad as ever. Seeing no
end to the dollar depreciation, Japanese institutional investors
began dumping large quantities of dollar bonds. Long-term
dollar interest rates soared past 10 percent.

On October 19, 1987, Black Monday, the New York market
broke. A victim of its own political cowardice and conceptual
poverty, the Reagan Revolution and its stepchild the Plaza Accord lay in shambles. The American Century had apparently
come to a premature end. But in the meantime the mandarins
of Kasumigaseki, the Keidanren, and Kabutocho were coping
the only way they knew how: adding more production capacity.

7. Coping with *Endaka*

Japan's "Bubble" Economy

J APAN'S BUBBLE ECONOMY of the late 1980s was the greatest bubble in history. At its peak companies listed on the Tokyo Stock Exchange accounted for more than 40 percent of the total market value of all companies listed on all stock exchanges around the world. The land value of Tokyo and its three surrounding prefectures exceeded that of the entire United States of America plus the net worth of every company listed on the New York Stock Exchange. Millions of ordinary middle-class Japanese families found themselves "rich"; cramped little houses described ten years earlier in a notorious European Community study as "rabbit hutches" turned out to be worth more than the palaces of Beverly Hills or the Côte d'Azur. Narrow slivers of property in central Tokyo served as collateral for the acquisition of vast estates overseas—Rockefeller Center, the Pebble Beach golf course, premier hotels from Sydney to Maui. Golf club memberships traded at hundreds of thousands, even millions of dollars. The market value of smallish regional banks in the Japanese countryside streaked past that of such New York banking giants as Chase Manhattan and Chemical Bank.

"Bubble," however, is a misnomer. The word has been so widely used to describe the Japanese economy of the late 1980s that we're probably stuck with it, but as with many other words used to discuss Japan, it distorts as much as it reveals. True, like the many famous bubbles of the past, from the Dutch tulip craze of the 1600s to the pre-1929 Wall Street boom, Japan's bubble economy ran on the fuel of easy credit. Like those earlier bubbles, it was accompanied by an ostensible collapse in prudential lending standards and saw prices soaring to levels that bore no relationship to fundamental values.

The surface glitter of late-eighties Tokyo also resembled what one reads of the Gilded Age or the Roaring Twenties. A frenzy gripped the city. Storefront brokerage offices were packed daylong with clients mesmerized by large screens trumpeting their snowballing wealth. Fashionable young people attired in thousands of dollars' worth of designer clothing thronged fancy French restaurants, where, if they so desired, they could have gold shavings spice up their consommé. Television programs poked fun at middle management fuddy-duddies, planning the family's three-day annual holiday at a hot springs near Tokyo, while their secretaries mapped out itineraries in Tuscany or Provence.

The literature of the bubble economy is filled with tales of wild excess, and they are not confined to profligate spending by youngsters or eye-popping deals by shady real estate brokers. The great names of Japanese banking—Sumitomo, Fuji, the Industrial Bank of Japan (IBJ)—shoveled vast amounts of credit at the flimsiest of ventures, often managed by *yakuza,* the Japanese underworld. In one notorious tale IBJ lent two billion dollars to the proprietress of a small chain of Osaka restaurants popular with gangsters and their molls. The woman was reputed to be a shrewd stock picker; she modestly attributed her success to guidance she received from the spirit world at midnight séances. The financing for her supernaturally directed trades came from IBJ; the collateral she provided was forged certificates of deposit from a local credit agency. The forgeries were not professional jobs detectable only by state-of-the-art technology; they were sloppy, handwritten pieces obvious to anyone.

IBJ is the bluest chip of blue-chip Japanese banks. With only slight exaggeration, one could say it financed the economic miracle of the 1950s and 1960s. It had been the principal provider of long-term credit to Japan's establishment companies— Nissan, Nippon Steel, Hitachi. It was second only to the elite ministries as a career choice for ambitious graduates of the crème de la crème of the Japanese educational system, Tokyo University. To understand its role in Japanese finance by using American comparisons, one would have to lump together leading wholesale banks such as J. P. Morgan and Brown Brothers Harriman with the investment banking departments of Wall Street's top firms—Morgan Stanley, Goldman Sachs, First Boston. The shock to Japanese sensibilities of IBJ's doings surpassed the notoriety in the United States of the scandals that destroyed Drexel Burnham and humbled mighty Salomon Brothers. These firms were, in the last analysis, outsiders, and particularly in the case of Drexel, they and their clients were loathed by the American establishment. But IBJ *is* the Japanese establishment, and the tale of its woes is evidence in and of itself that the bubble economy was a much more complex, much more fundamental phenomenon than facile comparisons with other speculative manias might suggest.

For one thing, the bubble had served as a conscious and deliberate instrument of policy. True, all speculative manias must be fed at some point by credit creation.[1] And at least since the invention in the last century of central banking, governments have been the ultimate source of credit. But what the Japanese financial authorities engineered in the late 1980s went well beyond loose monetary policy. It was not simply a reenactment of the Federal Reserve's notorious monetary easing in the summer of 1927 often blamed for the final excesses of the Roaring Twenties.[2] To understand this, one needs to remember that Japanese banks are the actual instruments through which money is released into the economy and that the banks' credit policies, accounting standards, capitalization, growth rates, even the value of the assets they hold are determined not by the market or a disinterested, independent accounting profession, but by constant consultation with Ministry of Finance officials. The extent of MOF's involvement in the day-to-day affairs of Japan's banks is unimaginable to foreigners unless they have actually worked as bankers in Japan. The MOF may not have known the precise details of IBJ's loans to the Osaka restaurateur, but MOF officials knew perfectly well the kinds of deals IBJ was doing. It was impossible for them *not* to know, and thus the officials were implicitly condoning them.

The same was true for Japan's securities firms. The Japanese stock market had been a sideshow in the country's race to catch up with and surpass the West. But it played a central role in the bubble economy. Securities firms, acting with the knowledge and thus the implicit support of the MOF, drove stock prices to previously unimaginable heights. In June 1991, after the game was over, the president of Nomura Securities, Tabuchi Yoshihisa, was forced to resign to "take responsibility" for having promised compensation payments to big investors on their market losses. Tabuchi did a very un-Japanese thing: Instead of leaving quietly like a good samurai, he acted the role of the little boy in the tale of the emperor's new clothes, shouting what everyone knows but no one will say. At a Nomura shareholders' meeting with journalists present, he said that the company had been acting with the advice and encouragement of the MOF.[3]

Tabuchi's successor, Sakamaki Hideo, tried to cover up the damage by claiming Tabuchi had spoken incorrectly, but he had not. Tabuchi was correct, in both a narrow and a wider sense. The bubble economy was deliberately manufactured by the Japanese Ministry of Finance and its sometime agents / sometime rivals at the Bank of Japan. The MOF and the BOJ first set about creating the macroeconomic conditions necessary for a run-up in asset prices with a loose monetary policy. They then condoned and encouraged Japan's banks and brokers at every step of the way in the ensuing credit explosion.

They were not doing this in order to crowd the streets of fashionable Roppongi and Aoyama with expensively dressed youngsters, to put thousand-dollar toilets within the reach of middle-class families, or to make gangsters rich. These were unintended and unwelcome side effects of a policy they thought was necessary. This forms another crucial difference with other famous speculative manias. Past governments whose easy credit policies lay behind most historical speculative manias generally had no intention of doing anything other than bringing about general prosperity. The Fed in 1927, for example, did not specifically aim to create a stock market boom. But Japan's economic mandarins did. They deliberately set out to inflate the prices of stocks and land with an unambiguous goal in mind: cheap financing costs to Japan's industrial corporations. These companies needed waves of capital investment to recapture a competitive edge endangered by the unexpectedly high yen rates in the wake of the Plaza Accord. As a senior BOJ official anonymously admitted in the pages of a leading business weekly, "We intended first to boost both the stock and property markets. Supported by this safety net—rising markets—export-oriented industries were supposed to reshape themselves so they could adapt to a domestic-led economy."[4]

Certainly the authorities made mistakes along the way. Their goals were muddied with other considerations after the October 1987 New York stock market crash. But none of this changes the calculated way in which the financial authorities created the bubble economy, nor does it obscure their success.

When other bubbles burst, the players were left holding worthless pieces of paper—property deeds to half-developed land and empty office buildings that no one wanted and that could not be rented, securities of bankrupt companies, commodity contracts at delivery prices many times those of the current market. The Japanese bubble differed in that it did not burst; rather it was slowly deflated. And when it was over, Japan had added to its GNP an amount equivalent to the entire GNP of France.[5] Most of its industries were fully competitive in world markets at rates of ¥110 to the dollar and beyond. Most important, Japan's administrators believed they had achieved the goal of a century, a wholly integrated industrial structure under Japanese control. Hardly a key manufactured component for any downstream manufactured product was not being made by a Japanese company.* Japan depended on foreigners only for commodities, commercial aircraft (for which most components were manufactured or could be manufactured by Japanese companies), and certain kinds of software.

It is true that millions of Japanese households and thousands of companies in the second tier of the economy speculated heavily in the late 1980s and lost heavily in the early 1990s. But the wealth did not disappear, as it had in most genuine speculative manias. It had been transferred. The bubble economy and its deflation formed simply the latest chapter in a saga begun more than a century earlier, when the Meiji oligarchs sold off their newly created industries to their ex-samurai colleagues for practically nothing. This saga was the continuous transfer of wealth away from the average Japanese household and the small-scale Japanese entrepreneur to large institutions under the direct control of Japan's administrators.

The bubble began with the post-Plaza recession. "Recession" is another loaded word to be used carefully in the Japanese context. It conjures up images of the unemployed, waves of bankruptcies, tottering governments, but anyone arriving in Japan during the 1986 "recession" would have seen little evidence of economic suffering beyond the screaming headlines in the newspapers. Part of the problem is definitional. A recession in the United States is pronounced when the economy shrinks for two consecutive quarters. In Japan, however, if the economy grows at less than an annualized 3 percent for three consecutive quarters, a *fukyō* (recession) is officially declared.

The sudden sharp and continuing rise of the yen after Sep-

---

* Japanese companies were to discover in the early 1990s that they had missed out on much of the telecommunications and data processing revolutions with unanticipated American superiority in the key areas of networking, software, and personal computers. But this was not fully understood until a good three years after the bubble economy was over.

tember 1985 did, however, throw the economy into "recession"—Japanese style. While it might have seemed only a mild setback in many countries, it was arguably the worst economic shock Japan had endured for some time, certainly since the OPEC-induced 1974 recession, perhaps since the early 1950s. GNP growth dropped below the stipulated 3 percent and in the first quarter of 1986 was actually negative, a phenomenon not experienced since the dark days of 1975. All the important business indicators from industrial production to machinery orders to surveys of business confidence dropped dramatically. Unemployment climbed steadily to graze 3 percent, the highest figure since the late 1940s.*

That this should happen was no mystery. The Japanese economy still depended heavily on exports, although not in the sense that they accounted for a huge percentage of GNP as they did in the economies of small trading countries, such as the Netherlands or Singapore. Rather exports still "closed the circle" of an economy that continued to be administered as if it were highly leveraged. Japan's leading industries were still geared to export: Electronics makers shipped 46 percent of their domestic production overseas in 1985; iron and steelmakers shipped 33 percent; for automobiles, the number was 55 percent.[6] But the declining dollar temporarily destroyed export profits in markets such as the United States. Companies had three choices open to them: They could pull out of markets that had become unprofitable; they could cede shares in these markets by raising prices to the point where they were once again generating profits, albeit on much smaller volumes; or they could hang on to the markets they had won by keeping their dollar prices the same, absorbing the losses.

Most companies chose the third course. As the CEO of a

---

*Unemployment statistics cannot be compared to those in the West. Not only are the criteria different, but informal labor market practices—sometimes backed up by subsidies from Japan's Labor Ministry—dictate that large companies hang on to workers when they have nothing for them to do. A 3 percent unemployment rate in Japan is probably the equivalent of 8 to 9 percent in the United States—potentially, a political problem.

leading Japanese firm admitted anonymously, "We don't export because we think it is profitable. We export because it is national policy." But when profits all but vanished, this national policy necessitated belt tightening. Holding on to markets recently won overseas had to be financed with what were effectively subsidies from the domestic Japanese market. So every conceivable means of cutting costs was put into effect: Orders were canceled; hiring was postponed; inventories were drawn down. As the effects rippled through the Japanese economy, the country slowed down.

An air of crisis hung over Tokyo. Everyone "knew" what was happening. The public was prepared for it by a generation of training to look upon upsurges in the value of the yen as trouble. The recession got its own name, the *Endaka Fukyō* (high-yen recession), and blame for it was placed squarely on the United States. As one Japanese journalist noted, "Neither the Japanese general public nor the business community in particular viewed the situation as just another recession in the usual sense. For them, the whole process was an affront to national identity, because it appeared that *gaiatsu* (external pressure) was trying to contain Japanese export might, upon which Japan had so heavily relied to catch up with Western countries."[7] The shriller weeklies labeled the Plaza Accord America's revenge for Pearl Harbor, a sneak attack on the Japanese economy.

This sense of an external challenge to Japan's national way of doing things gave the financial authorities a favorable climate to take extraordinary measures. These measures were not of the sort that Western economists would probably have recommended. Keynesians might have fingered sluggish domestic demand as the root cause of Japan's troubles and urged fiscal stimulus to solve it. Neoclassicists pointed to a structural stifling of market forces leading to "incorrect" price signals: Suppressing interest rates while inducing "excessive" savings kept markets from performing proper credit allocation functions. "Irrational" land policies precluded nice big houses stuffed with expensive gadgets. Rigid labor practices prevented the emergence of an upper middle class with lots of money to spend. Distribution cartels propped up prices and suppressed demand. Protectionism preserved inefficient industries—agriculture the leading but far from the only example—and raised prices for everyone. Using banks to subsidize corporate restructuring while the bureaucracy subsidized the banks kept alive first-tier companies that should have been allowed to fail. The result of all this market stifling: an unhealthy reliance on exports bringing recession in its wake when the cash flow from exports faltered.

This neoclassical, structuralist critique of Japan's economic methods found a lot of sympathy in Tokyo, particularly among some of the more internationally aware politicians and business leaders. Prime Minister Nakasone was a leading exponent of a structural overhaul; he had an acute understanding of the endless international tensions that would otherwise be Japan's fate. Resorting to his favorite tactic in his battles with the bureaucrats, he commissioned a high-powered *shingikai* (deliberative council) led by a former internationalist Bank of Japan governor, Maekawa Haruo, with instructions to produce a blueprint for restructuring. When news of the Maekawa Report began to seep out in the spring of 1986, it was greeted with accolades around the world. Here, finally, were a proper diagnosis of the "Japan problem" and a realistic plan for its cure.

But reports are not policies. Even the skilled and courageous Nakasone did not begin to have the power or mandate to translate the report's blueprint into reform. Virtually none of the report's recommendations was implemented.

It was sabotaged by the bureaucracy, savaged by the press,[8] and regarded by ordinary Japanese as window dressing for foreign consumption. Japan's administrators were not about to implement structural reforms that would destroy their power over fundamental economic decisions or jeopardize the security of their carefully calibrated domestic alliances, nor, as we saw in the last chapter, would the Ministry of Finance consider any fiscal stimulus. The public explanation: Japan was too deeply in

debt; official statistics showed that Japan's government liabilities as a percentage of GNP exceeded those of that latter-day
fiscal deadbeat the United States. But these statistics did not tell
the real story. In fact, Japan's savings rate and the MOF's control
of public pension funds meant that from a technical point of
view, an increase in the Japanese deficit would have been very
easy to implement and finance. But the official statistics were a
useful cover for what we saw in the previous chapter: Fiscal
stimulus works poorly because it tends to end up in unnecessary
"public" works,* and in any case it enhances the power of the
Construction Ministry and its *zoku* (tribe) in the Diet at the
expense of the MOF.

And so Japan's financial authorities, unwilling or unable
to use either "structural" reform or Keynesian fiscal stimulus,
turned to monetary policy. Their institutional memories told
them monetary policy was the best tool in times of trouble. It
had been a key element of the economic takeoff plan discussed
in Chapter 3 and had ended Japan's worst postwar inflation—
the OPEC-induced 1974–75 crisis—in one year instead of the
eight years it took the United States. Ultimately the mandarins
of the Finance Ministry, the Bank of Japan, and the leading
banks had confidence in monetary policy because they believed
they controlled it. Central bankers in most countries could influence the rate of monetary growth, but the Japanese authorities thought they could do more than that: They could control
where the money went.

Thus the monetary spigots were opened. Interest rates were
cut and cut again.[9] M2, the key money supply indicator, rose
sharply. Every statistical measure one cared to use pointed to
the sudden easing of monetary policy in 1986. But in all the
blizzards of statistics documenting the flood of liquidity let
loose into the Japanese economy, two stood out. And they sent
what appeared to be contradictory messages.

The first statistic was inflation. Good monetarists will tell

---

* In technical language, the Keynesian "multiplier" was quite low.

you that inflation is everywhere and always a monetary phenomenon. Yet in the face of a loose monetary policy, Japanese inflation was nowhere to be found in the aggregate numbers. Consumer prices hardly moved while wholesale prices actually declined.[10] Of course as a partial explanation the soaring yen helped make Japan's imports, mostly denominated in U.S. dollars, very cheap. But imports formed a pretty small percentage of GNP, and well over half of these were raw materials, foodstuffs, coal, and petroleum.[11] In a country where most manufactured products were produced domestically and most of the value in these products was added domestically, cheap imports did not explain the lack of inflation. Where was the excess liquidity created by the government going?

The second odd statistic was the growth of Japanese bank lending. Until the early 1980s the year-on-year growth of such lending tracked fairly closely the growth of Japan's nominal GNP—that is to say, GNP at current prices before subtracting for inflation. This is what one would expect, particularly in a country like Japan where banks had, until 1980, regularly met some three quarters to four fifths of all external financing requirements by Japanese industry. But beginning in the early 1980s, the growth rate in Japanese bank lending began to accelerate. By 1986, in the wake of the Plaza Accord, it was tripling nominal GNP growth.[12] This might seem to answer the question of where the excess liquidity was going, but it flew in the face of another very important development: the ongoing revolution in Japanese corporate finance.

This revolution had started back in the early 1980s. It was partly a result of the so-called liberalizations of those years— the revised Foreign Exchange Control Law of 1980 or the various measures in the wake of the Yen / Dollar Accord discussed in Chapter 5. But much more important than this superficial tinkering was a fundamental change in Japan's financial structure. Japan was deleveraging, capital no longer a scarce resource.

The entire Japanese system of corporate finance was built

around the scarcity of capital and the government's central role in credit allocation. As we have seen, Japan's financial administrators allocated this scarce good on the basis of either industrial policy or political pull, not on the basis of a capacity to generate profits. The instruments were the government banks serving as green lights, the long-term banks with their close connections with the Finance Ministry, and the great city banks, overlending to their favored customers and dependent on the central bank to fund their overloans. But this system began to implode in the early 1980s, when capital became more and more abundant. Rationing of a plentiful good is an empty exercise.

Japan's administrators had managed to postpone dealing with this threat to their control for more than a decade even though troubling portents were visible as early as the late 1960s. That was when Japan first began running large current account surpluses, the surest sign that an economy is generating more savings than it can use. But the various shocks of the 1970s kept putting off the day of reckoning. Then came the Reagan Revolution, which helped absorb much of the excess capital. But there was finally no escaping the revolutionary impact of the excess capital on Japanese corporate finance: Large Japanese companies no longer needed their banks. In turn the financial authorities that stood behind the banks saw their control over credit seriously threatened.

In a normal market economy, this maturing process and the coming of abundant capital would see capital markets take over many of the functions theretofore provided by banks. Companies would replace much of their debt financing with retained earnings or equity raised from stock markets and could deal directly with savers through bond and commercial paper markets for their debt needs. Meanwhile banks could direct their lending at smaller, riskier ventures, where their professional skills at credit evaluation were still necessary.

Many of these phenomena happened in Japan during the 1980s—large companies turned away from banks, banks went down market—but they happened in distorted forms because of the unwillingness of the authorities to give up their instruments of control. Take the matter of turning away from banks to bond markets. Japanese companies did flee comparatively pricey bank financing, but the domestic bond market was so shackled with restrictions and so expensive that it was unappealing or unavailable to most of those companies. The Japanese financial authorities had not yet figured out how to create a real bond market where they could be assured of certain outcomes. They could not bring themselves to adjudicate among the competing interests of banks, brokerage houses, and insurance companies. And so Japanese corporations turned for much of their debt-financing requirements to overseas bond markets, principally to the so-called Eurobond market centered in London and the Swiss capital markets.

A few Western academics have pointed to this sudden surge in overseas financing by Japanese companies as "proof" that low-cost Japanese capital is a figment of the imagination—else why would companies go overseas for financing as soon as they had the freedom to do so?[13]—but any bond salesman working in Tokyo could have told them that most of the paper in these deals ended up back in Japan. The bonds were issued overseas through syndicates of Japanese, European, and American investment banks and securities companies. Some of the paper would be bought by foreign investors, but most of it was intended for the Japanese market, and indeed the deals were carefully structured with the peculiar needs of Japanese investors in mind. Various petty restrictions imposed by the MOF meant that the bonds had to be "seasoned" for anywhere from twenty-four hours to six months before they could be brought back to Japan. Investment bankers and Japanese institutional investors were, however, adept at coming to private agreements on setting up dummy holding vehicles in Hong Kong or the Cayman Islands for the necessary period of time. Bankers coined colorful terms to describe the deals: sushi bonds, "black-eye" bonds. My favorite was JAL Pac bonds, named after the Japanese airline's quickie tours of Europe for vacationers with only a week to travel.

Why do things this way? Why have a Japanese company float bonds in London, with all the extra trouble that involved, when ultimately most of the bonds were bought by and indeed intended for Japanese insurance companies and trust banks? Why not allow the company to sell its bonds directly in Tokyo without all the rigmarole? For one thing, going overseas enabled the authorities, paradoxically, to maintain more control over the process. Changing a rule here and there over bond issues floated overseas was a simple matter of issuing "guidance" to the relevant companies and securities houses. Allow a deep and wide domestic bond market to take root, however, and changing the rules would no longer be so easy with the entrenched domestic constituencies that would inevitably develop. Then forcing the deals to make a Tokyo–London–Tokyo round trip kept most individual Japanese households out of the market and left important investment decisions in the hands of large Japanese institutions, which were closely monitored and supervised by the MOF. Running the deals through the Euromarkets also helped give the perennially whining foreigners something to do and a few crumbs off the table; many of the deals were lead-managed by foreign investment banks, and nearly all the foreign banks in Tokyo got, at one point or another, a piece of the action. It helped quiet these *gaijin* banks and gave them an incentive to continue to be quiet lest the MOF change a rule or two that would deprive them of business.

Irrespective of whatever odd forms it might be taking, there was no mistaking what was going on: Large, creditworthy Japanese companies were abandoning their banks. The phenomenon was a familiar one in much of the industrialized world, a function of maturing economies, on the one hand, and the computerization of the financial services industry, on the other. Historically, corporate treasurers had needed bankers' help to find and raise funds. Now treasurers could do much of the job themselves with a few thousand dollars of hardware and a subscription to a data service. Economists labeled the process "disintermediation." Banks had long stood as intermediaries between savers and borrowers, but by raising money directly from savers through capital markets, large companies around the world were circumventing—disintermediating, if you will—the banks. Japan was no exception.

Why, then, did Japanese bank lending suddenly start to soar in the wake of the Plaza Accord? One might have expected the reverse. And if major Japanese companies weren't borrowing from the banks, who was? The riddle of Japan's bubble economy lies in the answer to these two questions. Bank lending started to soar because monetary policy turned loose—banks were still the primary means by which the monetary authorities released money into the economy, and the banks had to do something with the money—and instead of lending money to their traditional corporate clients, the banks shoveled credit at second-tier firms, which used the money to drive up the stock and real estate markets.

In countries like the United States and Britain, authorities rely primarily on markets in government securities to manage the money supply. The Federal Reserve can, for example, increase the money supply by purchasing Treasury securities for cash in the open market or reduce the money supply by doing the reverse. But the Bank of Japan lacked such instruments—deliberately so. The Japanese government did not even begin to run deficits until the mid-1960s. Thereafter the MOF set interest rates on the deficit-covering bonds at low levels; the post office and the banks, organized in revolving syndicates, bought most of them. The composition of the syndicates and the allocation of the bonds were predetermined and had nothing to do with "market appetite." Among Japanese government securities, only the so-called benchmark bond—a ten-year security that changes every few months—could be said to trade in

accordance with market forces. And speculation, not investment, drove trading in this security; at any given moment other
Japanese government securities were effectively illiquid.

The authorities wanted it this way. An illiquid and controlled government securities market kept down financing costs
to the government itself. It was also essential in controlling the
overall level of interest rates in the economy—in any country,
the rate the government itself pays for funds is the foundation
for the whole superstructure of interest rates—and keeping interest rates low in turn served to ensure that "strategic" industries had priority access to funds at cheap rates.

But it did reduce money supply control options for the
Bank of Japan. The BOJ had effectively no alternative to the
commercial banks as instruments for releasing money into the
economy. Before the 1980s the monetary authorities would not
have regarded this as a problem. With their close supervision of
the banks they could steer capital into priority sectors. But with
big Japanese corporations now raising funds elsewhere, control
over credit seemed to be slipping from their hands. How were
the authorities to ensure that credit went into the enhancement
of Japanese productivity rather than simply end up as inflation?

The solution lay in Japan's two biggest asset markets, the
one for land and the one for stocks. As we saw, banks in the
1980s lent a great deal of money to small, second-tier companies to finance purchases of land and purchases of stocks. They
also lent money to developers and to the "nonbanks"—leasing
companies, housing affiliates, consumer credit firms—that
passed the funds on to borrowers for real estate and equity
deals.

To grasp how this kind of lending ultimately translated into
additions to Japan's stock of plant and equipment, one needs to
keep in mind the collateral principle of Japanese bank lending.
As we examined in Chapter 2, Japanese banks lend on the basis
of the value of underlying collateral. Unsecured medium- and
long-term lending is rare. Japanese bankers are not trained to
analyze loan projects by determining whether the assets to be

financed by the loan will generate sufficient cash to provide interest and principal payments. Rather they are taught to look at the collateral that secures the loan. And in Japan the most valuable collateral—far more valuable than any office building, machine, or factory—is land.

How, then, is the value of collateral—particularly the value of land—to be determined? In many countries one would look at the market or rely on the services of an impartial accounting profession. But the latter, as we have seen, does not, to all intents and purposes, exist in Japan. A few people call themselves accountants and are licensed as such, but they are organized into a professional association controlled by the Ministry of Finance. They are largely under the thumbs of the companies they are supposed to audit. They cannot easily make independent, disinterested professional evaluations of asset worth.

But what about the market? In the sense that land changes hands in Japan from time to time and buyers and sellers agree on a price, one can say there is a land market of sorts. But this "market" is hemmed in and stymied by a dense thicket of "irrational" rules and regulations, rules resulting in the devotion of prime urban land to the growing of cabbages and onions, rules making it difficult to evict tenants, rules restricting building size or height without rhyme or reason. Real estate is subject to a brace of taxes by different ministries and agencies that control vast tracts of land that they can release or withhold from the market at will. These bureaucratic bodies are in constant rivalry and arbitrarily set widely differing values on property. One scholar noted that "a given piece of land has four different assessed prices"[14]: one from the Ministry of Finance for inheritance taxes, one from the Ministry of Home Affairs for taxes handed over to local governments, one from the National Land Agency as a benchmark price, and one directly from the relevant local government. Thus extrapolating on the basis of the isolated sale to determine the "value" of particular plots of land is impossible. Doing so produces the absurd statistics so often seen in discussions of Japan's real estate: It accounts for

60 percent of the land value of the planet; Tokyo is worth more than the United States; the Imperial Palace grounds are worth more than Canada.

Yet this is what happened. Japanese investors and bankers began extrapolating. First, land changed hands at stratospheric prices, not because the land could be developed to generate cash, cover financing, and permit a profit but because purchasers believed it could be sold to someone else—sooner rather than later—at an even higher price. Or it could serve as collateral to finance purchases of stock, which could subsequently be sold at a profit into a soaring market.

Also, companies whose basic businesses were no longer making much money found they could use their landholdings to drive up their share prices. Take the steel industry. Steel had not been a money spinner for ten years or more, but steel companies such as Nippon Steel and NKK owned vast tracts of land, from office buildings in central Tokyo to waterfront docking properties to large factories in the suburbs. With the "values" of corporate landholdings spiraling, investors began taking positions in the equity of these companies as a real estate play. "One Japanese economist attributed a full 72% of the rise in stock prices between 1985 and 1987 to the real estate boom."[15]

Banks financed the entire process. At the peak of the bubble Japan's banks and financial institutions had lent $350 billion to real estate developers. With the printing presses at the Bank of Japan running nonstop, there was no lack of funding. As for potential credit problems, this hardly bothered Japan's bankers. They knew that they and their backers in the government controlled the parameters of the real estate market. They financed it; they assigned it collateral value; they determined the conditions under which trades would or would not take place. As Japan's greatest student of its banking system observes, "When the banking system engages in near total intermediation of savings, banks have control of asset prices independent of market assessment because of their discretionary ability to evaluate and price assets for collateral purposes."[16] That is to say, the value of land was what the banks, with the approval of the Finance Ministry, said it was. Japan's financial system was basing itself on a land standard, *tochi hon-i sei*.[17]

The stock market gave the banks even more confidence. Bank credit fed the equity spiral, driven in turn by the soaring "values" in the real estate market. The banks had huge positions in the stock market, linked through their *keiretsu* connections with the most highly capitalized Japanese companies. The soaring market was thus doubling and tripling the values of their holdings. Meanwhile the banks were seeing their own market values rise. Bank shares were no exception to the general run-up in prices. The market value of IBJ would stand at some eighteen times that of the J. P. Morgan with which it was often compared.[18] And no one worried about a loss of control. This was no U.S. market where "raiders" could attack established companies, throw out their managements, and sell off the pieces at a profit. Enough stock, held by the banks and their fellow *keiretsu* members, had invariably been tucked away to prevent this from happening.

Ultimately the brazen confidence of Japan's banks during the bubble years rested on their vast cushion of hidden assets. On the surface Japanese banks might look thinly capitalized, as if a few major loan losses could wipe out their capital. But Japanese financial reporting did not require that banks or companies mark their assets to their market values. They listed them at historical costs. Many of the great city banks had their roots in the late nineteenth century, when the yen traded at 2 to the dollar. Land that might be worth billions of dollars in 1987 had been acquired in those days for the equivalent of a few hundred. Equity that might be listed at tens of thousands of yen per share had been purchased at 3 or 4 yen per share. And there these numbers stood, on the public financial statements of the banks. Loan losses hardly seemed much of a problem when disguising them was a simple matter of selling a few hundred shares of stock now listed at ¥40,000 and carried on the books at ¥3. Or in a really bad situation, a bank could dispose for $50 million of a small parcel of land that was on the books at $300.*

In the perfect vision of hindsight, the bankers were making a fundamental error. If land and stock prices could ratchet each other up, they could also ratchet down.[19] The real estate market was showing the classic signs of a bubble: Money could be made only by selling to a "greater fool."

But it cannot be overemphasized that this was not a typical bubble. While some of the cash thrown off was dissipated on a spree of conspicuous consumption never before seen in Japan, most of it ended up as additions to the nation's production capacity. The drama of the bubble economy was staged, ultimately, to serve large industrial companies, which used the Tokyo stock market, directly or indirectly, to raise money. Some of this money came from straightforward sales of stock. With stock prices at sixty times earnings and investors happy with tiny dividends, equity issues were attractive enough for corporations. But then brokerage houses and investment banks began offering Japanese industrial companies something truly irresistible: large sums of money they were told they need never pay back. And to induce them to go ahead with the deals, they were offered bonuses as the deals matured. In other words, someone walks into the office of finance *buchō* (general manager) Tanaka and says, "Mr. Buchō, here's a hundred million dollars. You don't have to pay me back. And since you've gone to the trouble of taking the money, let me give you, say, an additional million dollars a year for the next seven years."

These transactions were called equity warrant bonds. A warrant is an instrument that gives its owner the right to buy an underlying share of stock at a predetermined price, called the exercise price. Investors buy such warrants for one of two

---

*This tactic was not limited to the Japanese banks. One quarter in the late eighties, when Chase Manhattan's earnings threatened to be worse than normal, the bank sold the Tokyo general manager's house, acquired in the late 1940s for a few thousand dollars, at something over $80 million. Several Third World countries retired substantial amounts of their national debts by selling their embassy properties in central Tokyo.

reasons: because the exercise price is lower than the current market price, allowing them to buy the stock at the exercise price, turn around, sell the stock at the market price, and pocket the difference, or, more commonly, because they believe the market will rise and bring the warrant "into the money"— in other words, make it profitable. Take warrants issued by a company whose stock is selling at 38. If the exercise price on the warrant is 36, then the warrant is worth 2 in today's market. If the exercise price is 40, the warrant may seem worthless today. But if the warrant isn't expiring for five years and it looks as if the stock is going to rise, many investors will want to buy the warrant anyway. After all, if you hold a warrant with an exercise price of 40 and the stock goes to 50, you can make a nice profit, particularly if you paid only 1 or 2 for the warrant.

This was the way the Japanese warrants were generally structured. Their exercise prices were a little higher than the current underlying prices, but everyone assumed the stock market would keep going up. Most investors, from small household saver to large insurance company, lay in the grip of a speculative fever common to manias. They had also convinced themselves that Japan could uniquely conjure up money out of nothing. In the 1960s overloan had funded the Japanese economic miracle. Now, in the 1980s, the authorities had apparently figured out a way to keep the stock market permanently high.

Demand for warrants soared. Companies would issue, say, $100 million worth of dollar-denominated equity warrant bonds carrying 2 percent coupons, or lower. Investment bankers would strip the warrants from the bonds. The stripped bonds would be sold to usual garden-variety bond investors, both Japanese and foreign, at discounts steep enough that the yields were similar to what other comparable bond issuers were paying. But the warrants were sold almost entirely to Japanese investors, who believed the Tokyo stock market would go in only one direction: up.

Corporations issuing the bonds also believed the market had but one way to go. They fully expected that before the bonds matured, the warrant holders would exercise the warrants—in other words, buy the company's stock at the exercise price. This would give the company the money it needed to repay the bondholders. Meanwhile, thanks to the swap markets, the extremely low dollar coupon payments could be swapped into yen receipts; in other words, instead of *paying out* interest, the company would *receive* interest.*

Things got dizzy. As Michael Zavelle, who headed Chase Manhattan's Tokyo corporate finance department during the bubble years, wrote later:

> The whole market was Pollyannaish. When dual tranche equity warrant bonds were issued with five- and seven-year tranches and with all other terms being the same (conversion price, everything), the five-year warrants and the seven-year warrants tended to trade at the same price. If anything, because five-year warrants were such a commodity, five-year warrants would trade on occasion at a slight premium to seven-year warrants. Option theory—and common sense—say that time has value, and thus seven-year warrants have to be more valuable than five-year warrants. I'm sure holders of worthless warrants would like those two extra years now. At the height of the market no one cared.[20]

As Zavelle remarks, most of the warrant holders found themselves holding worthless pieces of paper. The Japanese stock market began to drop dramatically in the early 1990s. The exercise price of the warrants ended up, in most cases, above the actual market price when the warrants expired. And the industrial companies that thought they need never worry about paying off the bondholders went scrambling for funds in the early 1990s, when the expected proceeds of stock sales to warrant holders failed to materialize.

All that was in the future. From the perspective of the Japa-

---

* Unlike the assumption behind the warrant market—that Tokyo stock prices would rise forever—the assumption behind the swaps—that the yen was sure to strengthen over time—turned out to be correct. A company could in the late eighties easily swap an obligation to pay, say, $100 million in the mid-nineties with intervening annual payments of $2 million (the example assumes the company had issued a $100 million five-year equity warrant bond with a 2 percent coupon) for an obligation to pay ¥150 billion at maturity and receive some yen in the interim. Issuers expected to fund the yen obligations with the proceeds of the stock sales to warrant holders.

nese corporate treasurer, capital raising in the late 1980s had become a matter of helping yourself to whatever you needed. In fact, the companies thought they were being paid to take it. Thus, in their view, it cost *nothing* to build a factory, acquire machinery, buy foreign real estate, or snap up foreign companies. All they needed to do was float an equity warrant bond. And floated they were—in amounts upward of several hundred billion dollars.

American finance theory argues that warrants are much more expensive than they appear. They do not represent "free" capital at all. Investors buy warrants because they expect to exercise them. If they are exercised, the company must issue new stock. The new stock dilutes the stake of the current equity holders in the company, who may see a permanent reduction in their pro rata claim on corporate assets and corporate profits.

But this analysis—perfectly valid in an American context and indeed used to "price" warrants—assumes that equity represents something. As we have seen, the outside shareholder in a Japanese company has no voice in the company's affairs: no right in practice to a pro rata share of profits, no pro-rata stake in the assets. At most such shareholders are entitled to small dividend streams. So this argument—tried by a few American investment bankers in useless attempts to persuade the Japanese to consider other forms of financing—carried no meaning for Japanese corporate treasurers or existing shareholders. It had no impact whatsoever on their financing or investment decisions. As far as they were concerned, the cost of equity meant the cost of dividends. As for dilution, dilution of what?

Thus the equity warrant bond market came on top of the booming stock and real estate markets, and all together financed the greatest wave of investments in productive capacity the world had ever seen. No other country could even begin to compete. The Toyotas and Nissans would build gleaming new factories enabling them to bring totally new cars—so-called full model changes—to market in less than four years, beating Detroit by a year. Toshiba would succeed in its announced goal of dominating flat panel displays without the ten years of losses the company's president had said he was prepared to accept. Matsushita would spend billions absorbing MCA while hundreds of small and middle-size American high tech firms would be snapped up by the Japanese. By the late 1980s Japan would be investing more on an absolute basis in plant and equipment than the United States; its per capita investment spending would be more than double that of America. Why not? American companies were paying 8 to 9 percent for capital. The Japanese were getting it for free; they were being paid to take the money!

The bubble lasted until the end of 1989, but by late in 1986 it was already clear the medicine had worked. The Japanese-style recession was over. The economic mandarins of Kasumi-gaseki—the Tokyo district where the great ministries have their headquarters—had not only created the economic miracle but figured out a new way to save it when threatened by the Plaza Accord. In the past they had created credit where none existed through the institution of overloan, and they had used exports to close the circle. Now, when these tactics could not work any longer, they had discovered new ones. In place of overloan, they latched on to unlimited bank credit to ratchet up the stock and real estate markets, and in place of exports to close the circle, they used investment spending. Waves of spending on plant and equipment would accomplish the twin feats of pulling Japan out of recession and fulfilling the century-old dream of an industrial structure fully under Japanese control.

Meanwhile another challenge arose. Japanese authorities were forced to keep the bubble going awhile longer. Pulling Japan out of recession, arranging free financing for Japanese industry, acting as midwives for a wholly integrated industrial structure were not enough. On October 19, 1987, the bureaucrats of the Finance Ministry learned they had to save the world.

8. Saving the World

Although most Japanese are too polite to make jokes about the American economics profession in public, the world has been fortunate during the 1980's that Japanese policy elites come out of a different intellectual tradition than the free market ideologues who have presided over American economic policy . . . future historians will probably note with more than ironic delight that at the end of the 1980's it was graduates of the University of Tokyo Law School presiding over the Finance Ministry of the industrial world's least deregulated economy who helped to rescue the Reagan administration and the international economic system from currency misalignments, trade imbalances, and financial crises produced by the fiscal and monetary policies of economics graduates of the University of Chicago.

DAVID HALE[1]

OCTOBER 19, 1987—Black Monday it was called. On that day, and through the following morning, it seemed that stock prices had no floor. Five hundred billion dollars simply disappeared. The market worth of companies listed on the New York Stock Exchange fell by nearly a quarter, the largest one-day drop in history. Several famous Wall Street names all but went under. Central bankers and financial regulators thought they were surely seeing the onset of their worst nightmare: a financial meltdown when no one can obtain credit and failure to meet obligations leaps from one bank or security house to another like fire in an ammunition depot. The leaders of the exchange almost shut its doors.

In Washington the government quaked. To the Reagan White House, Alan Greenspan's Fed, Jim Baker's Treasury, and both sides of the aisle in Congress, it appeared that the day of reckoning had arrived. Accounts were finally coming due for twenty years of reckless disregard by America's policy elites for the country's economic health.

Black Monday's eerie historical parallels greatly amplified fears that the jig was up, for October 29, 1929, Black Tuesday, had been the day in the popular imagination that marked the beginning of the Great Depression. Newspapers after Black Monday drew endless comparisons with that earlier October: DOES 1987 EQUAL 1929? was the pointed headline on the front page of the *New York Times* the day after the crash. Television stations ran grainy 1929 footage of the corner of Wall and Broad streets juxtaposed with current views of the same spot. The ghoulish sightseers and hordes of panicked investors in the two clips seemed to differ only in the way they were dressed. All the buildings that loomed overhead—the New York Stock Exchange, Federal Hall, the headquarters of the Morgan Bank, Trinity Church—were the same. The panic and fear, and their causes, were the same. Might not the consequences—a decade of misery followed by world war—be likewise similar?

Such comparisons were not surprising. An ostensibly conservative Republican administration presides over a decade of high living and conspicuous consumption. The administration cuts taxes on the rich and openly advocates trickle-down or, as it was called in the 1980s, supply-side economics. Income disparities grow more marked. Deregulation and lax oversight of the financial system lead to the amassing of fortunes from asset shuffling. A new class of rich vulgarians, fawned over in the popular press, becomes the object of emulation by millions. Sharp dealing, dubious financial practices—stock pyramids in the twenties; junk bonds, S&L boondoggles and LBOs in the eighties—and outright illegality become the norm on Wall Street. The excesses come to a screeching halt with a market collapse that in a matter of hours sees a large chunk of the country's wealth simply disappear. The collapse spreads outside the United States, taking stock markets around the world down with it.

These easy parallels were underscored by the writings of a group of America's most respected scholars, men such as Robert Gilpin at Princeton, Charles Kindleberger at MIT, Robert Keohane at Harvard. They hailed from that region of scholarship where international relations, history, and economics all meet, a region once called political economy. They fathered a notion we have briefly encountered several times in this book, the theory of hegemonic stability. Gilpin explains the theory with reference to the other two men as follows:

According to the theory of hegemonic stability as set forth initially by Charles Kindleberger (although he preferred the term "leadership" or "responsibility"), an open and liberal world economy requires the existence of a hegemonic or dominant power. In the words of Robert Keohane, the theory "holds that hegemonic structures of power, dominated by a single country, are most conducive to the development of strong international regimes whose rules are relatively precise and well obeyed. . . . [T]he decline of hegemonic structures of power can be expected to presage a decline in the strength of corresponding international economic regimes." The hegemonic power is both able and willing to establish and maintain the norms and rules of a liberal economic order, and with its decline the liberal economic order is greatly weakened.[2]

In other words, the world needs a country that will look after the world as a whole. When there is no such country, the global economy plunges into crisis. This theory seemed to offer the most satisfying explanation for the Great Depression. Great Britain had held hegemonic power during the seven decades preceding the First World War, the longest sustained period of global growth and prosperity in history. After the war Britain had tried to reassert its dominance but was no longer up to the task. It had been weakened by the war and a gradual loss of its industrial and commercial preeminence, first to Germany and then to the United States. The latter country had, by the early 1920s, fully eclipsed Britain as the world's premier economic power. But the United States did not understand that the continued health of the world economy depended on some country somewhere acting disinterestedly on behalf of the system as a whole, and the United States itself was, by that point in the century, the only country with an economy big enough and rich enough to do it. Its political elites, however, had little experience weighing policy choices with anything other than strictly domestic considerations. Thus it was that in the late 1920s the United States closed its markets to foreigners and demanded repayment of debts incurred by other nations while making it impossible for them to earn the dollars to pay those debts. Its financial authorities failed to provide so-called lender of last resort functions, thereby guaranteeing a global banking crisis as bank after bank, unable to obtain cash to pay off panicked depositors, closed its doors. With the United States unwilling and no other country able to undertake system-saving hegemonic functions, the liberal capitalist world order imploded.

Now, in October 1987, was history repeating itself? In the 1920s Britain had dropped the hegemonic baton, and it had lain in the dust of depression and war until the United States picked it up in 1945. Had the United States now dropped the baton? And who would pick it up?

That the United States had faltered seemed clear. It was not a matter anymore of unwillingness to exercise global leadership. While the Washington of 1929 may have been the stronghold of isolationists, the Washington of 1987 swarmed with "government officials, ex-government officials, think-tank denizens,"[3] CIA agents, Pentagon functionaries, pedigreed Foreign Service snobs, aid czars, senior congressional minions, development bankers, and hordes of "expert" journalists and academics all quite ready to arrange the affairs of the planet.

But the country had crippled itself. Chanting the mantra of free trade and laissez-faire, its senior officials had stood by while strategic industry after industry was lost to foreigners who had not forgotten that in order to consume, one must first produce. In the space of seven short years America had turned itself from the world's greatest creditor nation into the world's greatest debtor. Nor had the funds been borrowed to rebuild the nation's industrial might, overhaul its appalling primary and secondary educational system, or restore its crumbling and crime-ridden cities. The debts instead bought votes in key congressional districts, funded a vast military establishment, provided lavish and early retirements for America's upper middle class, and enabled hospitals to perform expensive miracles, keeping death at bay for a few weeks. In order to subsidize all this consumption and avoid the political discomfort of hard choices, the United States had debauched its currency, stretched its borrowing power to the limit, allowed the foundations of its wealth and power to rot. It need not have happened; for all the gains of its competitors, the United States had been dealt history's finest hand. Even as late as 1980 it had a far richer endowment in natural resources, human abilities, and inherited wealth than any country ever. This endowment had been squandered; the United States found itself in 1987 where Britain had been sixty years earlier. The costs of hegemony had become too high. Who would pay them?

Eyes turned to Japan. After all, Japan had financed the American deficits. Japanese companies were the ones muscling Americans out of key industries. In the reams of print comparing the two societies, every American weakness mirrored a Japanese strength: the twelve-year-old schoolboy in necktie and short pants doing American college-level math; the modestly paid company executive pouring funds into research and development; clean, crime- and pothole-free city streets; gleaming bullet trains and world-class factories; high savings rates and the sober brilliance of MOF bureaucrats, launching yet another revenue increase or scratching out one more piece of pork.

Yet what an odd country to stand as the hegemon heir apparent. Acting as a global hegemon is more than dollars and cents. It is something intangible as well, a fervent belief by its elite that its way is best, that the hegemon has gifts to be shared with humankind, that, as an American senator once put it, with enough effort we can raise Shanghai up and up until it reaches the level of Kansas City. It is funding Alliances Françaises around the world, teaching the Russian nobility to speak

French, welcoming black Africans and Algerians to Paris as cabinet ministers. It is the British doggedly showing "native" lawyers in the Federated Malay States how to don horsehair wigs in ninety-degree tropical humidity. It is the babel of Indian, Chinese, and Korean accents heard in the laboratories of MIT, the winning of literary prizes in Britain by people with names such as Ishiguro, Naipaul, and Rushdie, the American Historical Association's choosing a man called Iriye to be its head. It is expatriate teachers and missionaries, aid workers and development bankers.

And of course all those dollars and cents. It is an open market where foreigners can sell their goods and services without restriction or bureaucratic interference. Else, where will the foreigner earn the hegemon's currency? For being a hegemon is a matter of allowing one's currency to be earned and stored by foreigners, so that it becomes a universal means of payment and a universal store of value. It is a central bank that thinks on behalf of the health of the entire global economy, a political elite that can articulate to an electorate why it may sometimes be necessary to send hard-earned taxes overseas as unrestricted foreign aid or why the blood of its sons may be spilled in obscure conflicts fought with and against unknown people.

To anyone acquainted with the country, the idea of Japan as a global hegemon was ultimately preposterous. This was a country where an entire literary genre was devoted to proving that its inhabitants were fundamentally set apart from the rest of humanity, where an accredited scholar could maintain that the Japanese process language differently from everyone else and be given a serious hearing, where senior government officials could sit in international forums and announce that beef was unsuitable for the Japanese diet because Japanese intestines were a foot longer than those of foreigners or that American ski equipment not appropriate for Japanese sports lovers because the snow was different in Japan. It was a place where landlords routinely listed "no *gaijin*" in the specifications given to agents, where the alma mater of the emperor could, after years of hemming and hawing, finally offer tenure to one non-Japanese professor, only to fire him in violation of Japan's own labor laws three years later, all the while raising a massive new building to house a massive new program of international studies.[4]

This was not a country ready to run the planet. Its sole previous attempt at bringing "the eight corners of the world under one roof," to quote a widely used Japanese slogan of the 1930s, had ended in disaster. The disaster occurred not because of superior American armaments or strategy but because the Japanese could not integrate other Asians into the Greater East Asia Co-Prosperity Sphere except as low-grade laborers or outright slaves. Initially welcomed as liberators, the Japanese were soon hated and feared from Korea to Singapore.

Such lessons were not taught in Japanese schools,* but the postwar administrators knew full well how and why they had botched the opportunity to lead Asia out of colonialism. The fathers of the economic miracle had cut their teeth organizing the economy of colonial Manchuria. These men understood that in the power balances that constitute Japanese "democracy" there is no room to accommodate the outsider, that attempts to do so will simply lead to accusations of being "un-Japanese."

And so the Japanese elite settled for growing rich under American hegemony. America would manage the world's security and provide a global currency. Americans would run the GATT, the IMF, the World Bank. The American market would be open to all comers, while Japan would be left alone to build an industrial machine behind barriers that kept out foreigners, their investments, and their products. America would get unrestricted access to military bases in Japan, while Japan would be part of the global American nuclear network, although both countries would pretend otherwise. Japan would pay lip service in the United Nations and other international forums to American foreign policy goals. But Japan would not be asked and would not seek to play hegemonic functions.

---

*The history of World War II is usually treated in Japanese schools as something akin to the Great Earthquake of 1923, a sort of natural disaster visited upon Japan for inexplicable reasons.

In the wake of Black Monday, however, this was what the Japanese Ministry of Finance had to do, forced to act as a lender of last resort, supporting markets on the edge of collapse and providing a floor for the universal currency. It had to ensure that capital was recycled. The choice was stark: Either do what was necessary or watch the global economic order disintegrate.

Take the immediate reaction to the market crash. The Tokyo market had reached an all-time high the previous Wednesday but had then been badly shaken by the grim news coming out of Wall Street and gave a bit of ground on Monday before the New York market opened. But Tuesday morning in Tokyo, a few tense hours after the New York Black Monday close, was more than a case of the shakes. Prices went into free fall. Only built-in circuit breakers prevented a full-scale collapse.* Tokyo was gripped by a panic as great as New York's. Fortunately, however, Tokyo closes for two hours in the middle of the day. Tuesday happened to be the day of the monthly lunch at the Ministry of Finance between Matsukata Takashi, head of the MOF's secondary markets division, and the chiefs of equity trading at Japan's Big Four securities firms: Nomura, Daiwa, Nikko, and Yamaichi.[5] As one account of the lunch has it, "Matsukata is asked whether it is the wish of the Japanese government that the big four support the market. Matsukata leans forward and, almost imperceptibly, nods. Here, in a nod that is to give hope to the whole financial world, a tacit under-standing is reached: the big four will return from lunch to begin their buying operations. Wall Street has haemorrhaged; it is time for the Japanese single-mindedly to take over the controls of global finance."[6]

That afternoon mysterious buyers began returning to the market, seeking particularly the shares of such companies as Nippon Steel and Nippon Telephone and Telegraph, the gov-ernment-owned behemoth scheduled for "privatization" whose sale in late 1986 of 12.5 percent of its equity had been managed by Matsukata.[7]

---

*The most important of these closes trading in a share that falls by an average of 15 percent.

Tuesday's was a rescue operation. But the following day revealed the full might of the Japanese financial machine and just who was keeping the global order going. Although Monday had earned the sobriquet "Black," it was actually on Tuesday morning following the Tokyo Tuesday close that the New York markets came closest to complete disintegration. A manipulated rally in a Chicago stock index future had halted the fall just before meltdown, and the Dow Jones Average had staged a limp recovery, closing a modest 100 points above the opening. But the world waited breathlessly for Tokyo. Another 15 percent drop in the Tokyo market like the one it had had the previous day would spell the end of any chance that the global rout could be stopped. London was reeling; Hong Kong had already closed its doors.

Wednesday became the biggest trading day in the history of the Tokyo exchange. The panic sellers of the previous day switched into panic buyers. The parallels with 1929 turned out to be empty. Black Monday did not mark the beginning of the century's second Great Depression. Instead it was a brief pause before the greatest bull market in history, the Tokyo boom of the late 1980s.

The MOF-guided interventions that reversed the market rout were not driven purely by domestic concerns. Through no conscious design, these bureaucrats stood at the center of global finance, positioned so that their actions, or inactions, could determine the prosperity of the entire planet. It had happened for three reasons. The first was Japan's snowballing trade and current account surpluses. As these surpluses mounted—$31 billion trade surplus in 1983, $44 billion in 1984, $56 billion in 1985, $93 billion in 1986, $96 billion in 1987—Japan's exporters, usually acting through their banks, converted the surpluses mostly into dollar claims—U.S. Treasury securities, Eurodollar bonds. Second, the currency of Japan's trade was largely U.S. dollars, and the surpluses mostly converted into dollar instruments. Had the MOF encouraged the international use of the yen as a settlements and reserve currency and welcomed foreign financial institutions to Tokyo, giving them unrestricted access to yen funding, Japan would have been accumulating claims in yen rather than dollars. But internationalization of the yen would have undermined the MOF's control of the domestic financial system, so it was discouraged.

Inevitably, then, Japan's surpluses were steadily converted into a growing pile of dollar claims. Finally those dollar claims were mostly under the control of a small group of institutions— about twenty-five banks and trust banks, six or seven insurance companies, four securities firms, plus the Bank of Japan itself— all used to acting on the basis of what they thought the MOF would let them get away with. We looked at this in Chapter 2 in the context of the domestic market, but the result in the international arena was herdlike behavior of a particularly unsettling kind, unsettling because the herd had such a huge and growing position in the instruments of the universal currency.

The implications had first emerged during the 1984 breakdown of the Continental Bank of Illinois. Like a number of other American banks in the spring of 1984, Continental had been caught with a lot of bad loans in the wake of the collapse in the Texas and Oklahoma real estate and energy markets. While Continental hurt worse than its peers, the situation had persisted for several months. No one expected a run, but on the morning of May 10, when a series of inaccurate press reports culminated in two stories in the *Nihon Keizai Shimbun* about Continental's troubles and its supposed rescue by a major Japanese bank, Japanese money managers smelled trouble and pulled their Eurodollars out of the bank. Later in the day, when Washington opened, the comptroller of the currency issued a statement denying the rumors, but by that point it was too late. Continental, heavily dependent on the international market, could not fund its assets, and the Fed had to step in with an emergency bailout.

No individual Japanese investor thought his actions particularly remarkable. A mid-level manager at a trust bank or a securities firm reads in the morning paper that Continental is in trouble. He sells his institution's holdings of Continental's certificates of deposit and puts the dollars somewhere else. But the implications were stunning. If a handful of mid-level managers acting for unexceptional motives could bring about the collapse of a major bank, what could these same people do to the market for U.S. Treasury securities?

This question hung in the minds of both internationalist MOF and American officials. In the wake of the Plaza Accord, Japanese investors sustained staggering losses on their dollar investments. The top five Japanese life insurance companies alone in the 1985–88 period lost more than $25 billion. Yet during the same period Japanese investors *increased* their holdings of dollar-denominated securities from $82 billion to $235 billion.[8] These investors were not tripling their dollar holdings because they were stupid or perverse. Nor were they doing so only because they "had no place else to put their money." They were doing it because of moral suasion from a Ministry of Finance terrified over the implications of Japanese investors' all dumping dollar securities at once. As Nomura's chief international economist Richard Koo wrote in testimony submitted to the Joint Economic Committee of the Congress:

> During 1986 and 1987, the most difficult years of exchange rate adjustment, when the dollar and financial markets around the world came precariously close to total collapse, Japanese authorities tried to keep investors in dollars by telling them how much good the US had done for Japan after the war, and how important it was for Japan to stay with the dollar to prevent the total collapse of the world financial system. . . . In spite of mounting losses, therefore, the senior management of major insurance companies and trust banks refrained from selling dollar securities as long as they could.[9]

But while the MOF could control all Japanese investors some of the time and some investors all the time, it could not control all investors all the time. It could not, for example, stop the panic selling of the dollar in the spring of 1987 after the collapse of the Louvre Accord. And it could not keep Japanese investors in dollars the week before the stock market crash. As Koo went to write, "Although the Ministry of Finance's moral suasion was effective in keeping long-term investors such as pension trusts and insurance companies from selling dollars, it could not restrain relatively short-term investors such as securities investment trusts. During [the spring of 1987], securities investment trusts sold off nearly a quarter of their total holdings of dollar assets. They bought some of that back in the May–August period only to sell it all off again during the September–December period."[10]

Something else was needed in the wake of Black Monday. "Guidance" helped. The arms of big investors must have been exceptionally sore from MOF twisting after October 1987. No subsequent announcement of poorer-than-expected U.S. trade numbers comparable to that the week before Black Monday—and there were to be several—would see the kind of dollar selloff that had happened twice in 1987. But guidance itself was not enough; the stakes were too high.

At risk were both the global financial system and the basic structure of the U.S.-Japan relationship, political and economic. Markets such as Southeast Asia had grown in importance, but the United States was still taking the lion's share of Japanese exports. A cutoff in Japanese financing for the twin American deficits could spell the end of U.S. ability and willingness to continue to absorb the unending stream of Japanese products. And as the Reagan administration limped into 1988, the political noises from America sounded increasingly ominous in Tokyo.

The Japanese press has a way of amplifying every stray comment by a grandstanding member of Congress to make it appear that the bombs are about to start dropping again. Critical remarks about Japan made in an empty committee room on the Hill (empty, that is, except for Japanese reporters) and not bothered about by a single U.S. newspaper will be on the front page in Tokyo. But for all the hype the administrators knew that in reality things were getting worse. The summer of 1987 saw the Toshiba incident, in which a subsidiary of the electronics giant had been caught selling restricted military technology to the Soviets. A storm of criticism resulted, culminating in the public smashing of a Toshiba radio on the steps of the Capitol by several representatives. And the first stirrings of the 1988 presidential campaign suggested that the Democrats could seize on the administration's "softness" on Japan as an effective campaign issue. A Democratic administration coming to power on a wave of anti-Japanese sentiment, complete with protectionist legislation and tough trade negotiators, was a prospect that terrified Tokyo. Richard Gephardt, with his early successes in the Iowa caucuses and his critical remarks about the Reagan administration's Japan policy, was demonized in the Japanese press. Gephardt's prospects were never that good, he was not the "Japan basher" he was made out to be, and, as David Hale noted, despite its rhetoric, it was the Reagan administration that had in fact been the most protectionist since the 1930s.[11] But the Democrats represented unpredictability, and unpredictability is to be avoided by Japanese bureaucrats whenever possible.

So the Finance Ministry supplemented its direct guidance of Japanese institutional investors to give them a motive other than its approval to hang on to dollar securities. Working through its appointee Sumida Satoshi, governor of the Bank of Japan, it lowered yen interest rates to the point where putting any money into yen securities looked very unattractive.

The price exacted would be heavy; just how heavy became clear in the early 1990s. The deliberate low-interest policies pursued by the Japanese financial authorities to support the dollar translated into extremely rapid monetary growth. And this rapid monetary growth blew Japan's bubble much bigger than it otherwise would have been. The greatest excesses of the bubble economy happened after it had achieved its initial purpose of restoring the industrial competitiveness damaged by the Plaza Accord. They happened when the MOF and BOJ threw the gasoline of more liquidity onto an already briskly burning fire of asset inflation. The explosion in equity warrant bonds, the wildest real estate deals, the frenzied chase of too much money for too few assets all came after Black Monday. The Japanese investors driving around the posher Honolulu neighborhoods buying houses on the basis of glimpses from the car window, the developers throwing money at office buildings and hotels in Los Angeles and New York without so much as a glance at cash flow projections, the shoveling of credit by Japan's top institutions at shady gangster-related outfits—all happened in 1988 and 1989 in large part because the MOF was trying to save the world from the consequences of American profligacy.

Here was a real parallel with the Roaring Twenties. One reason the Federal Reserve had kept interest rates so low in the last years of that decade was to support the British pound,[12] and the policy had helped fuel the final roars of the era. Similarly, the MOF by late 1987 was as worried about the U.S. dollar as anything else, and with comparable results.

I happened to speak at a conference on Capitol Hill in the spring of 1990. The conference had brought together a number of people to talk about America's declining competitiveness vis-à-vis Japan. It was well attended by congressional staffers and some media representatives and produced a useful and sober look from a variety of different perspectives at the issues. At the lunch after the conference, however, one congressman and one congresswoman, neither of whom had bothered to attend the conference itself, began berating a Japanese conference participant from Sony about the company's recent acquisition of Columbia Pictures. They knew a little about the way the deal had been financed—Sony had issued an equity warrant bond with a coupon of less than 2 percent—and they were incensed at this "obvious" example of an insidious Japanese plot to buy up America. I didn't know whether to laugh or to cry. While it was about time that some people in Congress started worrying about the implications of selling off the national patrimony, these two seemed to have little grasp of their own role in the selloff. Didn't they have any understanding of why it was Sony could do deals at 2 percent interest rates? Didn't they realize that American deficits had largely driven the crazy currency movements of the previous decade? That MOF policies aimed at forestalling global financial meltdown had produced this great surge of Japanese liquidity? That if the United States ran deficits of $200 billion year after year after year, going hat in hand to Japan to finance them, ultimately the Japanese would turn their paper into real assets?

The MOF got no thanks. Perceptive commentators in the United States suggested half-jokingly that the ministry ought to register as a Republican PAC, but the Japanese buyup of American assets served to fan the flames of economic nationalism. Meanwhile in Tokyo Japanese businesses were attributing the rivers of money flowing into their coffers to their superior savvy, not to their luck at being in the midst of a deliberately engineered financial boom. Nomura Securities boasted in huge advertisements taken out in the global financial press that anyone concerned about the sustainability of Tokyo stock prices was the equivalent of a sixteenth-century astronomer refusing to accept the Copernican Revolution.

Japanese political life got sleazier and sleazier as flush new businesses tried to purchase influence on a massive scale. The biggest of these attempts, the Recruit scandal, helped bring down the government of Takeshita Noboru in the spring of 1989. The scandal was a typical bubble economy phenomenon. Recruit's founder, the gifted entrepreneur Ezoe Hiromasa, had made a fortune shaking up Japan's rigid labor market, providing real information to job seekers on market opportunities. His success stemmed partly from the bubble-fostered ethos of a younger generation, gradually becoming more interested in money than in status. But the administrators in the bureaucracy and the Nikkeiren (Employers' Association) reacted with visceral loathing to Ezoe's business. He threatened the informal norms of the labor market and encouraged youngsters to be "un-Japanese." The Ministry of Labor began preparation of a bill that would make it illegal to disseminate information on job opportunities without going through official channels. This would strike at the heart of Ezoe's business, and to forestall the bill, he began bribing every important politician in the country. He used the Tokyo stock market as the source of funds, offering shares in Recruit subsidiaries that were "guaranteed" to shoot up in value.

The Recruit mess could not have happened without the context of the bubble economy. The bubble created the conditions for Recruit's phenomenal growth. It gave Ezoe the means to bribe politicians. It made politicians even more desperate than usual for money; the costs of an election in Japan were soaring. It became one more blinking indicator warning Finance Ministry bureaucrats that the bubble's costs were climbing dangerously high.

As 1989 wore on, events overseas gave the MOF assurance that the dollar crisis had ended; the danger of financial meltdown and an unpredictable United States had been reduced. George Bush had been elected president with a decent majority. From a Tokyo perspective his people were even softer touches than the Reaganites. Carla Hills, his new trade representative, had had a speech prepared for her first trip to Japan in October 1989 with a suggestion that it would be healthy if Japan imported more. This was something even MITI was saying. But the office of John Sununu, Bush's chief of staff, insisted she take out the reference. After all, if she were to suggest the Japanese import more, the Japanese might ask how much more, and then we would be negotiating about targets, and that would be managed trade, something the Bushites would have nothing of.[13] The Bush people proved themselves skillful at managing protectionist pressures in Congress; when Congress got steamed up about one or another aspect of Japan's closed economy, the administration would home in on narrow targets that it knew the Japanese government directly controlled—satellite and supercomputer procurement policies, for example, or wood products standards. The administration took to announcing "get tough" tactics in public—e.g., the Structural Impediments Initiative—while privately telling Japanese government officials that they didn't believe the United States had a problem with Japan, but would the Japanese please cooperate in giving them some token victory so they could keep the barbarians in Congress and the Democratic party at bay?

Meanwhile on the financial front, as 1989 drew to a close,

the forecast called for much calmer weather. After a decade of turbulence the currency markets had finally begun to stabilize. The dollar gradually drifted back up against the yen from the low 120s into the 130s and then, in late 1989, into the low 140s. Japanese institutions in a very slow and orderly way began withdrawing from the long end of the U.S. Treasuries market, and while this depressed growth in the United States and ultimately helped perpetuate the U.S. recession of the early 1990s, no dramatic bond market panic of the kind seen twice in 1987 recurred.

One further crisis confirmed to the MOF that it had learned how to deal smoothly with such emergencies: the mini–stock market crash of October 1989. The '87 crash had many causes—Japanese doubts about the dollar being only one of them—but there was no ambiguity about the '89 minicrash. It clearly started in Tokyo. The crash came about because of the collapse of the United Air Lines leveraged buyout, which occurred when the bank financing essential to the deal fell apart. Japanese banks as a group suddenly withdrew from the syndicates of lenders that had been lined up by the likes of Citibank and Chase Manhattan because the Ministry of Finance told the banks it thought their exposure to the LBO market in the United States excessive. LBOs had been providing much of the "action" on the American markets. The collapse of the United deal spelled the end of the LBO boom, and the stock market promptly dropped—the New York market, that is.

This time Tokyo hardly blinked. It might have helped that the incident happened on a Friday in New York, giving players in Japan a chance to reassure one another over the weekend. Even this being conceded, the minicrash seemed clear evidence of how independent Tokyo had become. And it gave the financial authorities yet more assurance that they could take a little air out of the bubble.

The public puncturing of the bubble occurred on Christmas Day 1989 (not a holiday in Japan), when the Bank of Japan announced a sharp rise in interest rates and the market promptly began to tumble. A good deal of controversy still exists over the timing and reasons for the decision. Some maintain the end of the bubble came about through one of the Bank of Japan's periodic spasms of independence. By tradition, the bank's governorship alternates between a career BOJ man and an appointee of the Finance Ministry. Presiding over the BOJ during the bubble years had been Sumida Satoshi, widely identified as an accommodative tool of the MOF. His replacement, Mieno Yasushi, has been called a central banker's central banker. Mieno liked to boast that he had never owned a share in his life, and on being named governor in December 1989, he promptly and visibly attacked the bubble economy.

Conventional wisdom has it that the MOF wanted to spin out the bubble awhile longer and opposed at least the abruptness of Mieno's actions. But this may have been just feinting for public consumption. One journalist suggested the entire spat between the MOF and the BOJ in the fall of 1989 was deliberately staged.[14] Certainly, whatever their disagreements about tactics, the administrators were in broad agreement that the time had come to take some air out of the bubble. It had accomplished its purpose. But it had gone on too long. Too many inadequately submissive young people had too much money. Too many politicians, flush with campaign funds, seemed to think they had some business interfering in the way Japan was governed. Too many gangsters had stepped outside their tacitly approved jobs of intimidating leftist teachers, arm-twisting debtors to pay up, getting construction projects finished on time, and running the commercial sex and gaming trades. There was too much, in fact, of everything: brash banks, dubious deals, palatial office towers, swaggering brokers.

Confident of the tools they had developed to control emergencies, with friends in Washington who "understood" Japan, the administrators decided to slow things down a bit. But they found they had miscalculated.

III

Paying the Price

9. Bubble Jeopardy

IN THE FIRST MONTH after the Christmas 1989 interest rate hike by the Bank of Japan the Tokyo stock market fell from its 39,000 peak, as measured by the *Nikkei* stock index, to 37,000, a normal reaction by any stock market to a sharp rise in interest rates. Increased interest rates attract funds into bonds and deposits, reducing stock purchases; companies facing higher borrowing costs cut back on investment plans; price increases taper off or even decline; and the economy slows. It is to bring these things about that central bankers raise interest rates: to cool off an economy before overheating translates into inflation. According to the dictates of conventional wisdom, the BOJ had acted like any good, conservative central bank, and the market's response was unsurprising.

Although the market continued to ease that winter, by the normal standards applied in places like New York and London, Tokyo remained incredibly overbought. P / E ratios—the price of a share of stock as a multiple of corporate earnings measured on a per share basis—were still three to four times higher than in other major markets. One could choose from a variety of explanations. Popular with bullish foreigners was the idea that since most Japanese equity is locked away with long-term shareholders who never sell, the rump of stock that does trade attracts funds that in other markets would be spread out over several times the number of shares. Japan's bulls liked to argue that Japanese companies had established such dominance that they would be capturing the lion's share of future global profits;

the market simply reflected this reality. More critical voices contended that power holders in Japan had the tools to maintain the market at any desired level, and they had decided that stratospheric P / E ratios were in their interest. Whatever the various rationales on offer—and as usual there were elements of truth in all of them—Tokyo's equities in the winter of 1990 could hardly be described as in "decline." While the *Nikkei* average had fallen to 34,600 by the end of February, this level had been reached only six months earlier for the first time in history.

With so little to show for the first round of interest rate hikes, Governor Mieno of the BOJ raised rates a second time on March 20. He publicly announced his determination to puncture the bubble once and for all, and the market did indeed tumble to around 29,000. By this point it had lost 27 percent of its capitalized value in three months. Even so, Tokyo retained its status as the world's most highly valued market. And as the spring went on, it began to recover lost ground, climbing again into the low 30,000 range.

Much of the world looked on with a mixture of admiration and misgivings. Japan's financial authorities had engineered one of the greatest booms in history. Having steered most of the boom-bred funds into permanent additions to Japan's production capacity, the authorities were cooling off the economy just as it began to flash danger signals. Less money would flow into U.S. Treasury securities, dubious hotel projects in Hawaii, and sybaritic comforts for Japan's fledgling yuppies. But Japanese acquisition of high tech firms in the United States, its factory building in Southeast Asia, its domestic investments in production capacity continued unabated. Japan would be as formidable a competitor as ever.

As the summer approached, however, the view from inside Japan differed. The medicine didn't seem to be working. Japan's administrators had fretted over the social effects of the bubble economy, most particularly the fracturing of Japan's middle class into those with land and those without. They worried about erosion of both the work ethic and the will to save. Tokyo now counted close to a million families holding land that made them dollar millionaires. Meanwhile most of the rest faced housing prices so high that a lifetime of salary wouldn't buy even a small lot.

Many of Japan's financial administrators wanted to reverse this. In particular they wanted banks to stop fueling land price increases. Despite the higher interest rates, however, bankers were still shoveling money at property developers. Figures released in June by the BOJ showed that loans for land purchases had been up at the end of March by 15 percent over the year-earlier figure.

So, on August 30, Mr. Mieno announced yet another rate increase. The BOJ's discount rate now stood at a full 6 percent. Fifteen months earlier it had been 2.5 percent. This time Mr. Mieno had his way with a vengeance. In a few days the market lost nearly a fifth of its value, falling below 26,000. But while this latest interest rate hike finally killed both the stock and the real estate market booms, nasty surprises waited.

In September Japan's financial community got its first major shock: A large property–cum–trading company had effectively gone bankrupt. Not one of the new developers that had grown up like toadstools in the credit-rich muck of the bubble years, this was Itoman, a member in good standing of the Sumitomo *keiretsu*, a firm backed and partly staffed by the Sumitomo Bank. The bank's September 20 announcement of the $2 billion Itoman bailout struck Japan the way a Chapter 11 filing by a household name would hit Americans.

As news of the Itoman debacle dribbled out, the implications began to register. Itoman was overextended in the property market. The very month of the rescue announcement, the company had told securities analysts of its plans to construct twenty new golf courses. But with the latest interest rate hikes, Itoman's financing costs exceeded any conceivable cash flow from the golf courses, resorts, and so-called one-room mansions (blocks of single-room condominiums for mixed office-residential use) that had become the company's specialty. If the

Sumitomo Bank had to rescue Itoman, what about property developers less well connected and the loans these outfits had taken down from nonbanks and the *shinkin* and *shinyōkumiai*— the credit associations that stood in the bottom rank of the Japanese banking hierarchy? Could those loans be collected? And who in turn would bail out nonbanks and *shinkin*?

Historically the rescuers had been the big banks. With one small wartime exception, the MOF had not allowed a bank to fail since the 1927 banking crisis. An institution headed for insolvency was typically bailed out by one of its larger brethren. Already the previous fall Chiba Bank, Japan's second-largest regional bank, had been muscled into leading an ongoing rescue effort for a failing *shinyōkumiai*.[1] The troubles of the recently upgraded Taiheiyo Bank were an open secret.* The MOF had roped four city banks into bailing the bank out and was hoping to cram it down the throats of one of them.[2] Dozens more *shinkin* and *sogo* banks were said to be floundering. Could the big banks rescue all these problem small fry just as property developers started to totter?

Both the capacity to absorb bad loans and the way it was done were problematic. A bank facing a drain on its profits—a bad loan, a bailout, an acquisition of a failing *shinkin*—usually dipped into the hidden assets that constituted the real capital base of the Japanese banking system. Generally this meant selling shares the bank had purchased decades earlier, generating a capital gain to cover the profit drain. But because of the informal guidelines governing Japanese business life, the banks couldn't leave it at that. They had to buy the shares back at current prices, not reflected in the bank's profit and loss but costing the bank more money.† The hidden asset was gone, and the bank's real, as opposed to reported, capital cushion had

---

* Like a number of its peers, Taiheiyo had been upgraded from a *sogo* (mutual) bank to a full-fledged commercial bank, thus intensifying concern when so soon thereafter its troubles became common knowledge.

† Only a company itself in difficulty was "allowed" to sell the shares of a valued customer or fellow *keiretsu* member without buying them back, and even then the shares were supposed to be placed within the *keiretsu*.

shrunk. And with it went the ability essentially to create money out of that asset.

Making things worse was the tightening corset of the BIS guidelines. "BIS" is an acronym for the Basel-based Bank for International Settlements—the central banks' central bank— and the guidelines refer to agreements adopted in the mid-1980s about universal bank capital standards. Complaints from Western banks tired of being undercut by the Japanese had helped bring them about. The Westerners assumed that if the Japanese were forced to raise their capital ratios, they could no longer price loans as if capital were free. The world's major governments agreed that by March 1993 the ratio of a bank's reported capital to its total assets must be a minimum of 8 percent. The Japanese had argued that their reported bank balance sheets did not accurately reflect their banks' capital because of their huge cushion of hidden reserves. They believed they should be allowed to count a portion of these reserves as capital. In a compromise settlement Japan's banks got the right to count 45 percent of the market value of these assets toward their capital requirements.

But the events of September 1990 suggested that this compromise might have set a trap. Banks forced to sell their hidden assets brought on a double whammy: Selling the assets meant selling off the banks' real capital cushions, and the sheer volume of what might be sold could itself lower the value of the market, thereby reducing the capital value of what was left. By that September the falling market had pushed every major Japanese bank below the interim BIS guidelines. The banks would have to issue stock, with the potential for further depressing the market with a flood of new bank equity,* for Japanese bank

---

* One of the ironies of the whole BIS guidelines affair was that scores of European and Australasian banks (including virtually every solid bank in the U.K., Ireland, France, Scandinavia, Holland, Australia, and New Zealand), plus a few American names such as Chemical and First Interstate, satisfied much of their so-called Tier II capital requirements by borrowing indirectly from Japanese banks and insurance companies. (The guidelines required half the capital, Tier I, to be pure equity or retained earnings; the remaining half could be subordinated debt.) Regulators in most

shares make up some 25 percent of the total capitalization of the Tokyo market.

As analysts began to make these connections, the market took a frightening fall, dropping another 5,000 points to just over 20,000. In nine short months the Japanese stock market had lost nearly 50 percent of its value. Then, on October 5, came the biggest shock to that date. Police arrested a Sumitomo Bank branch manager, charging him with persuading bank clients to make $170 million in illegal loans to stock market speculators. The MOF demanded the resignation of Isoda Ichiro, the bank's chairman. Usually, when senior officials resign to "take responsibility" for mishaps involving their institutions, they continue to wield power behind the scenes.* But the MOF insisted that all links between Isoda and the Sumitomo Bank be severed. Isoda was widely admired as the quintessential Japanese banker of the 1980s. During that decade Sumitomo had become the most profitable Japanese bank, the number one choice of college graduates seeking careers in banking, and highly respected overseas. But Sumitomo had overstepped the norms of acceptable behavior in the Japanese system. And Isoda had offended the MOF. He had had the effrontery to state

---

countries will not allow banks to count one another's shares or subordinated debt as capital; otherwise banks could simply swap shares or debt, technically meeting requirements without bringing any new capital into the banking system. But the foreign banks raised billions of dollars of Tier II capital from Japanese nonbanks between 1987 and 1991. The nonbanks funded themselves either from Japanese banks or insurance companies. Meanwhile the MOF prohibited the city banks from raising subordinated debt until June 1990. As a result, money that could have gone to recapitalize Japan's banking system instead went to strengthen balance sheets in London, Sydney, Copenhagen, and New York. When the Japanese were finally allowed by the MOF to issue subordinated debt, most of it was bought either by *keiretsu* members, who were funded by the banks for that specific purpose, making a mockery of the whole exercise, or by life insurance companies, some of which had to sell shares to buy the subordinated issues, thus putting further downward pressure on the stock market and, therefore, bank capital cushions.

*Tabuchi Yoshihisa, for example, the president of Nomura who resigned in the summer of 1991 to "take responsibility" for the securities scandals, is still said to run the company. The same is true of his counterpart at Nikko, Iwasaki Takuya, who also publicly fell on his sword. Tanaka Kakuei was the most powerful politician in Japan *after* he resigned both from the prime minister's office and from the LDP. He effectively dictated the choice of four prime ministers.

publicly that the MOF and the BOJ were not legally empowered to boss Sumitomo around, and he had specified a time when Finance Minister Hashimoto Ryutaro should see him, rather than ask the latter's convenience. When he resigned to "take responsibility" for the arrest of the branch manager, he had first informed the Bank of Japan rather than the Ministry. MOF inspectors descended in droves on Sumitomo and stayed there until they were assured that Isoda was gone for good.[3]

It was a pointed demonstration of the power of the MOF to bankers who might have forgotten it during the euphoria of the bubble years. But as the stock market headed down toward 20,000 with no floor in sight, Japan's flustered bankers, brokers, and bureaucrats did not blame anyone in Japan. Instead they blamed the *gaijin*. The BIS guidelines were tagged as an insidious plot to gag Japanese banks, forcing them to issue equity into a weak market. American firms such as Salomon Brothers, Morgan Stanley, and Bankers Trust were cast as the villains of the market drop because they had brought derivative instruments to Tokyo.

Derivatives are financial instruments whose values derive from other, underlying financial instruments—thus the name. A put option, for example, gives the owner the right to sell a security at a certain price. A call option carries the right to buy at a certain price. Index-linked derivatives pay according to the value of an underlying index, such as the Dow Jones or the *Nikkei*. Derivatives had become increasingly important worldwide in the 1980s; the computerization of the financial markets had made it possible for investors and bankers to adopt complex hedging strategies using derivatives. Regulators in many countries worried, however, that derivatives had become the tail that wagged the market dog. Fingers pointed at derivatives in the wake of the 1987 New York stock market crash.

The Ministry of Finance and many in Japan's securities industry took a comparable tack to explain the Tokyo market slide. Blaming the Americans, however, was unconvincing. American banks did lead in derivatives technology, but the big

Japanese institutional investors—life insurance companies, trust banks—were using the instruments to hedge their portfolios. A trust bank would not openly sell shares of a leading Japanese industrial, but it could accomplish the same thing, locking in a certain price, by quietly buying a put from an American bank. Or, it could hedge its entire exposure by buying *Nikkei* index–linked puts.

The Ministry of Finance had, in fact, given Japanese financial institutions every incentive to use the derivatives. The BIS guidelines' special provision for the Japanese—counting 45 percent of the hidden value of their equity holdings as capital cushions—were an open invitation for the banks to lock in the value of those holdings. Life insurance companies were given a similar inducement when the MOF permitted them to include 25 percent of their long-term capital gains as income that could be used to pay policyholders.

The ministry made other mistakes. In December 1988 heavy selling in the futures market, where derivatives such as puts and calls are traded, worsened a temporary downturn in the stock market. Because the closing times in the two markets differed, buyers and sellers in the futures market found it difficult to settle. (In the exercising of an equity derivative, the underlying share of stock must ultimately change hands.) The MOF changed the closing times to make it possible to cover the futures market with the stock market. Doing so, however, knocked out from under high stock prices a key prop already tottering with the surge in derivatives trading: restricted supply. As noted, one of the hoariest explanations for high Tokyo stock prices was the paucity of equity that actually traded. The coming of derivatives to Tokyo and the creation of a genuine futures market had the effect of vastly increasing supply; trading in derivatives allowed investors to reap the gains (or suffer the losses) that would have accrued from trading the stock itself.

The MOF little understood what it had unleashed when it permitted the introduction of derivatives trading into the Tokyo markets. The decision appears to have been hasty, partly a result of loud foreign complaints about the inability to make money in Japan and partly a naïve belief that derivatives offered a means by which insurance companies could support the market without committing extra funds. While derivatives trading in the United States had grown up over a period of many years together with a market that was mostly rising, the MOF had allowed derivatives to enter Tokyo all at once at something close to a market peak. This practically guaranteed that investors would seek to use them primarily to lock in gains with the paradoxical effect of worsening what each individual sought to forestall: a drop in market value.[4]

The ministry's loss of control was not, however, a simple failure to master the highly quantitative skills that underlie derivatives trading.* MOF bureaucrats also confronted in the late 1980s an unprecedented phenomenon for them: uppity bankers who thought they were smarter than any bureaucrat. In the past, when an MOF man laid down the law to a supplicant from the Fuji Bank or Daiwa Securities, both parties had acknowledged that the MOF man possessed not only higher status and more power but a better brain. In the late 1980s, however, MOF officials had to deal with cadres of people who were their equals in intelligence, enthusiasm, and—most important—the opinions they held of themselves.

The first wave was young American and British bankers sent to intermediate the flow of capital out of Japan. The dignified expatriate lending officers of the 1960s and 1970s, skilled at building relationships with establishment Japanese companies in order to safeguard their banks' stable shares of a cartelized market, were replaced by brash yuppies, many of whom combined Japanese-language skills with the street smarts and trading mentality bred by Wall Street and the City of London. Even more significantly, by the mid-1980s foreign firms had begun pulling in top-drawer Japanese. Foreign banks and securities

---

*Derivatives trading, more than any other area of finance, is the arena of young computer jocks. A quick tour of the MOF, with its near-total absence of computers, makes it clear enough why the ministry had trouble staying on top of this business.

companies had traditionally encountered difficulties tapping into the best people at the entry and middle-management levels.* That changed with the floodgates of Japanese capital opening up in the 1980s. If the foreign firms waved around enough cash, they could get the sharp young Japanese they needed. Morgan Stanley and Salomon Brothers found they could even recruit at Tokyo University.

Most Japanese at the top foreign firms, particularly the younger ones, had absorbed the "master of the universe" ethos of 1980s-style American investment banking. To fawn before bureaucrats who did not understand one's business did not fit this ethos very well. Blissfully ignorant American managers would send young Japanese in their mid-twenties off to deal with the MOF, a task set aside in Japanese firms for the upper ranks of middle management. After all, the classic assignment for the first-year associate on Wall Street is the preparation and filing of documents with the SEC in connection with the issue of securities. Why should Japan be any different?

Thus MOF "guidance" tended to fall on deaf ears. Instead of the usual obsequious middle-aged bankers skilled at reading bureaucratic nods, grunts, and asides, the ministry had to deal in unfamiliar territory with insolent young traders backed by employers who had finally learned to make embarrassingly loud political noises when the MOF tried to discipline them in proper Japanese behavior. As far back as 1984 Citicorp had deliberately announced its acquisition of the British broker Vickers da Costa to coincide with a visit by table-pounding Treasury Secretary Donald T. Regan. Citicorp wanted Vickers as much for its franchise in Japan as anything else, but it knew

---

* At the senior management level, however, the problem was reversed. Foreign financial institutions found they needed to hire at least one retired MOF or BOJ official and provide him with an impressive title, a generous salary, an attractive secretary, a largish office, a car and a driver. In fairness, most of these men did earn their keep by informing management of the bureaucracy's thinking, telling management whom to talk to in the bureaucracy about what, and acting as an advocate for the institution with their former colleagues. They also, of course, provided the authorities with a way of informally keeping tabs on what the *gaijin* were up to.

it was getting something—the right to trade equities—no foreign or even Japanese bank enjoyed. Citicorp was sure the MOF would oppose the purchase, but by announcing it the day Regan arrived to demand "liberalization" of the Japanese financial market, Citicorp anticipated—correctly—that the MOF would not dare block the Vickers acquisition.

As the eighties progressed, American and British firms often got results when they complained to their governments. The most effective tool was the threat of retaliation against Japanese financial institutions in New York and London. Are British stockbrokers unable to obtain seats on the Tokyo exchange? Fine, then full licenses will be withheld from Japanese institutions in the City of London. Are Americans barred from capitalizing in Japan on their expertise in derivatives? Then Japanese securities houses will be ineligible for primary dealer status in the huge and lucrative U.S. Treasuries market.

These tactics began to work fairly well—among other things, they threatened to deprive the MOF of one of its more important carrots used in controlling Japanese financial institutions, permission to open branches abroad—and by the late eighties the American firms were doing pretty much what they wanted in the derivatives arena. Their skills and their competitive edge enabled the top performers to earn phenomenal amounts of money during the peak years of the bubble economy and indeed well into the slowdown that followed it.[5] The profitability of Salomon's Tokyo office may have saved the firm in the wake of the 1991 U.S. Treasury securities trading scandal that toppled its chairman John Gutfreund, and it is certainly the major reason why the Tokyo office head, the Englishman Deryck Maughan, was named the firm's president in the wake of the scandal.[6]

Once they grasped what derivatives had done to their ability to determine market outcomes, however, MOF bureaucrats strove mightily to bring them under control. They pushed the Monetary Authority of Singapore to suspend trading in Japanese derivatives on SIMEX, the Singapore futures exchange and the most important futures market in the world after the Chicago market, with which it was linked.[7] At the behest of the Finance Ministry, the *Nihon Keizai Shimbun* threatened to rescind its permission for the American Stock Exchange to use the *Nikkei* index, over which it had copyright control, unless the exchange ended trading in certain index-linked derivatives. Business hours on the Osaka futures exchange were cut back, and circuit breakers installed that closely limited activity. Both MOF bureaucrats and executives at Japanese securities houses fumed about how the Americans were "undermining" the Japanese market.

Much of this intervention was hamfisted and conveyed a sense of desperation that probably served to worsen the situation. Thus, when the *Nikkei* index dropped below the crucial 20,000 line in early October, something more was required. Finance Minister Hashimoto announced a splashy series of measures to buoy the market. Margin requirements were reduced to 20 percent. Life insurance companies were allowed to put more money into the so-called *tokkin* funds, or investment trusts. This was a significant concession by a MOF normally unwilling to consider anything that might reduce tax revenues and an indication of how seriously the ministry viewed the situation, for the *tokkin* funds enable life insurance companies to revalue an asset without creating a taxable capital gain.

More important than the specifics of Hashimoto's announcement, however, was the fact that it had been made. Most investors in the Tokyo market tended to believe that the best indicator of the direction of equity prices was the level where the ministry wanted them to be. The market had fallen so far in part because investors knew that the authorities had intended to end the bubble economy and that this involved bringing down the stock market. They were waiting for a sign that the MOF had decided things had gone far enough. This Hashimoto's announcement accomplished. Household investors poured back into the market, and the *Nikkei* index jumped to over 25,000.

Perhaps the market drop had well and truly ended and prices would stabilize in the 25,000–28,000 range. As the rally caught on and widened in the succeeding months, foreigners joined households in putting money into a market that looked like a genuine buy in comparison with the levels where it had been eighteen months earlier. Fears that the sharp market drop of 1990 would spill over into the "real" economy of factories and trade appeared unfounded. Economic fundamentals were robust. Capital spending continued at a blistering pace, growing in early 1991 at a real rate of more than 10 percent annually. Such spending had been the primary engine of GNP growth since the Plaza Accord, and it seemed to solidify the growing edge Japanese industry had over its foreign competitors. GNP growth for the first quarter of 1991 registered the strongest quarterly performance since the first quarter of 1988 during the height of the bubble economy. One well-known foreign economist was quoted in April saying, "The entire policy establishment is congratulating itself for being the first regulators in history to deflate an asset bubble without impacting severely on economic activity."[8]

But disquieting signs suggested the self-congratulation might be premature. The market had rallied on a narrow base, supported mostly by individuals buying on the margin and foreigners, such as the American pension plans that had poured a cool ¥1 trillion ($8 billion) into the market in the first six weeks of 1991.[9] More savvy players—banks, insurance companies, even the *tokkin* funds—continued to be sellers. Sporadic news of speculative losses still shocked. The steel trading company Hanwa announced in mid-October a ¥20 billion ($160 million) write-off in losses from bubble years–style *zaitekku* (financial engineering).[10] In a pattern typical of many companies in such aging industries as steel and textiles, *zaitekku*— a word marrying the Japanese for "finance" and the English "technology"—had come to dwarf Hanwa's original business. Rumors had the company involved in under-the-water trades many times the size of its write-offs. The second-biggest condominium developer in Japan, Asahi Juken, was said to be in dire straits, and a bailout operation undertaken by the giant trading firm C. Itoh.[11] Nissan Motors had to guarantee more than $800 million in loans to its car seat maker affiliate, Ikeda Bussan, because of the latter's *zaitekku*-related losses.[12]

As 1990 turned into 1991, a string of property companies went under.[13] Azabu Building, a large property and *zaitekku* speculator, was told by its banks to reduce its debt by the yen equivalent of more than $1.8 billion.[14] Another troubled *shinkin* had to be force-fed to a reluctant bank, this time to Nagoya's Tokai Bank.[15] Every day brought news of problems with the nonbanks. Esco Lease, the biggest leasing company in Hokkaido, had to be rescued by its parent, the Hokkaido Takushoku Bank.[16] The first actual bankruptcy of a nonbank occurred in April, when Shizushin Lease, a leasing company based in the middle-size city of Shizuoka, defaulted on liabilities of ¥256 billion ($2 billion), making it the fourth-largest bankruptcy in Japanese history.[17]

So far these stories were confined to developers, the second tier of the industrial sector, and the nonbanks and the *shinkin* rather than to Japan's core financial institutions, but would that last? Profits at Japan's largest banks had nose-dived in the fiscal year that ended March 31, 1991. An official from the Long-Term Credit Bank of Japan (LTCB) was quoted in *Institutional Investor* as saying his bank "would not be obliged to rescue Japan Leasing."[18] For the parent of Japan's second-largest leasing company, this was an extraordinary and reckless statement to make. Japan Leasing's name had been linked in the press to a troubled Janome Sewing Machine, which had had to shell out ¥30 billion in borrowed money to stock speculator Kotani Mitsuhiro, who was later indicted for extortion; there was, however, little evidence that Japan Leasing itself was in any serious difficulty. But the LTCB man's comments pointed to the naked fear on the part of many of Japan's bankers over their metastasizing credit problems and a rush to avoid getting stuck with the tab. The mess at Janome had already forced the resignation of Masuno Takeo, president of the newly merged Kyowa Saitama Bank.* The merger itself had been another shotgun wedding of the relatively healthy Kyowa and the tottering Saitama, traditionally the smallest and weakest of Japan's city banks.

Meanwhile the overhang from the equity warrant market we looked at in Chapter 7 loomed over the financial horizon. Most of the deals were not coming due until 1993, but if the market were not safely back over 30,000 by that time, most of the warrants would expire worthless. Corporate Japan would then have to scramble to raise hundreds of billions of dollars to pay off the bondholders rather than use the expected proceeds of stock sales to warrant holders.

Despite all the bad news, faith in the ability of Japan's mandarins to direct its economy did not really start to crumble until the summer of 1991, when a series of the biggest financial scandals in history hit Japan. The entire securities industry, several of the country's most important banks, and the Ministry of Finance itself were drawn into them.

The scandals came to light when the *Yomiuri Shimbun,* Japan's largest newspaper, reported in June that securities companies were deducting as entertainment expenses payments they had made to many of their bigger clients to compensate them for losses taken on stock market investments.[19] Promising such compensation is illegal in Japan, as it is in most countries, although the payments themselves were not.† The *Yomiuri* apparently obtained the information from an official of the MOF's tax bureau, later criticized by an ex-MOF vice minister for "violating his duty to keep the information confidential."[20] The official suggested that the tax bureau had been worried that Nomura would seek the aid of politicians in putting pressure on the ministry to hush up the matter and claimed the tax bureau had planted the leak to prevent this from happening.

---

*The bank is known today as the Asahi [Morning Sun] Bank.
† Such payments were finally made illegal in April 1992.

But it turned out not to be this simple. While the MOF was perfectly capable of planting different stories in the press to create a cloud of confusion, the idea that the tax agency would leak such important information without consulting other ministry officials strained credulity. The real problem lay in the conflicting "guidance" that the securities bureau of the MOF had given the industry. At the end of 1989, just before Mieno's first bubble-bursting interest rate hike announcement, the MOF had instructed the securities companies both to end compensation payments and to close so-called *eigyō tokkin* accounts. These *eigyō tokkin* differed from ordinary *tokkin* (investment trusts) because the securities companies themselves managed the funds. Securities companies had offered clients guaranteed returns to induce them to set up the *eigyō tokkin*.[21] As one study of the Japanese stock market written before the scandals noted, "The typical performance target of a *tokkin* fund is an 8 percent annual return. Although illegal, it is common practice for an investment advisory firm to guarantee such a return to its client. . . ."[22]

Once the market had started dropping, however, ending compensation payments while shutting down the *eigyō tokkin* would have put further horrendous downward pressure on the market; there were some ¥4 trillion (over $35 billion) in these accounts. Companies had opened the *eigyō tokkin* in good faith because they believed the promises of guaranteed returns. The securities firms sought guidance from the ministry and were told in so many words that wrapping up the *eigyō tokkin* in an orderly fashion took precedence over ending compensation practices, that the latter would, in effect, be overlooked for the time being.

When stories of the payments started appearing in the press, however, they outraged the millions of small investors whose participation was essential to a market recovery. While most such folks had long suspected a market rigged on behalf of insiders, they were happy to go along with the game when they too were making money. But when people who had been induced by fast-talking brokers to pour their savings into the stock market saw the value of their holdings drop by 50 percent, they were less pliable after they read that the big boys had been guaranteed against losses.

According to conventional wisdom at the time, word of the compensation payments had been leaked because honoring all the promises would have bankrupted the securities industry. The public wrist slapping delivered to the top firms was said to provide a convenient cover for reneging on the promises.

The way Nikko Securities handled the fallout tended to support the idea that the scandal had been staged to bail out the industry. Its president, Iwasaki Takuya, resigned to "accept responsibility," although he would naturally continue as a power behind the scenes in the role of "adviser." The company closed its business for a day. Instead of barking into telephones, hawking shares on the basis of the theme of the week, Nikko's salespeople assembled in a large auditorium where they listened to a lecture from a professor of ethics. This ritualized public show of contrition is the standard Japanese way of dealing with an embarrassing situation that has unavoidably come to light. Nothing really changes, but the air has been cleared, and everyone can agree to start over with face preserved and accounts settled.

Nomura Securities, however, flubbed its lines. Its president, Tabuchi Yoshihisa, resigned like his Nikko counterpart, Iwasaki, to "take responsibility" for the problems. But his famous remark that the company had been making the compensation payments with the knowledge—and thus the implicit approval—of the Ministry of Finance cast doubt on the idea of an explicit arrangement between the MOF and the securities industry. Tabuchi may have only said publicly what everyone knew, but for an insider simply to blurt out the truth is a deadly political act in Japan. Japanese political and economic arrangements depend on everyone's maintaining the appropriate fictions; there is a vocabulary for this dance in Japanese, the most well known of the terms being *tatemae,* or the fiction to which everyone gives lip service, and *honne,* or the real situation, which is understood, as it were, at the edge of consciousness.* But a single word spoken by the wrong person at the wrong time can tear the curtain of *tatemae,* forcing the *honne* into public view. Tabuchi's comment bears comparison in its impact with the remarks made the previous summer by Tanaka Kakuei's private secretary, Hayasaka Shigezo, when his friend Aoki Ihei committed suicide. Aoki had been, like Hayasaka, private secretary to a publicly disgraced prime minister; in Aoki's case, the prime minister was Takeshita Noboru, who had been brought down in the summer of 1989 by the Recruit scandal. Hayasaka was shown over and over again weeping on Japanese television and saying that Japanese politics was nothing but an unending quest for money. The *tatemae* of Japanese politics—that Japanese politicians govern Japan, that they contend for votes with competing visions of Japan's national interest—was for a moment ripped apart by Hayasaka's breakdown.

Similarly, Tabuchi's remark exploded the *tatemae* of the Tokyo stock market as an open market governed by transparent rules where risk capital seeks the highest returns on the basis of investors' judgments on the capability of companies to turn profits. Once Tabuchi's remark had been made, it could not be unsaid. The little boy had shouted, and there was no escaping the fact that the emperor was naked. The MOF had not hatched an elaborate and detailed scheme to bail out the securities industry. It had simply been caught trying to resolve too many contradictions at the same time: ensuring steady tax revenues while adjusting to market losses; keeping the big players on board while maintaining the confidence of outside investors; rescuing the securities industry from traps its own "guidance" had cre-

*The words are Japanese, but *tatemae* / *honne* is not a phenomenon limited to Japan. It is at work in the framing of ethnic, racial, and gender issues in the United States. From a Japanese perspective, the entire "political correctness" movement is an attempt to widen *tatemae,* to ensure, for example, that such issues as the links between family breakdown among urban blacks and violent crime cannot be discussed except in ritualized code.

ated. The MOF could never admit it had made mistakes, so it tried to make it appear as if others were at fault.[23] And the Tokyo stock "market" that accounted for 40 percent of total world equity capitalization was seen finally for what it was: a useful tool in the hands of insiders in the securities industry, the LDP, large companies, and the Finance Ministry to strip wealth from ordinary Japanese and concentrate it in a central core.

But for the game to work, it required the participation of these ordinary Japanese, and in the wake of the scandals this became more and more difficult to arrange—particularly so because in the weeks after the compensation scandal broke, worse doings came to light. By the fall of 1991 the stock market and indeed much of the financial system stood revealed as a cesspool of corruption. Those entrusted in the Japanese system with managing the savings of the Japanese people were not just scratching one another's backs; they were visibly in cahoots with the criminal underworld.

To begin with, Nomura and Nikko had financed an attempt by a well-known mobster, Ishii Susumu, to corner the shares of the Tokyu Corporation, a large railroad–cum–department store company. Ishii headed Japan's second-largest crime syndicate, and Nomura's assistance went beyond financing the raid. It was ramping shares in Tokyu, a company that was supposed to be its client. Meanwhile Nikko was helping Ishii conduct a similar raid on Honshu Paper.

Dealings with gangsters were not confined to the securities industry; even more egregious examples involved several of the great banks. Stockbrokers may have been regarded by large segments of the Japanese public as standing only a rung or two in the social hierarchy above cabaret pimps, but bankers were respectable pillars of the Japanese economic order. Yet we saw the Industrial Bank of Japan finance billions of dollars in equity deals by an Osaka restaurateur with links to the Osaka underworld, using nothing but visibly forged CDs as collateral. She was arrested and went bankrupt in August.[24] The saga of Itoman, the Sumitomo group company whose problems had sucked in the Sumitomo Bank, turned out to be more than a story of bad business judgment. To all intents and purposes, the bank had allowed a mobster to become the head of Itoman's property division and then a member of the board, from which position he had proceeded to loot the company of some half a trillion yen ($4 billion). Before the Itoman tale played itself out, much of Itoman's senior management was in jail, including its president, Kawamura Yoshihiko, seconded from the bank, while another Sumitomo secondee was dead by his own hand.

The Itoman affair tarred reputations other than Sumitomo's. It turned out that the Fuji Bank, Japan's third largest, had urged a number of its clients to deposit about a $1 billion yen equivalent with an Osaka credit union that then lent much of the money to Ito Suemitsu, the mobster Sumitomo Bank had allowed to become an Itoman director.[25] Fuji ended up having to dole out some ¥200 billion ($1.6 billion) toward the credit union's rescue.[26] Fuji's problems that summer did not end there. Three different Fuji branches were caught having issued forged certificates of deposit so that property companies with gangster connections had "collateral" to borrow some ¥700 billion ($5.6 billion) from groups of nonbanks.[27] Branch managers at two other city banks, Tokai and Kyowa Saitama, were also fired that summer for issuing fake CDs.

The scandals took a toll on the market, which slumped back below 22,000 in August, deserted now by households that believed they had been fleeced once too often. Mesmerized by their charts showing how far the market had dropped from its all-time highs of two years earlier, foreigners again came to the rescue. But the foreign buying was not enough to do anything more than prevent a rout. So on October 1, 1991, almost exactly one year after the previous market rescue package, the Bank of Japan announced a reduction in bank reserve ratios. It hoped to release more funds for lending as well as signal investors that the scandals had marked the bottom of the bear market.

The announcement worked for a few weeks, and the market jumped nearly 3,000 points. But it soon became clear that the

BOJ's actions had done little to cure underlying woes. It would take more than a reduction in bank reserve ratios to get banks lending again. Their bad debts formed too huge an overhang, and no one knew how bad it would ultimately get. Estimates of uncollectable debt varied wildly from ¥15 trillion to ¥60 trillion. One number was certain, however: the paltry ¥3 trillion (roughly $25 billion) in loan loss reserves that the banks had set aside. For the MOF had long discouraged the banks from setting aside sufficient money to write off loans that looked as if they might not be collectable. Labeling a loan "troubled" and setting aside money to write it off reduce profits and, therefore, taxes.

But it wasn't just taxes. Banks needed to maintain the pretense that loans that would clearly never be collected were still performing. Otherwise they ran the risk of bringing a great deal of real estate on to an illiquid, shaky market whose "values" underpinned the entire superstructure of Japanese finance. As we have seen, most loans in Japan are collateralized, and far and above the most common collateral is real estate. So in order to keep ruined property companies from putting land on the market at distressed prices or seizing and selling the land themselves, banks went on pretending that their loans were performing, the financial authorities went on pretending that the banks were just going through a rough patch in the road, and everyone went on pretending that a property market teetering on the edge of collapse was fundamentally sound.

But pretense could not pull money back into the stock market or convince investors fearing a rout to stay there. On December 2 alone the market dropped a frightening 700 points. The little rally in October might as well never have happened. As 1991 turned into 1992, many leading indicators, from industrial production to construction starts to the wholesale price index and the Bank of Japan's survey of business confidence, pointed to an economy headed into recession. Not a Japanese *fukyō* with a couple of quarters of slower-than-usual growth. This could be a real 1930s-style global depression as the world's two largest stores of wealth—the Japanese real estate market and the Tokyo stock market—shrank into a black hole of collapsing asset values.

The spurts of bad news were relentless. Apollo Lease, a large nonbank in the important north Honshu city of Sendai, was the subject in February of a rescue operation led by the Mitsui Taiyo Kobe Bank.*[28] It was the biggest nonbank bailout to date. America's office of the comptroller of the currency announced a full-scale examination of Japanese bank operations in the United States. The banks had more than $400 billion of assets in the country—one eighth of all bank assets in the United States and one quarter of all bank assets in California. But these assets were concentrated in some of the weakest sectors of a weak American property market, places such as downtown Los Angeles, where virtually every office building less than five years old had been built with Japanese money and the vacancy rate was over 22 percent.[29] In the winter of 1992 a new wave of scandals swept out of Kabutocho, Japan's Wall Street. These latest scandals involved parking—*tobashi* in Japanese— the practice of lending securities to a third party to escape the tax man or disguise ownership. Just this kind of illegal activity had brought down Drexel Burnham in the United States. A restaurant chain sued the middle-size broker Cosmo Securities for failing to buy back some depreciating American zero coupon bonds as promised.[30] Cosmo had to cough up the difference, wiping out a third of its capital. In order to boost its reported earnings, Daiwa Securities, Japan's number two stockbroker, had parked inflated securities with a major real estate company, promising to buy the securities back at a premium. When it reneged on its promise, the company sued—there was no alternative to litigation now that laws had been changed after the scandals of the previous summer—and the president of Daiwa joined his counterparts at number one Nomura and number three Nikko in resigning to "accept responsibility." Americans were distressed by Drexel's brazen violation of secu-

---

* Renamed the Sakura [Cherry Blossom] Bank that April.

rities laws; Japanese were frightened that Daiwa might have been unable to honor its promises.[31]

By mid-March the market was testing the key 20,000 level. Most players waited breathlessly for the last week of the month. March 31 marks the end of the fiscal year, for both the Japanese government and most Japanese companies. Surely the authorities would "do something" to get the market back up. If a rally could be sparked by March 31, then bank capital ratios would look so much better, big companies could avoid declaring capital losses on their investments in one another, and a virtuous circle could finally kick in with resumed lending, resumed investment, and a snuffing out of recessionary fears.

The authorities fed the expectations. The Economic Planning Agency leaked news of a planned March 31 announcement featuring a large dollop of public spending, interest rate cuts, and a slew of technical market-boosting measures. The authorities delivered on their promises. Among other things, $40 billion in public spending was brought forward six months. The Bank of Japan weighed in with a 0.75 percent discount rate cut, half again bigger than expected.

But the measures did no good; investors had already discounted them. On the first two days of the new fiscal year the *Nikkei* average dropped a sickening 1,000 points to 18,200. A week later it was well under 17,000, back where it had been in early 1986, before the bubble economy had gotten started. Even more ominous than the collapsing market was the composition of the collapse: Bank shares were plummeting like stones. The message was unmistakable: Investors believed that Japan's banks were in deadly peril. And these "investors" were not simply the stunned households and small-time speculators who had been fleeced and fleeced again. Nor were they just the shell-shocked foreigners who had poured some $45 billion into the market when it was up in the mid-20,000 range. Growing and unmistakable evidence pointed to certain central *keiretsu* companies dumping the shares of their banks. Indeed, a wish to avoid reporting the sale of "allied" bank shares in the fiscal year just closed partly explained the magnitude of the drop on

April 1 and 2. Was the very fabric of Japanese capitalism unraveling?

It was getting harder and harder to argue, as a few clued-in observers had done a year or two earlier, that this was all some kind of show staged by the authorities for the benefit of gullible foreigners and insufficiently submissive Japanese yuppies, entrepreneurs, and back-scratching politicians. A weak rally in May pushed the index back over 18,000 for a few days, but by mid-June the market was headed down again below 17,000. At the end of July it was scraping 15,000, and in August it plunged below that key number with no floor in sight.

Hard news of financial distress could no longer be confined to comeuppance stories of nonbanks and arriviste developers. The *Mainichi Shimbun,* one of Japan's top three serious newspapers, wrote openly about the perils of the Nippon Credit Bank, one of Japan's three long-term banks.[32] For the first time ever investors began to discriminate between Nippon Credit's debentures and those of the other long-term banks, a very serious sign in Japan, where investors rarely bothered to specify among the long-term banks when placing orders, assuming the government would always stand behind them. Meanwhile the *Asahi Shimbun* printed detailed lists of the many huge loans made by a wide cross section of banks to Japan's seven-largest housing companies. The newspaper noted that nonperforming debt at these companies totaled more than $40 billion.[33]

It was enough to give even seasoned Japan hands pause. The history of the country since it had embarked on modernization 125 years earlier seemed to contain one overwhelming lesson: Never underestimate Japan. The country had crushed the Russian Navy, ended Western colonialism in Asia, risen phoenixlike from the ashes of the Second World War, come storming out of the OPEC-induced mid-seventies recession, financed the Reagan Revolution, and created, with the bubble economy, the greatest wave of peacetime plant and equipment investment ever seen. Its companies dominated the world's basic manufacturing industries. Its banks and brokers had gloated over the biggest cash hoards ever assembled. Developing country elites had no time anymore for the free market sermons coming out of Washington and Chicago; they wanted to understand and emulate MITI and the Japanese miracle. Yet by the summer of 1992 faith in Japan was wavering. The fathers of the economic miracle, the creators of the bubble economy could not have wanted this. They couldn't have wished for a stock market losing 60 percent of its value, core financial institutions tottering, an economy headed into a long, intractable recessionary trough. What had gone wrong?

There were a lot of different explanations on offer. The MOF had underestimated the impact of swaps and derivatives. Unending waves of investments in productive capacity without regard to profitability had finally created an undigestible glut of plant and equipment. The coming of surplus capital in the early 1980s had undermined bureaucrats' power, weakening their sway over banks and brokers. An illiquid property market had set a trap: If a few transactions at stratospheric prices could undergird a whole superstructure of asset values, a few transactions at down-to-earth prices could bring that entire superstructure down. Japan too was prey to the winds of change transforming economic structures around the world, but the stifling of market mechanisms meant that the necessary adjustments were happening in one explosion rather than drawn out over a generation of corporate restructurings and work force redeployment, as they had been in the United States.

Each of these explanations is plausible; taken together, they suggest that the administrators at the MOF and the BOJ were cracking under the strain of maintaining the facade that Japan's was a market economy, all the while doing what was expected of them in the Japanese system. Their roles in the Japanese power structure, their very sense of legitimacy, were bound up with their skill at providing a macroeconomic framework for economic strength, at propping up stock and real estate "markets," at allocating credit when and where required, at underwriting the soundness of every bank and every broker. In other words, they were responsible for *socializing and managing risk*. The essence of a market system, however, is risk taking by individuals and private companies. A company that makes the wrong investments loses money and goes under. A bank that exercises poor credit judgment cannot collect money it has lent and closes its doors. A person whose skills are no longer needed is fired.

But these things are not supposed to happen in Japan, and in the end it is up to the Finance Ministry to ensure that they don't. Banks are to be protected from their poor credit judgments, or, to be precise, it was never really up to them to make credit judgments in the first place, so it is not "their" fault when loans go sour. Large companies are supposed to invest and export not on the basis of their assessments of where money is to be made but as part of their particular roles in the grand push to ensure that Japan need not depend on foreigners, so it is not their responsibility when the cash flow to cover their investments is insufficient or they find they are suddenly expected to pay back the financing for these investments that they had been told was free. The male heads of households who have played by the rules, sacrificing their childhoods to get "good" jobs, sacrificing their spiritual and family lives to keep those jobs, cannot now be dumped on the street and told to "retrain." Large investors who had put money into the stock "market" with promises they would be made whole cannot now be ruined.

At the same time Japan's administrators could not turn around and say to the outside world—or even to themselves— "We don't want foreign brokers in Japan because our market is rigged, and they might not understand that, and we're not sure we can control them," so the foreign brokers were let in and given something to do in the hopes that it would be a minor sideshow that would make them a little money. It turned out they significantly reduced for a while the administrators' ability to control the market covertly. Japan's negotiators in Basel could not say, "Look, it makes no difference what the reported capital bases of our banks are. They are going to price loans at whatever it takes to get business, and we will support them in that. None of them will ever fail, and what's more, we control the value of their assets and the extent of their real capital cushions," so they ended up agreeing to capital adequacy guidelines, even with a lot of exceptions for Japan, that gave the banks incentives to do things the authorities wish they hadn't done. Japan's spokesmen could not sit in international forums and say, "We have no intention of ever allowing any important technology now under Japanese control to go back under the control of foreigners. And we intend systematically to gain control of all remaining technologies not now under Japanese management. Thus no foreign company will ever take over an important Japanese company, but we must make sure our companies have the tools to acquire foreign firms when they need to." Instead Japan's negotiators agreed under pressure to various "liberalizations," most of which weren't worth anything but that now and again—letting Americans trade Japanese derivatives; allowing swaps to be attached to Eurobonds—tended to undermine control. Japanese government officials could not say publicly, "It's much more convenient for us for the time being to have the dollar serve as our de facto second currency. We need payments and settlements mechanisms for our trade and investment flows, but we don't want large quantities of yen outside the country, where we can't control them. So we're going to conduct most of our business with the outside world in dollars and discourage foreigners from accumulating yen." Instead the Euroyen market was "freed" up, and various foreign governments and multilateral institutions were implored to borrow yen in splashy transactions. But these borrowers would try to hedge their yen obligations because the normal opportunities to earn yen by selling to Japan were so few; thus the prices of the hedges rose, making yen borrowing that much more unattractive.* Meanwhile most borrowers who sought financing from Japan did so in dollars, and Japanese institutions were accordingly forced into dollar investments that progressively lost value in yen terms.

By the summer of 1992 the administrators' dilemma of

---

*In the language of the currency swap markets, there was a perennial imbalance between yen payers and far more numerous yen receivers.

maintaining the illusion of Japan as a market economy all the while desperately trying to put out more and more fires had become intolerable. With the stock market in free fall and the growing grip of a recession that promised to be be the longest in postwar history, many suggested solving the dilemma by turning Japan into its *tatemae,* a market economy. Serious proposals emerged for an independent financial market watchdog modeled on the U.S. Securities and Exchange Commission that would end the ability of the MOF and the Big Four to manipulate the stock market. Laws were passed forbidding such tools of manipulation as compensation payments. Stories on the coming end of lifetime employment popped up everywhere. Morita Akio, the president of Sony, wrote a widely discussed article effectively admitting that Japanese corporations were so formidable because they were not subject to the market disciplines of their foreign competitors.[34] He advocated a wholesale overhaul of Japan's management methods, complete with realistic supplier pricing and corporate concern for profits rather than market share. But all this advice ignored two critical points: First, no bureaucracy has ever voluntarily surrendered power or face, the price of turning Japan into a genuine market economy, and, second, no conceivable outside entity had the political weight to bend the bureaucracy to its will.

Indeed, Japan's political facade was crumbling even more rapidly than its stock market. Prime Minister Kaifu Toshiki, plucked from obscurity in 1989 to serve as a surprisingly popular prime minister in the wake of the Recruit scandal, had been unceremoniously dumped by the leaders of the Liberal Democratic party when he made some injudicious noises about reform in October 1991. In his place they installed the former finance minister Miyazawa Kiichi, who had had to sell the equivalent of his political soul to the party leaders for a job that turned out to be "not worth a pitcher of warm spit," to borrow a phrase once used to describe the American vice presidency. By the summer of 1992 a new and even bigger scandal, this time involving the trucking company Sagawa Kyubin and its whole-sale bribery of practically every important politician in the country, was deflecting the attention of both the politicians and the public from the momentous choices their real leaders in the Finance Ministry were making. Sagawa Kyubin was to bring down most of the leadership of the Liberal Democratic party, end Miyazawa's term prematurely, and help split the LDP.

Meanwhile the press was off baying about this latest round of scandals instead of digging into the biggest scandal of them all: that unelected bureaucrats, in order to protect their reputations, were condemning Japan's population to years of recession, crushingly high prices, tax increases, and growing hostility from the rest of the world. The bureaucrats solved their dilemma by jettisoning once and for all the illusion of Japan as a market economy. They openly and defiantly propped up the stock market, no longer pretending they were doing anything else. They would order banks to support their affiliates, irrespective of the nominal size of the banks' "equity" stakes in these affiliates. They would do whatever it took to keep every bank afloat.

It may have been an act of desperation, but at least in the short term it worked. On August 18 Finance Minister Hata Tsutomu* held a press conference to announce a list of technical market support operations featuring a number of accounting changes and ideas for something like the American Resolution Trust Company, into which the banks could dump their bad debts.[35] The underlying message: The MOF would spend however much of the taxpayers' money it took to bail out the banks. Governor Mieno chimed in two days later with supportive remarks. Rumors had the MOF prepared to pour funds from the postal savings system into the market.

The reaction was explosive. In ten days the market jumped a full 25 percent, back over 18,000, one of the biggest rallies ever. The press and market observers cynically dubbed these

---

*This is the man who served briefly as prime minister in the spring of 1994.

tactics "PKO," playing on the abbreviation for "peace keeping operations" by which Japanese soldiers were sent under UN auspices to Cambodia, but in this instance meaning "price keeping operations." Banks and other financial institutions were ordered to buy shares, while industrial companies were prevented from any more dumping of bank shares. Accounting changes further muddied the real financial state of the banks. The MOF diverted some $150 billion from the postal savings system into the market.

Over the next few months the market bounced around in the upper teens until finally eking its way past 20,000 again. Households had been scared off for the foreseeable future, but savvy foreigners and Japanese insiders could recognize a no-lose offer when they saw one. The ministry slowly and painfully started the process of working the banks out of their bad debts.

The "real" economy, however, didn't do so well. With Japanese households squeezed to pay for PKO and bank bailouts, domestic demand could hardly lead the economy out of its trough. And with the huge overhang of bad debts, underutilized capacity, and some $200 billion in bonds from the equity warrant deals to be paid back, Japanese companies were in no position to launch another mid-eighties–style investment boom.

Predictably the financial administrators turned to the two tactics that had always worked in the past to get the Japanese economy out of such jams: controlled inflation and exports. Japan's trade and current account surpluses started to soar to new records. In the midst of a classic *de*flation of a kind encountered since the 1930s only in textbooks, the bureaucrats busily set about raising every price over which they had direct control: bus, subway, and taxi fares; expressway tolls; casualty insurance premiums; telephone and utility charges. In an effort to flood the country with liquidity again, the Bank of Japan belatedly started slashing interest rates until they were even lower than they had been during the height of the bubble.

But the medicine wasn't working. Exports could not close the circle. Loose monetary policy turned out to be pushing on the proverbial wet noodle. A general inflation that would finally wipe out the bad debt on the books of the nation's banks simply could not be created. In the press conference following his fall from office, Miyazawa Kiichi effectively admitted that the authorities had been unable to reinflate the economy.[36] Political heavyweights such as Kanemaru Shin—the so-called shadow shogun of Japanese politics and the most powerful politician in the country until his downfall in the wake of the Sagawa Kyubin scandal—tried to place all the blame on Mieno. At the probable instigation of the MOF, Watanabe Michio, who had served as both foreign minister and deputy prime minister, went so far as to call for Mieno's head.

Independent and strong-willed as he surely is, Mieno had only been doing what was expected of him. The real problem was that Japan's administrators were denying to themselves how radically the country's position had shifted in the context of the global economy. Over the preceding twelve years Japan had become the world's premier creditor country, and a creditor country cannot easily engineer inflation. The many years of trade surpluses that turn a nation into a net creditor inevitably spell a strong currency. If the country follows a free trade regime, cheap imports render attempts to raise prices difficult or impossible. In the case of Japan, which eschews free trade and instead accumulates claims on foreigners in the form of promises to pay in currencies other than the yen, inducing inflation becomes paradoxically even more difficult, because the foreign promises to pay appear as (usually dollar) assets on the books of Japan's financial institutions. The countries that have imported Japanese goods do not have the means to work off these promises by selling into the Japanese market. Because the yen rises relentlessly as a result, the holdings of foreign currency assets on the books of Japanese financial institutions shrink in value. These shrinking assets stymie any attempt to increase money in circulation, what inflation is ultimately all about.* Thus, instead of boosting inflation, the ratcheting up of those prices directly controlled by bureaucrats had the opposite effect: forcing financially strapped households to cut other spending, pushing up the yen as consumers bought even fewer imports, and further deflating the economy.

Japan's administrators had set an economic trap for themselves. The methods they had used so brilliantly to create the Japanese economic miracle no longer worked in predictable ways once Japan had moved to the center of global finance and industry. The administrators had left, as it were, the Newtonian world of absolutes—such as a stable dollar and a huge and seemingly infinite American market—in which they had grown up. They had entered instead the kind of space that modern physics describes where their own actions shifted the parameters of the economic universe. For ten years they had managed to avoid the implications by propping up the dollar's hegemony and financing American consumption.

But this was no longer possible. And thus the economic trap became a political trap. For the legitimacy of Japan's economic mandarins was ultimately rooted in their ability to deliver results. As long as they could provide steady increases in growth and income, sustain both jobs and the institutions that provided them, and buy off potentially disruptive elements—e.g., farmers—with pork and / or protection, serious challenges to the existing order were unlikely. But once the bureaucratic mandarins faltered, things might slip out of their control, exposing them to outside scrutiny and demands for accountability. One more time, however, they would receive help from an unexpected quarter, the West Wing of the White House.

* Central banks create money by creating liabilities on the books of a nation's financial system. Principles of double-entry bookkeeping require financial institutions thus to create assets to match those liabilities. Japanese banks did this during the high-growth years with overloan. But by the early nineties the volume of foreign assets had become so great that their constantly shrinking value (i.e., the continuous rise of the yen), together with the huge overhang of bad debt, kept pushing down the overall asset position of the financial system, forestalling any attempt to create new liabilities. Thus monetary policy had become an exercise in wet noodle pushing.

10. The Turn of the Screw

IN 1992, FOLLOWING a twelve-year hiatus and an additional $2 trillion in national debt, the federal deficit slipped back to the center of American political debate. Neither Democrats nor Republicans were happy about it—among other things, neither party had any credibility on the issue—but they had little choice. The political maverick Ross Perot had forced the parties' nominees to give at least some lip service to deficit reduction. Perot had converted the vague fears of millions into political dynamite and the most successful third-party candidacy since 1912. Few voters could have described precisely how the deficit threatened the country's future, but they suspected that the United States could not year after year borrow 5 percent of its GNP without heavy bills coming due someday.

The deficit had also become harder to finance. Most voters did not grasp this directly, but they certainly felt the effects, and those effects influenced the way they voted. The "economy" of the famous slogan that helped put Bill Clinton into the White House referred to a recession lasting a lot longer than it was supposed to—in part because real long-term interest rates (the nominal rate minus the rate of inflation) stayed puzzlingly high. Economics textbooks will tell you that interest rates, particularly long-term rates, should be very low in recession. Recession, after all, means that people aren't investing or consuming. With the demand for money falling, the price of money—interest rates—ought to fall as well. During the recessions of the 1960s and 1970s, for example, real long-term rates had been under 1 percent. But during the recession of the early 1990s, real long-term rates topped 4 percent, delaying the recovery that should have started in plenty of time to reelect George Bush comfortably. People do not start borrowing and investing when money is that expensive.

The phenomena of a drawn-out recession and stubbornly high real long-term rates were puzzling, however, only so long as one forgets the connection between long-term rates and the government's financing requirements. The most important long-term interest rate in the U.S. economy is the yield on the thirty-year Treasury security, the long bond. The biggest buyers of these bonds during the 1980s had been Japanese life insurance companies.

No more. The Japanese Ministry of Finance had persuaded Japanese institutions to buy long-dated U.S. Treasury securities through the late 1980s, but in the wake of the bubble economy collapse it could no longer do this. We saw Japanese exporters in the 1980s taking the dollar proceeds of their export sales and reinvesting them, either doing it themselves or having their banks do it for them. The dollars were converted into Treasury securities or other forms of dollar investment. But by the early 1990s many of the dollars were needed to repay the equity warrant bonds discussed in Chapter 7. Many more were used to bail out the half-empty Los Angeles office buildings and other questionable investments made abroad during the bubble years. And most of the rest of the dollars were brought back to Japan and exchanged for yen to discharge some of the enormous volumes of bad debt on the books of Japanese banks and nonbanks. Not much was left over for long bonds.

That was too bad for George Bush and the Republican party. They had enjoyed twelve years in the White House, borrowing some $2 trillion to stay there. But the money had run out.* Their lenders now had big problems of their own. The party was over, and the voters showed them the door.

---

*The deficit was of course still being financed. But the dry up of Japanese interest in long-dated Treasury securities forced the Treasury to shorten the average maturity of

When Bill Clinton took office, he discovered the true legacy of the Reagan-Bush deficits. Maybe the Republicans would have the last laugh after all. For Clinton's grandiose plans—middle-class tax cuts, waves of public investments to revitalize the country's economic base, health reform, "ending welfare as we know it," the information superhighway—ran straight into the brick wall of accumulated deficits.

All the choices Clinton faced were unappealing. Draconian measures—steep tax increases; taking a meat-ax to spending—would have killed the fragile recovery just under way as Clinton took office. In any case they were not politically feasible. Some of his advisers suggested ignoring the deficit and going full speed ahead with his programs on the theory that once the economy was booming, it would be a lot easier to deal with the deficit. The first Reagan administration—whose tactics, if not ideas, the Clinton people had closely studied—had managed to pull off something similar. But this time around, the financial markets would not let it happen. No Japanese insurance companies with wads of cash stood eager to buy Treasury securities. Any sign that Clinton might launch another round of fiscal profligacy would be met by an economy-killing bond market crash. So would any attempts to inflate the country out of its debt. When Clinton's top economic advisers laid out for him the brutal numbers at a meeting before the inauguration, the president-elect exploded: "You mean to tell me that the success of the program and my reelection hinges on the Federal Reserve and a bunch of f***ing bond traders?"[1] James Carville, Clinton's chief campaign manager, remarked ruefully that in his next life he wanted to be reincarnated as the bond market; then he could intimidate everybody.[2]

Clinton was stuck. He squeaked through Congress a budget bill that pleased no one. It promised some slowing of deficit growth in the medium term, but nothing close to a real resolu-

new securities being issued; monetary, fiscal, and exchange rate policies were thus more subject than ever to the whims of volatile markets. And the yield curve remained stubbornly high right into the mid-1990s.

tion of the problem. The bill's modest tax increases alienated supply-side theologians, still influential in Republican circles. They squawked at the Clintonites from the editorial pages of the *Wall Street Journal*. Meanwhile core Democratic interest groups felt betrayed to be getting so little out of only the second Democratic administration in a quarter century.

Clinton raged in frustration. He had been elected to rebuild the country. Virtually every serious program he contemplated, however, ran into a bond market groaning under trillions of dollars in accumulated debts. But one visible course of action would cost the government nothing. If successful, it would boost employment without boosting inflationary, deficit-feeding consumption. The course of action: cutting the trade deficit.

Understanding the trade problem was simple; doing something about it was not. One country accounted for more than 50 percent of the U.S. trade deficit: Japan.* The equation that had held true through the 1980s—U.S. trade deficit = Japanese capital outflows to the United States = percentage of federal deficit financed by non-Americans—had broken down. After ten consecutive years of exporting long-term capital in the tens of billions of dollars annually, Japan in 1991 had actually *imported* close to $40 billion of long-term capital. My friend Mr. Saito of Sumitomo Life would be moving to London to run the company's securities subsidiary there. His new job involved raising money, not investing it. The tired old warning that American measures to reduce the trade deficit with Japan would threaten the flow of Japanese money into the Treasury market had lost its power to intimidate; there wasn't much of a flow anymore to threaten. Inevitably the new administration began to consider an overhaul of Japan policy that would put trade issues squarely at its center.

Budget constraints and deficits had pointed to an overhaul,

---

*Estimates that the U.S. trade deficit with Japanese companies, thanks to their operations in such places as Southeast Asia, was 50 percent higher than the deficit with Japan as a country suggested that more than 75 percent of the U.S. trade deficit could be explained by Japanese competition.

but the end of the Cold War made it possible. From as far back as the late 1940s no other factors in the U.S.-Japan relationship had been permitted to interfere with the primacy of security and anti-Communist considerations. Japan's strategic significance was obvious. Military control of the Japanese archipelago meant military control of all warm-water access by the Soviet Pacific fleet to the open ocean. Huge U.S. bases on Okinawa supplemented by U.S. installations dotting the rest of Japan formed the linchpin of the American military presence in East Asia. The waging of the Korean and Vietnam wars would have been unthinkable without them, and they were central to any confrontation scenario with the Soviets, the Chinese, or the North Koreans.

The implications for other areas of Japan policy—trade disputes, market access, financial deregulation—were thus pretty clear. They were not ultimately important. James Fallows, once Jimmy Carter's speechwriter, explains:

Anyone who has dealt inside the U.S. government understands how its hierarchy of rank and respectability runs. The upper end of the totem pole is for people who can take the big, strategic picture—people who can go to foreign summit meetings, who can say "Sorry, that information is classified." . . . The U.S. secretaries of state or defense are viewed as potentates all around the world. The U.S. secretary of commerce is viewed as just another arm-twister for American business. . . . The Cold War reinforced this natural hierarchy. Within the U.S. government, the Pentagon and the State Department were almost guaranteed to win any argument about how to deal with Japan.[3]

Japan's diplomats and public spokesmen in the United States had long used security considerations to combat any reexamination of the fundamentals of the U.S.-Japan relationship. They played upon Pentagon and State Department fears that too much pressure on Japan in trade or other arenas would arouse anti-American sentiments in the Japanese population that could result in a closure of the U.S. bases and other unimaginable horrors.

In fact, the U.S. security umbrella formed a vital part of the postwar sociopolitical order in Japan. It had enabled the administrators essentially to forget about defense; foreign policy had become a matter of giving lip service to American goals and sustaining American misperceptions of Japan while doing everything possible to maintain access to important markets and sources of supply. Freed of the usual responsibilities of governance—providing for a nation's security and managing its foreign relations—Japan's administrators had built a vast industrial machine in the shadow of the U.S. military umbrella.

Many Japanese, left and right, in the 1950s believed this abdication of foreign policy control to another country had mortgaged their national soul. Opposition to the 1952 U.S.-Japan Security Treaty that formalized the lopsided arrangement had been searing and intense; the renewal of the treaty in 1960 had seen upward of a million people take to the streets in protest. But this kind of opposition had long since disappeared or ceased to matter. Japan's administrators had come to regard the U.S. military umbrella as part of the natural order of things. Aside from ritualistic noises by the Socialists that no one took seriously,* it had not been a make-or-break political issue since the 1960 riots.

Japan's skilled diplomats and public spokesmen had for years disguised this obvious fact from America's foreign policy elite. The U.S.-Japan relationship, an essential pillar of Japan's political order, was portrayed as a fragile achievement in perpetual danger from a volatile Japanese public opinion that might be stirred up if too many American cherries, woodchips, or piles of soda ash were to appear in Yokohama Harbor.

The collapse of the Berlin Wall, however, reduced the scare value of such traditional warnings. A responsible American government might have felt it needed to take seriously arguments that efforts to pry open the Japanese market for American window glass would start a chain of adverse reactions that could

---

*The essentially hollow, ritualistic nature of the Socialist party's opposition to the U.S. military presence was confirmed when a member of that party finally managed, after a forty-seven-year hiatus, to become prime minister in June 1994. The party had for decades practically defined itself by its anti–Security Treaty, anti–U.S. military stance, but when the opportunity to grab a bit of power finally presented itself, the party managed to overlook this history, cutting a deal with the nominally "pro-American," pro–Security Treaty Liberal Democrats.

lead to the closing of the vital installations in northern Hokkaido that monitored Soviet fighter planes; with the Soviets
gone, the reaction was more likely to be "So what?"

The supposedly fragile character of the U.S.-Japan security
relationship was not, however, the only illusion that had
blocked an overhaul of Japan policy. Another was the tangled
legacy of the occupation, the Communist revolution in China,
and the ideological battles of the 1950s. The occupation had
started off with a pronounced leftist hue. Japanese Communists
and labor activists were released en masse from the jails where
the militarists had confined them. American New Dealers at
SCAP pushed for a wide-ranging program of land reform, trust
(zaibatsu)-busting, labor union empowerment, women's
rights, and democratization more sweeping than anything they
had been able to accomplish back in Washington. But in reaction to a string of Communist victories in both the wider world
and Japan itself, the occupation "reversed course"—the term
used by the Japanese. General Douglas MacArthur forbade the
general strike planned for February 1, 1947. "Reds" were
purged from a Japanese officialdom they had only just begun to
penetrate, and the positions went back in many cases to wartime
bureaucrats fresh from prison. A Detroit banker, Joseph
Dodge, arrived to impose an orthodox economic program of
tight money and fiscal austerity.

It was nonetheless important in the minds of people like
MacArthur that the occupation be understood as an exercise
in the democratization of Japan, particularly after the 1949
triumph in China of Mao Zedong. It requires some effort now
in the wake of the worldwide collapse of communism to put
ourselves back into the mental universe of the late 1940s. Forty-
five years ago Marxist models of development appeared irresistible to developing country elites. They held a good part of the
Western intellectual world in thrall, and they evoked fear, even
hysteria, on the part of American power holders, a backhanded
acknowledgment of how compelling they were. The pressure
for an alternative paradigm—an alternative that would, like
Marxism, incorporate the logic of development but, unlike

Marxism, point to the United States as a model—grew intense, and when it appeared, it acquired the pretentious label "modernization theory." And Japan played the starring role. Very obviously a "modernizing" society, Japan was following a course that seemingly had nothing to do with the Communist world.* Instead, aided by an occupation that had supposedly gotten Japan back on track after an unfortunate deviation, Japan was said to have learned how to do it largely by studying and imitating the United States.

The key figure linking the modernization theorists with the actual conduct of Japan policy was the Harvard professor Edwin Reischauer. Reischauer did not give birth to modernization theory—credit for that usually goes to Walt Rostow—but he became an enthusiastic champion. Indeed, as early as 1949 Reischauer had explicitly called for an ideology to counteract Marxism, an ideology that would answer the aspirations of Asia's elites.[4] Following the McCarthyite purges of Asian studies in the United States,[5] Reischauer emerged as the dean of American Japanology, and John F. Kennedy appointed him ambassador to Japan.

Reischauer saw himself as a "missionary" on behalf of Japanese-American understanding. Once in Tokyo as ambassador, he launched what one scholar dubbed the "Reischauer offensive" and another "an attempt to discredit Japanese leftist intellectuals by offering modernization theory as a more correct mode of analysis for the Japanese to use in interpreting their own experience."[6]

Playing skillfully on the sensation made in Tokyo by a Japanese-speaking ambassador with a Japanese wife, Reischauer performed prodigious labors in defusing Japanese hostility to the United States. To a lesser extent he helped loosen the stranglehold of Marxism on Japanese intellectuals. A gifted teacher, he introduced to Japan two generations of Harvard undergrad-

* In fact, as noted in Chapter 3, the architects of the Japanese economic miracle were steeped in Marxian thought, most important the notion that the pace and structure of economic change drive human history.

uates—and many more outside the confines of Cambridge when his students became professors themselves. But in his tireless championing of modernization theory and Japanese democracy,* Reischauer promulgated a perspective that implicitly saw Japan as a pupil, following a trail blazed by the United States. For this perspective to work, fundamental differences between Japanese and American economic methods had to be treated as mere deviations from an American norm. The institutional links between the Japan of the 1930s and that of the 1950s had to be thrown into deep shadow. Indeed, the entire history of Japanese militarism had to be explained away as an unfortunate detour, a "relapse" in the otherwise exemplary tale of Japan's modern history.

Although Reischauer's perspectives on Japan dovetailed nicely with the primacy of security considerations in Washington, they never conquered academia. Younger scholars, alienated by the Vietnam War and the radicalism that swept American universities in the late 1960s, questioned the claims of modernization theory and its untroubled view of Japan's development. The establishment of the Committee of Concerned Asia Scholars, which drew in many outstanding younger academics of that time, directly challenged the hegemony of modernization theory and Reischauer's interpretation of modern Japan.

But the country's stunning debut in the 1980s as an economic superpower finished off the teacher-pupil perspective more thoroughly than leftist academics could ever hope to. Old Japan hands in Washington might still fuss over "the Relationship" and wring their hands at any imagined threat thereto, but out beyond the Beltway people were reading novels about sinister Japanese businessmen-cum-samurai, thronging to employment offices in Japanese-owned factories, and grumbling that Japanese interests were buying up the country. It was only

---

*Like the hundreds of other Harvard undergrads who took Reischauer's and John King Fairbanks's famous course on East Asian civilization every year, I myself got a hefty dose of modernization theory.

a matter of time before some analysts would begin a systematic overhaul of the old occupation/Reischauer–fostered views of Japan. When in the late 1980s a group of writers launched this overhaul, they were, predictably enough, called revisionists.

The revisionists represented no coordinated movement; only one was at all widely known before the appearance of the "revisionist" writings: James Fallows.* They enjoyed no significant funding or publicity beyond that which publishers would ordinarily provide for trade books expected to sell a few thousand copies.† But they gave voice to an idea whose time had come: Japan was not a junior United States; the problems in the U.S.-Japan relationship were structural in nature and likely to get worse unless fundamentals were reexamined. And they were read by policy makers in Washington.

The revisionist label was first used about a group of writings that surfaced between the summer of 1988 and the spring of 1989.[7] The most important of these: a book by Clyde Prestowitz, a former Commerce Department official and trade negotiator[8]; a long, searching cover article in the *Atlantic* by James Fallows[9]; and a book by the Dutch political philosopher and longtime Japan resident Karel van Wolferen.[10] The revisionists disagreed about many things. University of California Professor Chalmers Johnson, tagged "revisionism's intellectual godfather"[11] for his 1982 study of MITI,[12] emphasized that Japan's economic development had been state-directed; van Wolferen, maintaining that the country lacked a center of political accountability, questioned whether Japan could properly be called a state at all. Prestowitz advised giving up efforts to change Japan and advocated policies to protect America's national interest, while Fallows argued that the world needed a program to "contain Japan."

Many of the revisionists' ideas had been seen before, most

---

* Karel van Wolferen was well known in Holland for his prizewinning journalism with that country's leading serious newspaper *NRC Handelsblad*, but before his 1987 article for *Foreign Affairs*, "The Japan Problem," virtually unknown in the United States.

† Both Prestowitz's and van Wolferen's publishers seriously underestimated the demand for their books *Trading Places* and *The Enigma of Japanese Power*.

notably in the writings of the Japanese political philosopher Maruyama Masao[13] and the largely forgotten work of the Canadian E. H. Norman.[14] Norman had been the most important prewar Western Japanologist; his leftist sympathies led the modernization theorists to consign his work to that limbo reserved for graduate students deemed reliable enough ideologically to withstand direct contact with essential but uncomfortable writing. Whatever their differences and the origins of their ideas, however, the revisionists agreed on points sharply at odds with the conventional view of Japan as a market economy. They contradicted the propaganda of Japan's diplomatic–public relations establishment in the United States. And they undermined the "democratic pupil" image of Japan dear to the cluster of old Japan hands—or the Chrysanthemum Club, as they came to be known—so visible in the floating foreign policy establishment in Washington.

Much of revisionism simply pointed out the obvious: that, for example, a continuation of the trends of the 1980s would make Japan the world's preeminent economic power within a decade or two. Other points were more uncomfortable. The revisionists argued that explaining Japan's success because of its "culture" was no explanation at all; it was simply a tautology. A proper study of Japan begins with its institutions. Dismissing talk of Japan's "unique culture" made the revisionists unpopular with Japan's public spokesmen; a revisionist emphasis on institutions spotlighted the glaring failure of the economics profession to explain the nation's rise to economic superpower. What really drew brickbats, however, was the revisionists' portrayal of Japan's unchecked bureaucratic authoritarianism, which challenged two of the most cherished notions America had about Japan: that the occupation had given Japan a "clean slate" and that Japan was a functioning democracy. While the economic merits of such Japanese institutions as industrial policy and centralized credit allocation might be the subject of debate, it is not possible to square with genuine democracy the control of taxes, budgets, interest rates, prices, foreign trade, school curricula, medical care, and public works by unelected bureaucrats who cannot be dismissed by the citizenry or its representatives.

Labeled "racists" and "Japan bashers," the revisionists provoked a spasm of hysteria from the American foreign policy establishment. George Packard, the dean of Johns Hopkins's School of Advanced International Studies, denounced them for "carrying on germ warfare."[15] Diplomats in the Bush administration organized a speech for Dan Quayle at the Council of Foreign Relations in which the vice president called for "revising the revisionists."[16] The U.S.-Japan Friendship Commission, an agency of the U.S. government led by John Makin, another prominent old Japan hand, rejuggled the criteria by which American universities receive funding for purchases of Japanese-language research materials to eliminate one campus, the University of California at San Diego, to which Chalmers Johnson had recently moved from Berkeley.* Makin wrote nastily and inaccurately of Fallows that he "doesn't like Japanese people very much."[18]

But by the time Clinton became president, the old Japan hands had lost the intellectual battle. Several of Clinton's key advisers came from Wall Street; on the basis of their firms' experiences in Japan, these men instantly got the point when the revisionists talked about informal guidance and unchecked bureaucratic power. Even more important, the revisionists offered a credible explanation of the persistence of the huge trade deficits with Japan. Their analysis pointed to a way out of the

---

*The Japanese diplomatic establishment in the United States enthusiastically joined and sometimes led the smear campaign against the revisionists. Van Wolferen's American agent had, for example, predicted a long and lucrative speaking tour for him on the basis of the sales of his book and the many favorable reviews it had received. But his appearances were blocked virtually everywhere because of Japanese pressure. Inside Japan, however, things were different. MITI officials had regarded Chalmers Johnson's book as a public relations coup while its great éminence grise, the late Amaya Naohiro, was publicly complimentary about Prestowitz's *Trading Places* and agreed to serve on the advisory board of the think tank Prestowitz established. Van Wolferen became a well-known commentator in Japan, writing best-selling books and magazine articles for publication there. Many of his ideas, particularly his diagnosis of the "Japan problem" as one of a lack of a center of political accountability, became conventional wisdom among at least a section of Japan's political elite. The architect of the Hosokawa and Hata coalition cabinets, Ozawa Ichiro, wrote an influential book of his own with ideas clearly drawn from the revisionists.[17]

endless cycle of acrimonious negotiations, the fanfare of trade packages that were going to solve the problem, the pathetic results, the buildup of political pressure to do something, and the resumption of the cycle with more acrimonious negotiations. The revisionists suggested that Japan's swollen trade surpluses were structurally embedded into its political and economic system and could not be dissolved with yet one more market-opening package. They also implied that American presidents, commerce secretaries, and trade representatives had been talking to the wrong people in Tokyo. Japanese prime ministers had little or no power to implement the kind of fundamental change that real reduction in Japan's surpluses would require; if it lay anywhere, that power lay with the bureaucrats.

Early signs from the president-elect on an overhaul of Japan policy were encouraging. Everything about him, from the way he talked to the books he read as well as to the men and women around him, spoke of a willingness to challenge orthodox wisdom, a tacit understanding that problems could not be separated into neat little boxes labeled "economics," "politics," or "foreign policy." He clearly grasped that the economic challenges facing the United States were beyond the powers of either the usual Republican recipe of getting government out of the way or the usual Democratic recipe of throwing borrowed money around. He seemed to understand that the competition American industry faced from Japan could not be met by simply trying harder and listening more closely to customers. The press had correctly labeled the Clinton presidency "the first post–Cold War administration," more than just a trivial observation that Clinton was the first U.S. president in two generations to take office without facing a Soviet nuclear threat. Most of Clinton's people had no personal memory of the turmoil of the late 1940s, when the containment of communism had become the guiding principle of American foreign policy; they were starting from ground zero, and this would surely apply to Japan policy.

Some of Clinton's initial appointments suggested a new approach. Laura Tyson and Ira Magaziner, who both had written knowledgeably about Japanese economic methods, received senior-level positions. Harvard Professor Ezra Vogel, whose 1979 book *Japan as Number One: Lessons for America* represented the first serious effort to alert Americans to the challenge from Japan, joined the National Intelligence Council. The embassy in Tokyo went to former Vice President and Democratic presidential candidate Walter Mondale.

But as the winter of 1993 turned into spring and scores of key positions went unfilled, many observers on the ground in Tokyo began to wonder if the administration really understood what it was up against. A handful of advisers who had studied Japan without preconceptions; a healthy skepticism about traditional tactics; a suspicion that Japan's success had been achieved by methods not listed in economics textbooks—all these were well and good but inadequate to the task at hand. Japan's leading ministries could field scores of experienced negotiators who represented the intellectual cream of the country's elite. These men possessed an institutional memory that stretched back a century or more; many had graduate degrees from American universities; most were fluent in English and conversant with the minutiae of American politics, economics, and business. At their disposal was what amounted to a vast intelligence-gathering network in the form of the large, well-placed Japanese expatriate business community. This network was in turn amplified by the most formidable political–cum–public relations machine ever operated by a foreign power in the United States, financed to the tune of $400 million annually.[19]

The entire weight of Japanese political and economic might was typically brought to bear on trade negotiations with the United States. Japan's economic mandarins reacted to American trade pressure as a challenge to the very existence of their system, which in a sense it was. Japan's postwar system of national leverage had depended upon bureaucratic control and unlimited access to the U.S. market. American pressure for "liberalization," "market opening," "results-oriented trade," however halfhearted and ham-fisted the implementation and however empty the threats of retaliation, carried the whiff of deadly peril. Like an animal fighting for its life, Japan's administrators had deflected, fought, and neutralized American trade pressure for a quarter century by every resource, tactic, strategy, and weapon at their command. A politically weak, poorly managed administration distracted by scandals and pulled every which way by foreign policy crises around the world, able to field in Washington and the Tokyo embassy only a handful of people experienced with Japan, could not cope with what it faced.

The clearest sign that the Clinton administration had little inkling of what it would take to overhaul Japan policy and bring down the trade imbalances occurred within a few weeks of taking office when its officials resorted to that cheap old moonshine trashing the dollar. Calls for a stronger yen to reduce Japan's trade surplus could be counted on to elicit howls out of Tokyo, turmoil on the foreign exchange markets, and a satisfying sense of having done something. They so painlessly replaced the tortuous search-and-confirmation process involved in fielding a team of credible trade negotiators or the stamina needed to face down the inevitable campaigns against any serious trade initiative with their lobbying blitzkriegs by former government officials on the Japanese payroll, "open letters" from teams of useful (to the Japanese) fools in university economics departments, and "free trade" sermons by famous columnists whose wives served as lobbyists for the Japan Automobile Manufacturers Association.[20]

In its eagerness to talk down the dollar, however, the Clinton administration showed a reckless disregard for recent history. Every previous administration that had used dollar-trashing tactics to reduce "politically intolerable" trade deficits with Japan had had the tactics blow up in its face. Each had gotten no improvement in the trade numbers and the worst economic crises of its administration. Richard Nixon had suspended the convertibility of the dollar into gold, primarily to force Japan to revalue the yen. Two years later he got the OPEC oil cartel determined to restore its real earnings eroded by depreciating dollars. The Carter administration announced a policy of benign neglect of the dollar in order to bring down Japan's trade surpluses. Instead it got a full-fledged currency crisis that could be cured only with double-digit interest rates and a recession that cost it the 1980 election. In its second term the Reagan administration went after the Japanese surpluses with the Plaza Accord's concerted attack on the dollar. As a reward it got the 1987 New York stock market crash.

The Clinton administration fell right into the same trap. Lured by arguments that a yen / dollar exchange rate that would finally force a rapid reduction in the Japanese surplus was not far off, seduced by the seeming ease with which it could be done, the Clinton people acted as if it were 1977 all over again and the intervening sixteen years had never happened. Now, it is true that a theoretical yen / dollar exchange rate exists at which the Japanese surplus would disappear. If, for example, the dollar were worthless, the deficit with Japan would vanish because Americans would be unable to pay for any Japanese goods, and naturally the rate that would finally end that deficit is well above zero. We do not know, however, what it is. A few short years ago it was thought to be ¥180 / $1. But with the yen having broken the ¥100 / $1 barrier at a time when Japan's trade surpluses stood at record highs, pundits claiming that this or that rate will force an end to Japan's surpluses are just shouting in the wind.

We do know that the Japanese economy does not react the way classical and neoclassical economists since David Hume's time have said a market economy should react to changes in the exchange rate. Its companies do not give up markets won overseas, even when exports lose money. Imports do not pour into Japan even when they cost a half or one third of comparable Japanese products.

The turn of the currency screw that began at ¥125 when Clinton took office and took the dollar to ¥79 twenty-seven months later had no chance of bringing a final resolution to America's trade problems with Japan. But by harping in its early days on the need to pump up the yen, the Clinton administration did accomplish one thing: handing Japan's economic mandarins their biggest public relations coup since the Japanese economic miracle. Thanks to American whining, Japan's bureaucrats escaped the political heat for a soaring yen almost entirely their responsibility.

The latest surge of the yen against the dollar did not require any unique insight to understand. As noted several times, in the 1980s Japanese exporters had generally either reinvested abroad the dollar proceeds of their export sales or deposited these proceeds with Japanese banks overseas. Neither the exporters nor the banks exchanged many dollars for yen. Instead the banks reinvested these dollars overseas, in Treasuries or in other securities, in funding Japanese companies in their purchases of American firms and their building of factories in Southeast Asia. In fact, the banks went out and borrowed more dollars than even their exporting customers deposited with them.[21] They did so much of this that financial regulators in Hong Kong actually launched an investigation of just why Japanese banks were raising so much money in Hong Kong's short-term dollar markets. All this borrowing and investing propped up global demand for dollars and kept the dollar much stronger than it otherwise would have been.

But the crises that hit the Japanese financial system in the early 1990s made it impossible to prop dollars up and keep them out of Japan, where they would inevitably be presented for yen. Japanese companies needed every bit of cash they could lay their hands on to keep production lines running at home, while their bankers, groaning under a mountain of bad debts, could ill afford more spending sprees abroad. We have already seen the effects on American long-term interest rates as the Japanese abandoned the market for long-term American government securities. The effects on the yen / dollar exchange rate were equally pronounced. The dollars formed a huge overhang in the Tokyo foreign exchange market. The prolonged slump following the end of the bubble economy and the Ministry of

Finance's veto of any stimulative measures to bring Japan out of that slump translated into a debilitating sluggishness in consumer demand, particularly in the demand for imports. A United States beginning to recover from recession would, conversely, suck in more Japanese exports, sending more dollars to Tokyo, increasing the dollar overhang.

Beyond the trade fundamentals lay PKO—the so-called price-keeping operations noted in the previous chapter, which the Ministry of Finance had instituted in August 1992 to prevent a collapse of the Tokyo stock market. When American investment bankers in Tokyo realized what the MOF was doing—that it had effectively committed the lion's share of Japan's households savings to uphold a floor underneath the market—they urged their clients to invest in Japanese equities. Additional waves of dollars poured into Tokyo in pursuit of "no-lose" Japanese stocks. That was what the MOF had intended. But another ratcheting up of the yen would follow inevitably.

Knowing what was coming, MOF officials set about ensuring that the Americans got the "credit." David Asher, member of a rare breed of Washington insider well clued in to Kasumigaseki's machinations, maintains that Clinton administration statements on the need for a higher yen were "closely coordinated with and, in fact, strongly encouraged by, Japanese Ministry of Finance officials."[22] Asher notes that Treasury Secretary Lloyd Bentsen's first remarks calling for the higher yen were immediately preceded by a briefing from Finance Minister Hayashi Yoshiro and Vice Minister Chino Tadao, and he quotes a "foreign researcher stationed in the MOF at the time" as saying that " 'the Clinton Administration was full of suckers waiting to be manipulated from the word go.' "[23]

Little of this could be gleaned from reading the Japanese press or watching Japanese television.[24] The press trumpeted every stray remark from an administration adviser to give the appearance that exchange rate policy was determined entirely in Washington. Indeed, there were in the spring of 1993 days when a reader of Japanese newspapers might believe that one man acting alone, C. Fred Bergsten, set the yen / dollar rate.

Bergsten, a former Carter administration official and the head of a prominent Washington think tank, had come to sound like a broken record on the subject of the U.S.-Japan trade imbalance and could be counted upon at every point to call for a cheaper dollar to end it. He may or may not have had the president's ear, but his comments invariably got front-page play in Tokyo. "Why are you Americans pushing up the yen?" was a question that any American living in Tokyo often heard. "Don't you realize it will hurt your country too?"

With great skill Japan's economic mandarins had deflected domestic political heat away from themselves and onto the duped Americans. The early 1990s were not an easy time for these bureaucrats. Not only did they have to contend with the woes of the collapsed bubble, but the end of unchallenged LDP "rule" in the summer of 1993 tore away the curtain of politics behind which they had busied themselves running the country. Actual, if sporadic, analysis in the Japanese press discussed how the bureaucrats determined policy. Ordinary Japanese in the millions knew the name of Saito Jiro, the MOF's administrative vice minister and surely the most powerful man in the country. His equally powerful predecessors had gone about their business—cutting deals with other ministries and politicians, setting fiscal, monetary, and tax policies—under the cloak of anonymity. But Saito had to move in the glare of publicity, leading him to snap angrily that he only carried out the will of his political superiors, this at a time when Japan had had three finance ministers in two months.

The soaring of the yen hurt a lot of people in Japan. It bankrupted thousands of small second-tier companies. Large, well-connected firms might not face bankruptcy, but a yen stronger than ¥110 / $1 made it impossible for many of them to generate any kind of profit on exports. As long as export revenues had been sufficient to cover the additional costs in labor and supplies necessary to make one more item—what economists call variable costs—low or nonexistent profitability had been a manageable problem, even if the numbers showed that exports no longer paid for their share of investments in factories and machines—i.e., fixed costs. Yet when a company actually lost money on each additional item it made for export markets, it either had to stop producing in Japan or swallow the losses—with recessionary effects on the economy as a whole.

But when ordinary Japanese read in their morning papers about the bankrupt utensil makers that couldn't sell their knives and forks abroad anymore, the major electronics firm that was not hiring this year and was moving production to Malaysia, the tens of thousands of middle managers pressured by their companies with demeaning make-work to take "voluntary retirement," what did they say to themselves? Whom did they blame? The Finance Ministry, whose blind zeal for fiscal "rectitude" and higher taxes was blighting the economic prospects for millions of Japanese? Did they fault MITI, whose mulelike resistance to American trade requests meant that no one could see any natural demand for dollars to buy the imports that might remove the pressure on the yen? Or the cozy cartels run by the Transport, Post and Telecommunications, Health and Welfare, Agriculture, and Construction ministries for blocking imports and, by extension, the natural corrective for a high yen rate? To be fair, from time to time ordinary Japanese did blame the bureaucrats in an unsystematic and uncoordinated fashion, but mostly they blamed the Americans.

As tensions mounted, in February 1994 Clinton directed his people not to sign a trade agreement without substance, and as a result, for the first time in the postwar era, a U.S.-Japan summit ended with no written document. In the long, sorry history of the trade agreements, the only one that had ever produced measurable results was a 1986 agreement that called for American semiconductor companies to reach a 20 percent share of the Japanese market. Arm-twisting Japanese companies to reach this target had been an unpleasant experience for MITI bureaucrats, particularly when a few short years earlier they had been prodding the same companies to invest billions in semiconductor manufacturing plants in order to wrest market leadership from the Americans. So when the Clinton team

sought similar sorts of agreements in other sectors, the bureaucrats vowed "never again." They pulled off one of the cheekiest
propaganda coups in history (with the help of a predictable
chorus of mainstream economists), posing with some success
as fierce opponents of "managed trade," proclaiming they were
"shocked, *shocked*" to find Americans wanting to repeat their
modest success with the semiconductor agreement. In fact, the
growth and dominance of the Japanese semiconductor industry
had been a textbook case in the application of the nation's
industrial targeting methods. And the Americans had, for once,
managed to obtain a bit of modest redress for the politically
driven economic onslaught launched against their firms.

In the buildup to the February summit the two sides took
tough positions because neither expected the other could tolerate a situation that produced no agreement. In the past Americans had relied upon such strong-willed Japanese politicians as
Tanaka and Nakasone to intervene at the last moment, pressur-
ing bureaucrats to avoid putting Japanese prime ministers in
serious face-losing situations. The Japanese, for their part, had
believed they could always get to the American president with
the national security argument. This time things were different.
The LDP's summer 1993 fall from power removed virtually all
leverage that politicians had over the bureaucracy. Shortly before Prime Minister Hosokawa's February trip to Washington,
the two most powerful bureaucrats in the MOF and in MITI,
respectively the administrative vice ministers Saito and Ku-
mano Hideyaki, were said to have agreed with each other that
irrespective of what Hosokawa might want or whatever pressure the Americans applied, Japan would sign no agreement
that had any kind of "test" to it. Meanwhile Clinton had read a
memo written by Glen S. Fukushima, a former American trade
negotiator and an architect of the 1986 semiconductor
agreement. The memo had arrived without the author's knowledge on Clinton's desk, but the president was so impressed
by it he sent copies to all his key economic advisers with the
handwritten note "worth reading and often accurate. Should

discuss." The memo predicted that an ambiguous, weaselly agreement would be signed, that it would not "yield the expected results," and that another crisis in U.S.-Japan relations would ensue. To avert this crisis, Fukushima advocated that "the agreements reached in February [be] tight enough and unambiguous enough to prevent each side from attaching its own, different, interpretation . . . a thorough review of the Japanese texts of the agreements to ensure that they are identical in meaning to the English text . . . a full explanation of the agreements by both sets of negotiators together, in front of the U.S. and Japanese mass media to ensure that . . . each side does not tell its public only its own interpretation." All these passages were underlined by the president.

Many hoped that Clinton's refusal to sign another meaningless agreement with Japan would mark the beginning of the long-awaited overhaul of Japan policy. These hopes were reinforced when copies of the Fukushima memo complete with the president's handwritten asides made their way into the hands of journalists. Clinton had underlined a passage that read, "The Administration also lacks an understanding of where, when, and how much pressure should be applied to achieve the maximum result while minimizing Japanese resentment" and had written "agree with this" in the margin. Yet over the next few months, while record trade imbalances persisted and the dollar sank below 100 yen, it seemed almost as if the administration were determined to prove Fukushima's allegation correct. The only substantive achievement the administration could boast that spring was winning for Motorola access to the lucrative Tokyo–Nagoya corridor for its cellular telephone network, and this was simply a matter of forcing the Japanese government to abide by an agreement made back in 1989.

An agreement finally signed in September 1994 turned out to be largely empty. Automobiles and auto parts, accounting for more than half the bilateral trade deficits, were left out entirely. The clauses dealing with Japanese government procurement procedures in telecommunications excluded Nippon

Telephone and Telegraph, which accounted for two thirds of such procurement, on the ground that it was a "private" company.* American electronics companies had been muscled by U.S. Trade Representative Mickey Kantor into putting a brave face on the results, but in private their people in Tokyo were scathing.

Why would an administration that had taken office promising to halve the deficit with Japan cave in so easily? The answer lay with the looming midterm elections and the weight of conventional wisdom. Scared that a failure to reach an agreement would roil the foreign exchange markets, fearful that a plummeting dollar could trigger a bond market panic as the Fed found itself forced to raise interest rates to protect the currency, the White House sent out the word that any agreement was better than no agreement. With their unrivaled intelligence networks in Washington, the Japanese knew that the Clinton people were desperate to stave off what appeared to be a possible Democratic loss of both houses of Congress, that they dreaded a rise in interest rates in the run-up to the election. The Japanese stonewalled, and once again the Americans reverted to type, settling for a largely meaningless piece of paper.

The administration's assumptions all turned out to be wrong. The Democrats lost the midterm elections anyway. Early in 1995 the dollar dropped further against the yen for reasons that had nothing to do with stalled trade talks. The dollar sell-off started with the collapse of the Mexican peso and accelerated when Japanese companies that had been hanging on to dollars in the vain hope they would strengthen had to convert them to yen to close their books by the end of the Japanese fiscal year on March 31. But the effects in Washington were barely noticeable; interest rates didn't move. The cries of anguish as the dollar sank straight through ¥90 to breach ¥80 came from Japanese industry, not from the Americans.

---

*The president of this "private" company was an ex–Ministry of Post and Telecommunications bureaucrat. Two thirds of the company's shares were held by the Ministry of Finance.

This time there was no setting up administration officials to take the blame. After the midterm losses Bentsen had resigned as treasury secretary to be replaced by Robert Rubin, a former cochairman of Goldman, Sachs with decades of experience on trading floors and arguably the last person on earth who could be tricked into making silly statements on the dollar. Indeed, the dollar rout stopped only when trade talks on autos and auto parts broke down in May. When the administration announced that it would impose sanctions on Japanese luxury car imports unless the Japanese came back to the table with measurable plans to boost purchases of American auto parts, the dollar promptly rallied.

The sanctions shrewdly threatened to inflict maximum pain on the Japanese industry with minimal disruption to the U.S. economy. The Japanese propaganda machine lumbered into action, blanketing the media with preposterous claims about the tens of thousands of American jobs at risk and the potential wreckage of global trade, but the campaign got nowhere, at least with ordinary Americans. Clinton's fiercest Republican opponents muttered their support for the president; they knew where the votes were on this issue.

But talk of sanctions turned out to be more empty bluster. American journalists and Japanese negotiators contradicted Clinton's June 28 boast that a last-minute agreement was "specific" and "measurable" before the words were scarcely out of his mouth. The agreement was not a total farce—Japan pledged to review its notorious vehicle inspection system that had blocked foreign replacement parts—but it did not begin to live up to the president's hype. The Japanese industry's simultaneous announcements of increased American parts purchases and investments in the United States had been in the works for months. And the explicit American promise to eschew its only proven weapon—sanctions—even if Japan failed to live up to the agreement's terms mocked any claim of an American victory. One side had caved, and it wasn't the Japanese.

Some smelled a brilliant MOF disinformation campaign over the supposed meltdown of the Japanese financial system lying behind the American capitulation. Whatever troubles large Japanese banks might face, they were not of the sort likely to lead to a major bank run catching the MOF unawares; none-theless, for weeks rumors of such had been flying among the world's financial regulators. Coming on top of the war-of-attri-tion tactics used by MITI's trade negotiators, these rumors with their implied threats of a Japanese flight from dollar markets had sapped the White House will to act on trade. Instead, the administration put the formidable market skills of Robert Rubin to use extracting the MOF from yet one more bind. Seemingly convinced of the need to avert a supposed Japanese collapse, the treasury secretary masterminded a series of coordi-nated interventions by the world's major central banks that drove the yen down to 98 by August.

Pressure on Japan's administrators eased; with a currency back below the break-even point for many companies, the stock market rose, restoring a bit of a capital cushion to the banks. Meanwhile, Clinton's Japan policies, trade policies—indeed, the whole of his campaign commitment to make America's engagement with the world work for ordinary Americans—lay in ruins. The president had thrown away the only issue that might have stemmed the wholesale defections of white blue-collar workers from the Democratic party. The skill with which Japan's public spokesmen manipulate American elite opinion cannot be the sole explanation, for this skill derives from some-thing more fundamental: the tyranny of the orthodox econom-ics fraternity over policy debates and intellectual life.

During the half century following the depression, econo-mists achieved a certain pride of place among social "scientists" and established a priesthood that enjoyed remarkable success intimidating politicians and other lay practitioners of public policy. The reasons for this seem pretty clear. Of all the social "sciences," economics presents the most plausible imitation of real science. It deals with dollars and cents and thus lends itself most readily to quantification. It is so thoroughly laden with unexamined values and assumptions that it paradoxically gives the appearance of being value-free. The economists' great forebears—Hume, Smith, Ricardo, List, Marx, Schumpeter, Marshall, Keynes—had used the normal tools of intellectual discourse—acute observation, coherent reasoning, lucid prose—to influence their fellow humans on the pressing questions of the day. Contemporary economists speak to one another in a dense, highly quantitative jargon that can be mastered only by several years of intensive study in an accredited Ph.D. program. They issue oracular pronouncements to the great unwashed. It is, alas, all very impressive to insecure politicians, journalists, and a public that has long been far too awestruck by "experts" and "professionals."

But the deafening silence on East Asia produced by economists began to be a problem for them. A naïve outsider might assume that the rise of a few East Asian countries from abject poverty and devastation to growth and prosperity in thirty years would be the most intellectually challenging economics topic of the postwar world. If economics is supposed to help us understand how to get the most from what we have—what its name implies—then surely the examples of Japan, Korea, and Taiwan would be of intense interest by its practitioners. One imagines swarms of assistant professors in Seoul and Taipei poring over archives and pestering retired bureaucrats and businessmen with "How did you do it?" sorts of questions or perhaps hordes of economics Ph.D. candidates crowding into Japanese-language programs.

The humor in these images shows how far they are from what really goes on. In fact, the rise of East Asia seemed to challenge a central tenet of at least Anglo-American economic orthodoxy: the holy status of free trade and the concept of comparative advantage. Since the days of David Ricardo, economists of the Anglo-American tradition had made the ability to understand and articulate the arguments for free trade the central test of economic literacy. Someone who understood basic economics understood that a country that blocked cheaper foreign imports was hurting itself, irrespective of what other countries did, that tit-for-tat protectionism meant bashing oneself when someone else was stupid enough to do so.

But the East Asian success stories all practiced protectionism, and with the publicity given to trade conflicts, it was impossible to prevent ordinary Americans from finding this out.
Many wondered if the protectionism didn't have something to
do with these countries' increasingly well-known wealth. So a
few economists began looking into two questions: Had Japan
done something not part of the normal development prescrip-
tion? Was it possible for governments to raise living standards
by proactively intervening to help ensure that high value-added
industries were established in their own countries as opposed
to others?

A group of economists including the likes of MIT's Paul
Krugman* and Robert Lawrence of the Brookings Institution
concluded that well, yes, Japan did seem to do some things that
orthodox Ricardian economics would regard as no-no's, and
what was more important, some of these things did seem to
lead to "unexpectedly small imports."[25] Others in this group
suggested that under certain circumstances governments can
boost national wealth by intervening to support domestic companies in international competition.

This kind of thinking came to be known as the "new international economics" or "strategic trade policy."[26] But Krugman
and his colleagues squirmed when this work was cited and used
by such "policy entrepreneurs"—to use Krugman's term—as
Clyde Prestowitz and Lester Thurow. Ultimately they seemed
to fear that strategic trade policy might legitimize modes of
discourse that were not under the control of properly creden-
tialed economists, and they quickly retreated to Ricardian orthodoxy, scolding and mocking those who advocated any kind
of similar policy response from Washington.

Krugman, sometimes described as "one of the most brilliant
economists since Keynes," obviously cares what people think
about economics and economists. He takes seriously the charge
that if economists don't go to the trouble of translating ideas
into language ordinary people can understand, they have no

---

*As of this writing, Krugman has moved to Stanford.

one but themselves to blame when ordinary people ignore their ideas. He has written two wonderfully argumentative, scintillating "ordinary-language" books that are feasts for anyone who enjoys the cut and thrust of policy debate.[27] But while the books clarify dominant trends in orthodox Anglo-American economics and include send-ups of supply-siders, Krugman cannot admit that noneconomists have anything to say. The "misuse" of strategic trade policy that so exercises Krugman in the closing pages of his *Peddling Prosperity* is presented as a poorly informed response by confused outsiders to debates that originated with economists.

It is nothing of the sort. It is a response to work like Chalmers Johnson's exhaustive study of MITI, to Karel van Wolferen's laser beam–like analysis of the way power is exercised in Japan, to Prestowitz's history of the U.S.-Japan trade relationship. And perhaps even more important, it is a response to what the eyes see and the ears hear: that something has been happening in Japan that we do not understand, something for which our conceptual framework is inadequate.

Orthodox economists have failed to provide this framework,* but they retain their capacity to intimidate. A group organized by Columbia's Jagdish Bhagwati sent an "open letter" to Hosokawa during the weeks preceding the February 1994 summit urging him not to accept any agreement that had any kind of test to it. The letter accomplished its purpose in hardening Japanese trade negotiators, who assumed correctly that over time Clinton could not muster the political support necessary to withstand a barrage of propaganda that could be unleashed at any potential trade agreement with substance. Later that year economists were largely responsible for foisting

---

* A homegrown American school of economics rooted in the thought of John Dewey, Thorstein Veblen, John Commons, and Clarence Ayres does offer a conceptual framework that could greatly improve our understanding Japan—so-called institutional economics. The school refuses to accept as a given the utility-maximizing behavior of individuals and corporations and argues that questions of purpose and value cannot be eliminated from economic discourse. Institutional economics has, however, been almost completely driven out of American universities by the neoclassical, monetarist, and neo-Keynesian orthodoxies.[28]

off on an insecure and frightened administration the notion that the foreign exchange and bond markets were "nervous" because of U.S. trade pressure on Japan.*

The clearest sign that ivory-tower economists were still framing the agenda of Japan policy was the widespread notion that American pressure for results-oriented trade was somehow propping up the bureaucrats. After all, went this view, a results-oriented trade agreement would need bureaucrats to implement it. With the bureaucrats themselves proclaiming their opposition to managed trade and eschewing the bad old ways, better not to interfere with Japan's "rapid convergence to the United States today,"[31] to quote one of Bhagwati's comments. The administration had enough experience with Japan's trade bureaucrats to recognize the naïveté behind such thinking when it came to the Japanese government's procurement procedures or access by American auto parts makers to the Japanese market. Away from the specifics, however, they all too easily fell back into the complacent view that impersonal economic forces were slowly changing Japan in ways that would in time make it easier for the United States to cope with the country. The Clinton people had, unlike their predecessors, finally grasped that real power in Japan did not lie with its elected officials. But they could not conceptually grasp the more elusive reality that the kind of decisive power necessary to take decisions in Japan's national interest—decisions to repair its relations with the United States, to put money in people's pockets and thus lift Japan out of recession—did not really rest with the bureaucrats either. Clinton and his advisers could not bring

---

*In fairness, most of this destructive intimidation came from orthodox university economists. The more practical sort who were paid by private companies to analyze what might actually happen—Deutsche Bank's Kenneth Courtis, Kemper Financial's David Hale, Salomon's Robert Feldman, J. P. Morgan's Jesper Koll, Jardine Fleming's Richard Werner, Nomura's Richard Koo—had much of interest to say. Hale had predicted the coming of managed trade in an influential article for the *Harvard Business Review* in the late 1980s.[29] Koo made the sensible observation that if Japanese officials were serious about bringing down the yen, they would institute a massive campaign of targeted imports. He argued that real as opposed to cosmetic deregulation would take at least five years to implement and another five years before the world believed it had taken root in Japan. Thus the only way to get the yen down fast was to organize a credible program to raise imports sharply.[30]

themselves to believe that since Japan's traditional economic methods posed a threat to the global economic framework, its rulers, whether prime ministers or unholy coalitions of MOF and MITI civil "servants," wouldn't move to change things.

Such moves involved basic changes in the Japanese political economy. They might look like economic changes, but they were fundamentally political in nature, political because they involved decisions on who had the power to require what of whom. Japan lacked the political infrastructure necessary to make these kinds of decisions. The political framework within which its administrators applied their economic methods had been constructed so long ago—forty years—that it had become almost invisible. At the time Japan accounted for an insignificant percentage of global economic activity. Japan's economic methods relied on external demand to compensate for the deliberate and systemic suppression of domestic demand so necessary to assure priority access by industry to cheap, socialized long-term capital. But as Japan's share of the global economy grew, the methods ceased to work in predictable ways. The clearest signs were the fourfold increase in the value of the yen against the dollar since 1971 and the failure in the early 1990s of the largest trade and current account surpluses ever run by any country in history to restart the engines of growth. The single experiment in an alternative to external demand—the bubble economy—had resulted in a formidable one-time jump in Japan's productive capacity and the competitiveness of Japanese industry. But it could not be duplicated for the foreseeable future.

The many suggestions that cropped up in and out of Japan to bring the country out of its slump—deregulation, cartel busting, targeted imports, allowing stock and land prices to fall to market-clearing levels, vigorous Keynesian pump priming financed out of the postal savings system—amounted to a call for fundamental change, for dismantling the postwar political framework on which Japan's economic methods had depended and the building of a new one. And they all had one fatal flaw:

There was no one to carry them out. The men who staffed the economic ministries did not see their responsibilities in terms of structural overhaul, and no other entity in the system possessed the political legitimacy to force bureaucrats to reflect on where their actions led and to redefine their mission. Bureaucrats at MITI saw their job as protecting Japanese industry's access to markets overseas; they demonstrated "sincerity" by resisting American trade pressure. Bureaucrats at the Ministry of Agriculture thought their responsibilities lay in fighting for Japan's farmers and fending off cheap foreign produce, and the bureaucrats at Health and Welfare were there to protect Japan's pharmaceutical companies, even allowing them to sell stocks of imported blood products that they had been warned were contaminated with the HIV virus, thus infecting scores of Japanese hemophiliacs with AIDS. Bureaucrats at the Finance Ministry believed they were entrusted with the sacred task of safeguarding the country's fiscal integrity from rapacious politicians and counterparts in other ministries and, in a widely used Japanese metaphor, to act as a "warship" shepherding and protecting the "convoy" of the nation's banking system (*gososen-dan*). Indeed, in the early 1990s, as the Finance Ministry fought off demands for economy-stimulating tax cuts and deficit spending, it was being true to its heritage. It had a long history of blind allegiance to fiscal rectitude irrespective of external circumstances. The MOF had helped drive Japan deep into depression with its orthodoxy in the early 1930s. The famous proto-Keynesian methods of Takahashi Korekiyo that brought Japan out of the depression some years before the West had been instituted only after the assassination in 1931 of the orthodox minister Inoue Junnosuke. The economic miracle of the 1950s might never have gotten started if the establishment gadfly Ishibashi Tanzan* and Ikeda Hayato, finance minister

---

*Unlike most other members of Japan's elite, Ishibashi was not a graduate of Tokyo University; he came from Waseda. A courageous dissident, he opposed both the MOF's fiscal orthodoxy and the militarism of the 1930s and was editor of Japan's most important economic newsmagazine, *Tōyō Keizai*. After serving in 1946–47 as finance minister, he was purged by SCAP in one of the most questionable and vindic-

and then prime minister in the crucial economic transition years of 1957–63, had not succeeded in overruling MOF opposition to their tax-cutting income-doubling plan.

But in the early 1990s assassinations were no longer an option in resolving policy disputes, and the times did not permit the rise of an Ishibashi-Ikeda–like combination of brilliant outsider and strong-willed politician sufficient to get a grip on a ministry increasingly unreachable. Ozawa Ichiro, the architect of the Hosokawa and Hata coalition cabinets, had hoped that an informal agreement worked out with the MOF's Saito before Hosokawa's inauguration might give the politicians a measure of leverage over the bureaucracy. But the agreement failed, and the rapid succession of weak coalition governments that followed the breakup of the old LDP in the spring of 1993 removed one of the last tenuous political checks on these rampaging bureaucrats.

In private conversations, I began in 1993 to hear from both Japanese and foreign observers comparisons with the final years of the Second World War. The Japanese military had gone berserk, leading the country into certain disaster, while powerless civilian governments in Tokyo formed and fell every few months. One close Japanese friend remarked when Hosokawa became prime minister that it was like 1940 all over again. That year Prince Konoe Fumimaro had headed a weak coalition government vainly trying to rein in an imperial army that had become a power unto itself; now, fifty-three years later, his grandson was heading a weak coalition government vainly trying to rein in the Finance Ministry.[33]

Of course the Finance Ministry was not shooting people, running history's largest experiment in forced prostitution, or murdering naïve Japanese boys by sending them off on suicide missions. But there were distressing political parallels. The Japanese Army had had no strategy beyond simply running amok

---

tive of such cases. He reemerged politically as MITI minister in 1955 and then served as prime minister for less than three months before falling ill and having to resign. His was arguably the most important intellectual contribution to the Japanese economic miracle.[32]

over all Asia, something that American investigators for the
Tokyo War Crimes Tribunal had been unable to believe and
kept looking for. At one point the army seemed to think it
could fight the Chinese, the British, the Americans, and the
Russians all at once. There was no one to hold its generals to
account, to force them to explain and justify exactly what they
were doing.

Similarly, the economic bureaucrats of the 1990s seemed to
think that Japan could simply run its economy forever the way it
had since 1955. They desperately wanted to believe that wicked
speculators and American Japan bashing explained the rise of
the yen, that Japan could always run huge current account surpluses, all the while continuing to use the dollar as a de facto
second currency. They did not factor into their reasoning two
contradictions. First, these methods would work only so long
as the rest of the world (particularly the United States) did
not adopt them—that is to say, if every nation tried to run
its economy so as to produce current account surpluses, there
would be no such surpluses; a surplus must have its deficit
counterpart somewhere. Secondly, if other countries continued
to eschew Japan's methods and ran their economies to max-
imize short-term consumer welfare, Japan with its higher levels
of investment and endless external current account surpluses
would end up controlling an ever-greater share of the global
economy. Thus the day would come when other countries
could not pay for Japanese goods.

Long before these contradictions were fully manifest—long
before, that is, the rest of the world duplicated Japan's economic
methods or before other currencies became worthless vis-à-vis
the yen—"reality" was likely to intervene, forcing adjustments
that would end these contradictions. In fact, many maintained
that this process had already started with the long slump of the
early 1990s and the fallout of the bubble collapse. Some saw
this process as relatively benign. They pointed to factors slowly
undermining bureaucratic control. For one thing, the soaring
yen had created such a gulf between domestic and foreign prices
that imports were by hook or crook finding their way into

Japan, where they had begun to force prices down in a growing number of sectors. Evidence could be found in everything from men's suits to whiskey to personal computers.

Even services were not immune. Northwest Airline's Tokyo office sends mail across town to my apartment by routing it via Hong Kong because it costs less. When I called the airline to reconfirm a flight recently, I heard a series of clicks and whirs; then a voice with a strong Cantonese accent came on the line. Northwest was saving money by routing my call to somewhere in Southeast Asia rather than deal with it in Japan.

The long resistance to big stores in Japan by distribution cartels had led retailers like the innovative Ito-Yokado*—now the majority owner of the 7-Eleven franchise in both Japan and the United States—to open chains of small convenience stores, where everything from delivery and financial services† to underwear, box lunches, packaged foods, and magazines are available twenty-four hours a day. Because shelf space is at such a premium in these stores, the balance of power is shifting from manufacturers and distributors to retailers; unless a product moves very fast, it is withdrawn. The financial authorities began hinting that they could not bail out every bank forever,[34] and at least one bank merger concocted by the Ministry of Finance collapsed when the healthy Kita-Nihon Bank balked at absorbing two of its smaller, ailing brethren.[35] With signs that monolithic government support for the banking system might be cracking, investors began discriminating among bank securities. As riskier banks thus paid more for funds, banks had to be more attentive to the quality of their own assets; in other words, they had to worry about the cash flow and credit standing of their borrowers.

---

*Ito-Yokado is probably the most innovative retailer in Japan. Significantly it lacks ties to any single large established bank that can influence its pricing and marketing strategies.

†In Japan you do not pay bills by check. Until recently you had to take the bill to a bank or a post office and pay it in person unless you had made arrangements for automatic account deduction. Now you can also take bills to convenience stores at any hour of the day or night and pay them. Japan's equivalents of Federal Express and UPS also operate through convenience stores.

Meanwhile political reforms held out the prospect of change. Historically Japan's multiseat-per-district system meant that the surest electoral strategy involved homing in on a relatively small number of voters, then plying them lavishly with public pork and private handouts. To raise funds for this largess, politicians ran a sort of racket in which they charged companies very high prices in the form of campaign donations for the service of running interference with the bureaucrats whose approvals were necessary to do business. But by moving to a single-seat system, politicians might have to learn to compete for large numbers of votes, and some of them could conceivably master ways of forcing the bureaucracy to pay more attention to the wishes of Japanese households. The MOF's passion for getting a substantial increase in consumption taxes passed as soon as possible stemmed in part from the fear that politicians might appeal to voters by promising to block an increase in this deeply unpopular tax. Without a consumption tax increase, the ministry would almost certainly be forced to issue deficit-covering bonds that could lead to higher long-term interest rates, which would work to reduce Japan's external surpluses as companies were forced finally to pay attention to the profitability of their exports, the costs of their supplies—leading to greater use of cheaper imported components—and the financial burdens of investments in capacity.

These scenarios were comforting. But they typically ignored Japan's lack of a market economy's infrastructure necessary to replace any conceivable crumbling of bureaucratic control. For the country to function as a genuine market economy, it would require an adequate and functioning judiciary that could settle disputes in reasonable time,* an honest market in corporate control where real ownership of assets could be

---

*Whether or not Japan's courts can be regarded as fully independent of bureaucratic interference—and there are those who have demonstrated convincingly that judges are subject to considerable intimidation[36]—Japan does not begin to have the number of lawyers necessary to cope with economic disputes. These are handled today mostly via informal "guidance" from the relevant bureaucrats, by lavish contributions to the appropriate politicians in order to run interference, and by widespread use of the services of criminal organizations.

traded and valued, functioning and transparent money and
bond markets, and adequate dissemination of economic information through disinterested accountants, independent ratings
agencies, and a fully independent financial press.

There were also much less comforting scenarios than a gradual loosening of bureaucratic control, scenarios that saw Japan's
power holders resort to more desperate measures to maintain
their ability to control economic events. As the buying power
of the United States dwindled, measured by the relentless rise
of the yen, Japan would need markets elsewhere to keep its
economic methods going. Only one plausible substitute for
the American market existed: the great arc that stretches from
Korea and Taiwan through the coastal provinces of China to
the ASEAN countries. If the trends of the last fifteen years
continued, by early in the next century some six hundred million people in this arc would enjoy living standards and buying
power comparable to those in southern Europe and portions
of the United States. Japanese institutions already dominated
much of this arc. Their cars and trucks, electronics, department
stores, and machine tools and other capital equipment were
visible everywhere and in overwhelming predominance. Japanese construction companies did most of the region's big projects. Much of the region's financing came from Japanese banks
and securities companies, and Japanese companies led its plant
and equipment investment. The *sōgō shōsha* handled most of the
region's foreign trade. Japanese popular culture had gone a long
way toward displacing American. The Japanese had cultivated
economic and political elites throughout the region. Governments looked to Tokyo as a model for economic management,
and the Japanese in turn discreetly joined many Asian governments in promoting the notion of a group-oriented, authority-
worshiping Asian value system as an alternative to the individu-
alism and human rights orientation of the West.

Indeed, Japan appeared to be building a more benign version of its wartime Greater East Asia Co-Prosperity Sphere.
Some contended that Japanese agitation over the soaring of the

yen and the heroic efforts to forestall a serious American trade policy could best be understood as delaying tactics. Japan was said to need the United States for a few years longer until it had achieved the necessary critical mass in Asia and would no longer be dependent for a continuation of its methods on the United States.

A scenario that saw Japan emerge as the de facto leader of a new economic empire—a "headquarters nation," in the words of one scholar who had argued this was happening[37]—would of course make things uncomfortable for Washington. The United States would be relegated to the periphery of the global economic system; the terms upon which it could trade, fund, and invest would be decided in Tokyo.

Many obstacles, however, lay in the way of a glide by Japan to regional dominance. The dollar continued to function as the primary reserve and settlements currency in the region. The yen could not supplant the dollar without wrenching changes in the Japanese financial order, despite talk about the emergence in Asia of a "yen bloc."* Japan might be the number one investor, the number one financier, and the number one exporter to the region, but the United States still imported more finished manufactured goods. Japan would have to find ways of supplanting crucial U.S. buying power, taking us right back to the same contradictions that bedevil its economic relations with the wider world: the loss of bureaucratic control implied in moving Japan from a country running external surpluses to one running external deficits. Moreover, while the Japanese were admired in much of the region and respected everywhere, they were still widely resented and feared. Memories of wartime Japanese brutality in Korea, China, Vietnam, and the Philippines had not disappeared. Ordinary Thai and Burmese farmers, hill tribes in

---

* According to an important article in the October 31, 1994, issue of the authoritative *Nikkei Business*,[38] the MOF has been quietly discussing steps to replace the dollar with the yen as the region's key currency for ten years, but only now is such talk surfacing publicly among key current and former ministry officials. As recently as early in 1994, according to the piece, an article advocating such a step that was supposed to have appeared in the Bank of Japan's monthly research report was suppressed.

Malaysia's Sarawak and Indonesia's Kalimantan, fisherfolk in the Philippines and Cambodia knew that their corrupt leaders were clear-cutting their countries' forests and destroying fisheries by selling them off to the Japanese. Koreans, North or South, would never acquiesce to Japanese dominance, and the Chinese had repeatedly demonstrated that they understood how to outnegotiate and intimidate Tokyo whenever it suited them.

But low probability of success did not deter the Japanese struggle to obtain the upper hand in Asia. The logic of the situation demanded it. Japanese companies faced with rising domestic production costs and a soaring yen had no choice but to move production abroad, and Asia captured a steadily greater share of those moves. Important political consequences would inevitably follow. As Japan accumulated assets in Asia, it would be forced to take steps to protect them. Never in history had a country accumulated substantial external assets without doing something to ensure their security.

At present Japan's physical investments and lines of supply in Asia are protected by the U.S. military. But the very presence of these investments undermines both the will and the ability of the United States to continue such protection. Japanese-owned companies in Asia and those that feed one way or another into the Japanese industrial machine have emerged as fierce competitors of American industry. With an uncertain American stake in Asia, it stretches credulity to think that the political will to maintain the region's security will remain unchanged, even if the costs of an American presence can somehow be financed. The moment the yen replaces the dollar as the region's preeminent settlements and reserve currency, for example, the costs in dollar terms of maintaining a U.S. military presence will zoom out of sight. Even if this does not happen, the mounting trade surpluses of the region vis-à-vis the United States will force currency realignments that will greatly increase the dollar tab for the U.S. presence.

It is common knowledge that thanks to Japanese contributions, the U.S. government actually spends less to maintain a soldier in Japan than in the United States. If the purpose of the U.S. military in Japan is to prevent a resurgence of Japanese militarism, then the Japanese are paying for their own occupiers. If the purpose is to provide for Japan's security, then American soldiers have effectively become mercenaries. Neither interpretation can be squared easily with long-term stability.

An American departure will create a security vacuum. Almost every government in the region, with the notable exception of the Philippines, faces a legitimacy problem of one kind or another, and the countries that are potentially the most powerful—China and Indonesia—are those where the succession problem looms largest. Cambodia, Burma, and North Korea all are potential powder kegs. The absorption of Hong Kong into China, Islamic fundamentalism in Indonesia and Malaysia, the unending jockeying for power among clusters of current and former Thai military officials who effectively control their country, a grab by Taiwan for de jure independence, the separatist movement in East Timor, three- or even four-way struggles over the Spratly Islands in the South China Sea: any one of these could erupt so as to pose a security challenge to Japan's economic lifelines.

Coping with this challenge will be the acid test of U.S.-Japan relations. One can hope that when the day arrives, Japan will have a fully accountable, responsible government enjoying sound political legitimacy and able to work with the United States in taking the painful measures necessary to deal with this challenge. But it is, alas, more likely that Tokyo will be paralyzed with indecision, as it was during the weeks after Saddam Hussein's invasion of Kuwait, unable to answer a direct U.S. request that American bases in Japan be available for any military response or that Japanese troops risk their lives with Americans. An enraged American public may demand a U.S. withdrawal, leaving a great but embittered Japan, convinced of the world's enmity, to embark again on desperate measures to protect itself against what it sees as a deadly threat.

America can help tip the odds. To start with, Washington should stop wistfully hoping that the bureaucrats will take the necessary steps if they are jawboned sufficiently. The United States stands a better chance of success impressing upon Japan's politicians, its opinion leaders, and its ordinary people—still startlingly sensitive to American opinions—the need to get a grip on these bureaucrats.

Even more critically the United States must ease its financial and industrial dependence on Japan with its corrosive effects on U.S.-Japan relations. While Tokyo may be whistling in the dark about a new order in Asia and living without the American security framework, we Americans are doing the same if we think our furtive dependence on Japan has ended. Japanese institutions may have withdrawn from the long end of the Treasury market, but since 1992 they have been replaced by an ominous surge of short-term, unstable Japanese money. The lenders today are chiefly nervous Japanese commercial banks rather than life insurance companies. The banks are buying the shortest-term Treasury securities directly or funding their American counterparts in the interbank market that in turn are purchasing the notes. To connoisseurs of the financial markets the meaning is clear: While Japanese institutions go on financing a lot of American national debt, they are no longer willing or able to bear the currency and interest rate risks of American profligacy.

Meanwhile the loss of so much of America's industrial base means that despite relatively healthy macroeconomic numbers, American demand cannot translate into enough good American jobs and orders for American companies. The production capacity in industry after industry is gone. Volatile bond markets and high real long-term rates impede the restoration of that capacity. Whether it is Detroit's resurgence or America's thriving computer and telecommunications companies, the dirty little secret of the mid-nineties recovery is that it depends more than ever on Japanese components and Japanese money.

Conclusion
Seriousness and Accountability

To know and not to act is not to know.

WANG YANG-MING

REMEMBER Sato Eiji from Chapter 3, the typical young salaryman who had joined prestigious Mitsutomo Metals in 1977 full of hope and ambition? He is now forty-three years old. He has devoted the best years of his life to that company, but he has not made it past *kachō* (section chief) level. He has a staggering mortgage on a small house that eats up a quarter of his salary, and he spends three hours a day in packed, sweltering trains going back and forth between this house and his office. He feels he hardly knows his wife, and they barely speak now except about essential household affairs. She has invested all her emotional energy in getting their twelve-year-old son into a middle school that offers a leg up on the "educational escalator." Mr. Sato rarely sees the boy, who is either in school, studying, or at a special cram school *(juku),* and on the few Sunday afternoons Mr. Sato has suggested they play catch or go to a ball game, the boy has listlessly refused, plopping himself down in front of a video machine with mindless pop music blasting through his earphones.

Mr. Sato's health is not good. He has stomach trouble and is drinking more now, even though his expenses budget has been cut and he doesn't take out customers or subordinates as often as he used to. Many evenings he stops at a seedy little bar near the station on the way home and gulps cheap whiskey served by an older woman who was once a hostess in a second-class Ginza nightclub. She listens sympathetically as he pours out his fears. He is being passed over for promotion. The company's business is not in great shape. A large factory is being opened next month in Malaysia, but this year in Japan salary increases were the smallest ever, and there is a freeze on new hires. Two men in Sato's class have taken "voluntary retirement," and five others who refused it were transferred abruptly to remote parts of Japan or sent to be travel agents at the company's new subsidiary. Mr. Sato often wakes up from a nightmare in the wee hours with his heart pounding and his stomach churning, wondering what he would do if he got "the tap on the shoulder." He doubts he could find a job anywhere on his own. Who wants a has-been forty-three-year-old with a shallow mix of "general management" skills? But the money from voluntary retirement would last only two years, even with the modest way his family lives. Could he bear living in a squalid little apartment by himself in Kita-Kyushu or, even worse, smirking in front of office ladies at a travel agency?

When Mr. Sato turns on the evening news, the first ten minutes are devoted to the foreign exchange markets that have seen the yen gain another 2 points against the dollar. Reporters on-screen talk to currency traders and Bank of Japan officials, who explain that the White House seems not to be serious about supporting the dollar. This is followed by the network's Washington correspondent interviewing C. Fred Bergsten, identified as one of Clinton's top informal advisers, voiced over into Japanese. Bergsten explains that the yen must gain another 5 points to reduce Japan's trade surplus.

The next segment features Mickey Kantor emerging from the latest trade talks. Sato grimaces with distaste as Kantor is shown lecturing the Japanese side on what Japan must and must not do. The next day on the way into work he picks up a popular weekly magazine. Hanging on to his train strap, he reads an article describing how a cabal of Jewish bankers financed the Clinton campaign and now control economic policy in Washington. There are prominent pictures of Alan Greenspan, Robert Rubin, Mickey Kantor, and Jeffrey Garten. These Jews are described as hating Japan, determined to break Japan's economic power once and for all. *Chikishō*—something like "the goddamned shits"—Sato murmurs under his breath.

These emotions are political dynamite. Sato's loathing is not confined to Americans or a mythical Jewish cabal. It is, in fact, unfocused and general. He reads about corrupt, money-grubbing politicians living lavishly on huge bribes and wonders, disgustedly, why he bothers to vote. He curses the bureaucracy when he hears of plans to raise all the public utility charges. He bows obsequiously at passing managing directors in the hall while inwardly entertaining fantasies of murder. He chews out the young freshmen assigned to his section, with their designer haircuts, their fashionable Italian-cut suits, and their soft demeanors barely hiding insolence. He tosses inwardly between lust for and rage at the young women in his section with their short skirts and aerobically conditioned bodies.

Mr. Sato knows in his guts that he has been on the receiving end of a raw deal. Whom will he blame? What will he do to get redress? Will he vote for a politician who tells him that this way of doing things cannot go on? A politician who promises credibly to bring the bureaucracy to heel? A politician who can make Mr. Sato believe—really believe—that the superior skill of another forty-three-year-old in regurgitating a mass of unrelated facts for a few hours twenty-five years ago when he sat for the entrance examination of Tokyo University does not make that man better than Mr. Sato? And that it certainly does not give that man the right to make unexamined decisions that determine the kind of life Mr. Sato leads?

Or will Mr. Sato come to the conclusion, as his grandfather did, that America hates Japan and does not want to make room for it, that if it weren't for whining, bullying Americans, his job would be safe and his future assured? Alas, this is likely, for perhaps the biggest difference between today's officials in the West Wing of the White House and their predecessors is that they regard Japan with disdain and distaste. All the diplomatic niceties in the world cannot hide this. And the disdain and distaste go way beyond the inner circle of one shaky Democratic administration; they embrace most of official Washington.

It is understandable why American officials view Japan this way. They see a rich, parasitical, deceitful country unwilling to make the slightest effort to support or protect a system from which it has benefited more than any other. They see power resting with a bureaucracy that is unwilling to make any concession, no matter how small, without interminable and acrimonious negotiations, that uses every chance to backslide on agreements when it thinks it can get away with it. They see and resent influence buying on a massive scale, even when many of them profit from it personally.

It may be understandable, but it is not responsible. Japan is too important. It has the second-largest economy in the world. It helped bring about the Russian Revolution and was the direct progenitor of the Chinese. It ended Western colonialism in Asia. It is the first non-Western country in five hundred years to become a great power. Its economic methods pose a fundamental intellectual challenge to our entire understanding of institutions, markets, and the process of development. The sun is not going to set on it, and it is not going to go away.

Fifty years after World War II many of the factors that brought that horrible conflict about are again at play. The United States and Japan are as dependent on each other as ever, but the dependence is denied or twisted. Each sees the other as more and more of a threat, and Americans and Japanese stare ever more balefully and incomprehendingly at each other across a widening chasm dug with misconceptions, shibboleths, and sheer irresponsibility.

Japan and the United States are about as different as two

large and powerful countries can be. But they have in common an ambiguous relationship with the wider world and a dangerous use of the mechanism of denial to avoid dealing with the world as it is. Japan's history is marked by a deliberate turning away from the rest of the world; America's, by a flight from it. In modern times Japan has sought to keep the world at arm's length, to be in it but not of it; Americans have insisted on treating the world as if it were an extension of the United States, coping with contrasts and complexities by resolutely refusing to see them.

Both countries also show the symptoms of denial—albeit in very different ways—on questions of power. The Japanese have long treated power the way Victorians treated sex: It exists, but polite people don't talk about it. Americans confuse inevitable exercises of power with exercises of morality and are thus driven to dress them up in the language of uplifting tracts.

In an interconnected and interdependent world neither country can afford these illusions. If we are to avert another catastrophe, Americans must come to grips with Japan as it is, not as we would like it to be. Washington must learn to negotiate quietly, skillfully, and firmly, reacting to intransigence not with hectoring and cheap talk but with measures based on painstaking, detailed study designed to achieve "the maximum results with the minimum resentment." This is not an easy or one-time task, and it cannot be accomplished as an aside after the latest tin-pot dictator in the Middle East, the Balkans, or the Caribbean has succeeded in mesmerizing Washington for weeks. It requires the construction of an institutional memory bank on the functioning of Japan, a dedicated cadre of specialists who have devoted much of their lives to the study and analysis of Japan's political economy, and a mixture of support from and access to the highest levels of any administration for these specialists.

This is the sort of infrastructure we built to cope with the Soviet Union. Japan does not threaten our existence, but its historical impact on the United States surely matches even that of Russia and will continue to do so. Indeed, the ready availability of Japanese finance in the early 1980s was an absolutely essential ingredient in the massive American defense buildup that seems finally to have convinced Soviet leaders that they could never win an arms race with the United States.

In the closing pages of his book *Diplomacy,* Henry Kissinger writes: "World leadership is inherent in America's power and values, but it does not include the privilege of pretending that America is doing other nations a kindness by associating with them, or that it has a limitless capacity to impose its will by withholding its favors."[1] No sounder advice could be given with respect to Japan policy. American leaders can never escape the necessity of dealing with Japan. Its companies, its products, its money, even its culture are now interwoven into every aspect of American life and American interests. Tokyo is and will remain one of the world's preeminent power centers—the city alone accounts for a good 5 percent of global GNP—and it has the potential to be a valuable ally and force for stability or, in a worst-case scenario, to become again an implacable and deadly adversary.

Coherent Japan policy starts from understanding and accepting that the interests of the United States and Japan will inevitably, from time to time, clash. Statesmen of goodwill, steeped in history, wary of but not intimidated by the power at their disposal, can reach an accommodation that respects the interests of both sides. But American leaders cannot allow their vision to be clouded by fantasies of a borderless economic world or of laissez-faire democracy as the norm to which all development necessarily aspires. They must come to see, for example, that America's ability to borrow some half a trillion dollars from Japan was due not to the workings of an eternal, unchanging market standing above and beyond human affairs but to a framework built on the correlations of national power and the conscious political arrangements of half a century ago. Japan's ability and willingness to lend stemmed directly from the institutional developments that have occurred there during that half century. We are fooling ourselves if we regard either the framework or the developments as anything other than ephemeral.

Americans have paid a high price for choosing to borrow money rather than face up to the need for far-reaching debate on the hard decisions that are the genuine stuff of an honest politics. A realistic, sober, and serious Japan policy could help create the conditions for such a debate, thus bringing ancillary benefits beyond averting another tragedy in the Pacific. Serious Japan policy could help force us as a society to bring the amount of government service we want into line with what we are willing to pay for. It would make us think about the need to support a dollar whose role as a universal medium of exchange and fundamental store of value we have too long taken for granted. It could focus our attention on the alarming decline of our primary and secondary educational systems, our penchant for fretting more over our children's self-esteem than their mastery of the disciplines, academic and otherwise, that provide an objective basis for self-esteem. Certainly it would highlight the scandal of our universities, swarming with games-playing model builders who have driven to the margins of intellectual life the disciplines necessary to cope with the world in all its complexity—geography, narrative history, institutional economics, area studies.[2] Thinking about Japan might help us think about our miserable savings rate and how we are to finance the infrastructure necessary to provide opportunity and a decent standard of living for the tens of millions of Americans who see the market power of their labor in relentless decline.

Realistic Japan policy from the United States would also help Japan. A policy that assumes as givens periodic clashes of national interests and the necessity for men and women of goodwill to work out an accommodation calls for leaders on both sides with a clear view of their respective countries' needs and wants and the authority to negotiate. Such a policy would remind the Japanese that their country desperately requires a political infrastructure with the legitimacy and support sufficient to cope with fundamental contradictions that have been denied too long. The Japanese too have paid a high price for avoiding the debate they must have on resolving these contradictions. Japan cannot both be a great power and rely on and even fund another country to make for it decisions on national security and international relations, it cannot be an economic superpower while hiding behind a foreign currency to denominate its trade and investment flows, and it cannot be the world's premiere creditor nation and expect to run unending trade surpluses. Its companies cannot enjoy unimpeded access to technology and markets around the world while running a controlled, cartelized, mercantilist economic regime at home. Japan cannot expect peaceful, untroubled relations with its neighbors until it has first demonstrated real understanding of the basic historical lesson of the 1930s—that its aggression in Asia was a product of unchecked and unaccountable bureaucratic power—and then provided clear proof that such aggression cannot and will not be repeated by bridling that power and bringing it to heel. A good first step would be to break up the Ministry of Finance, lodging tax collecting, bank oversight, and securities market regulation in independent agencies that report directly to the prime minister, monetary policy in the Bank of Japan, and fundamental decisions on taxes and budgets in Japan's elected representatives in the Diet.

Here, perhaps, is where we Americans, who, after all, bear much historical responsibility for the pathologies of Japanese political life, can perform our greatest service, by doing our best to make clear to the Japanese whenever we can and as politely as possible that it is up to them, finally, to get a grip on their institutions. The tremendous effort needed to bring this about may seem all too much for a citizenry that has been exploited, abused, and victimized for centuries, that has worked like dogs and gone without for decades and feels it deserves, as it does, a bit of a breathing spell. Alas, history is neither kind nor fair. Ordinary Japanese will not enjoy the full fruits of their labors, and they risk all that they have worked for, unless they demand accountability and transparency from those entrusted with power over them. The schoolteacher beating up children in the name of order; the Construction Ministry bureaucrat damming Japan's last free-flowing river; the Finance Ministry official squeezing money out of households to bail out bank loans to gangsters; the company *jinjibuchō* (personnel department manager) tearing a man away from his family, transferring him to a remote city with one week's notice: these people must be made to explain and answer for what they do to skeptical and demanding citizens. Japanese people must insist—individually, collectively, repeatedly, relentlessly—that their companies, their banks, their bureaucracies, their schools, their politicians serve them and not the other way around.

While the Japanese demand accountability from their institutions, we must insist on seriousness from ours. A number of our companies with their backs to the wall have, it is true, shown an ability to get serious and restructure themselves from the inside out. But most other institutions in our society are driving thoughtful observers to the point of despair. Our universities, our schools, and our media are manifestly failing in their jobs to inform and educate. And political discourse has become so vicious, so degraded, and so fantastic that American citizens are going to have to resort to desperate measures to get the serious debates we simply must have. Somehow we must force Congress, our political parties, and their electoral candidates to quit their infantile games of character assassination, pork barrel bribery, and scapegoating. We must to learn to jeer at any political "contract" or crackpot intellectual that pretends we can have Swedish-style social welfare financed with Hong Kong–style taxes. And we must take power back from the slick political operators, campaign consultants, and talk show louts who fiddle while our heritage burns.

Notes

1. The Japanese Company
Ownership, Control, and Competition

1. Hoashi Kei, quoted in Karel van Wolferen, *The Enigma of Japanese Power: People and Politics in a Stateless Nation* (New York: Alfred A. Knopf, 1989), p. 356.

2. Itami Hiroyuki, *Jinpon Shugi Kigyō: Kawaru Keiei; Kawaranu Genri* (Peopleism Enterprises: Changing Management; Unchanging Principles) (Tokyo: Chikuma Shobo, 1987). Itami is a professor at Tokyo's Hitotsubashi University who has written a number of books on management and control systems.

3. Matsumoto, a former MITI official, wrote an influential book setting forth his concept of *kigyō shugi*. The book has been translated under the title *The Rise of the Japanese Corporate System: The Inside View of a MITI Official*, tr. Thomas I. Elliott (London: Kegan Paul International, 1991).

4. Okumura, a prolific and influential writer, has been a journalist for the conservative daily *Sankei Shimbun*, researcher at the Japan Securities Research Institute, and professor at Ryukoku University. He has written a number of books on the Japanese corporation; he describes his concept of the Japanese economic system in *Hōjin Shihon Shugi: 'Kaisha Hon-i' no Taikei* (Corporate Capitalism: A "Company Standard" System) (Tokyo: Asahi Bunko, 1991).

5. Imai Masaaki, *Kaizen: The Key to Japan's Competitive Success* (New York: McGraw-Hill, Inc., 1986), p. 27. Imai is admittedly more of a management guru than a bona fide intellectual; he has, however, been one of the most successful salesmen abroad of Japanese management techniques.

6. Nakatani Iwao, "The Economic Role of Financial Corporate Grouping," in *The Economic Analysis of the Japanese Firm*, ed. Aoki Masahiko (Amsterdam, New York, and Oxford: North Holland, 1984), pp. 227–58. See also his *The Japanese Firm in Transition* (Tokyo: Asian Productivity Organization, 1988). Nakatani specifically discusses his concept of network capitalism in his latest Japanese-language book, *"Japan Problem" no Genten* (The Roots of the Japan Problem) (Tokyo: Kodansha, 1990), pp. 109–14. Nakatani is a well-known commentator and professor at Tokyo's Hitotsubashi University.

7. Sakakibara Eisuke, *Beyond Capitalism: The Japanese Model of Market Economics* (Lanham, Md.: University Press of America, 1993), p. 4. This book contains a useful summary of Japanese scholarly views on the na-

ture of the Japanese economic system; see particularly pp. 4–11 and pp. 143–62.

8. Robert Ozaki, *Human Capitalism: The Japanese Enterprise System as a World Model* (New York: Penguin Books, 1991).

9. In fairness, Nakatani, *"Japan Problem" no Genten,* loc. cit., p. 112, is forthright on the ease with which corruption and bribery become endemic to network capitalism and also discusses the conflicts this brings with the rest of the world. Sakakibara's latest book, *Bunmei toshite no Nihongata Shihon Shugi: Tomi to Kenryoku no Kōzu* (Japan-Style Capitalism as Civilization: A Sketch of Its Wealth and Power) (Tokyo: Tōyō Keizai Shinpōsha, 1993), is, however, a disappointing compendium of clichés about Japan's "unique" system: the modern company's descent from the traditional *ie;* the *sarariman* as the contemporary embodiment of samurai virtues; the entrepreneurial heads of smaller firms reincarnating the ethos of the old Osaka merchant class.

10. This basic premise of *Nihonjinron*— that the Japanese differ from others in ways far more profound than the ways in which, say, the English or the Greeks or the Sinhalese differ from others—is explained with a variety of absurd theories: Japan's supposedly unique four season–wet monsoon climate, the "single race" origins of the Japanese; the rice paddy economy of traditional Japan, which fostered warm communitarian values as opposed to the savage "hunter culture" of the West; the way in which the Japanese alone among all humans process language through the instinctive, artistic, creative right half of the brain rather than the cold, mechanical, logical left half; Japanese psychological makeup stemming from manipulative behavior toward first the mother and then the superior *(amae);* the special characterization of Japanese society

by vertical rather than horizontal bonds; the extra length of Japanese intestines, giving rise to the distinctive diet; so on and so on. That *Nihonjinron* is so widely disseminated and to a greater or lesser extent believed by large numbers of Japanese—including many scholars who ought to know better, vide Sakakibara's *Bunmei to shite. . . ,* loc. cit.,—is something of an indictment of Japanese education. For a thorough discussion of *Nihonjinron,* see Peter Dale, *The Myth of Japanese Uniqueness* (London: Routledge, 1988); Roy Andrew Miller, *Japan's Modern Myth* (New York and Tokyo: Weatherhill, 1982); and Karel van Wolferen, op. cit., Chapter 10.

11. Robert Zielinski and Nigel Holloway, *Unequal Equities: Power and Risk in Japan's Stock Market* (Tokyo and New York: Kodansha International, 1991), p. 209.

12. Aron Viner, *The Emerging Power of Japanese Money* (Tokyo: Japan Times Ltd., 1988), p. 173.

13. Van Wolferen, op. cit., 134–35. See also Gerald L. Curtis, *The Japanese Way of Politics* (New York: Columbia University Press, 1988), pp. 82–83 and 103–04.

14. In a paper on Japanese bankruptcy practice, Frank Packer and Mark Ryser note that "Private out-of-court settlement of business failure is the dominant practice in Japan," and refer to the "pervasive role that organized crime plays in the handling of corporate financial distress in Japan." See "The Governance of Failure: An Anatomy of Corporate Bankruptcy in Japan," *Working Paper #62.* Working Paper Series (New York: Center on Japanese Economy and Business, Columbia University, 1992) pp. 20 and 26 respectively.

15. Interview with Monden Akihiro, editor of the *Asian Autotech Report* and managing director of A. I. Publishing, a firm specializing in publications

about the auto industry.

16. See the account of life in a Toyota factory written by one of its employees, Kamata Toshio, *Japan in the Passing Lane*, tr. Akimoto Tatsuru (New York: Pantheon Books, 1982).

17. James Sterngold, the business-financial Tokyo correspondent for the *New York Times*, wrote at the time of the scandal: "Nobody would be questioning Japan's regulatory system, of course, if the [MOF] relied on laws rather than guidance. Japan has securities laws . . . but they are rarely if ever invoked. For instance, although a variety of penalties have been meted out for the improper compensation—from pay cuts and resignations to fines and suspensions—there has yet to be a formal charge of wrongdoing or an open legal process in which evidence was presented." "Regulation, Japan Style," *New York Times,* (September 9, 1991), p. D-2.

18. Frank K. Upham, *Law and Social Change in Postwar Japan* (Cambridge, Mass: Harvard University Press, 1987), p. 16.

19. See Michael L. Gerlach's exhaustive study of the *keiretsu* in his *Alliance Capitalism: The Social Organization of Japanese Business* (Berkeley and Los Angeles: University of California Press, 1992), especially Chapters 3 and 4.

20. Among works in which these views can be found are Ozaki, op. cit.; Sakakibara, *Bunmei to shite . . . ,* loc. cit.; Ronald Dore, *Taking Japan Seriously* (Stanford, Calif.: Stanford University Press, 1987); William G. Ouchi, *Theory Z* (Reading, Mass.: Addison-Wesley, 1981); and Ezra F. Vogel, *Japan as Number One: Lessons for America* (New York: Harper and Row, 1979).

21. See William J. Holstein, *The Japanese Power Game: What It Means for America* (New York: Charles Scribner's Sons, 1990); Edward J. Lincoln, *Japan's Unequal Trade*

(Washington: Brookings Institution, 1990); Nakatani, *"Japan Problem" no Genten,* loc. cit.

22. As usual, van Wolferen, op. cit., is an exception. See particularly Chapter 13.

23. See account in Upham, op. cit., pp. 176–84.

24. Van Wolferen, op. cit., p. 342.

25. The incident was related to me by a journalist who had attended the conference. The journalist requested anonymity.

26. Alan Wolff, "U.S.-Japan Relations and the Rule of Law: The Nature of the Trade Conflict and the American Response" in *Japan's Economic Structure: Should It Change?,* ed. Yamamura Kozo (Seattle: Society for Japanese Studies, 1990), p. 152.

27. The Japanese weekly *AERA,* published by *Asahi Shimbun,* ran a series of articles in the spring of 1994 on teacher-instigated violence at a number of schools throughout Japan. A summary of the articles, "Schools Turn a Blind eye Towards Violence," ran in English in the *Asahi Evening News,* August 9, 1994. Although many parents and other concerned Japanese, not to mention the children involved, are deeply distressed at the widespread use of intimidation, humiliation, and corporal punishment in Japanese schools, the articles point out that there is no institutional means by which anyone can get a grip on the situation. While such incidents are by no means universal in Japanese schools, they seem to have escalated sharply with the Ministry of Education's clear victory in recent years in a decades-long struggle with the leftist Nikkyōso, the Japanese teachers' union.

28. Michael Jablow, quoted in Joel Kotkin and Kishimoto Yoriko, "Theory F," *Inc.: The Magazine for Growing Companies* (April 1986), p. 53.

29. Mikuni Akio, "The Vitality of Japan in a Comparative Perspective," remarks at conference in Tokyo, March

26–27, 1992, *Transcript of Proceedings* (Luxembourg: Luxembourg Institute for European and International Studies), p. 54.

30. James C. Abegglen and George Stalk, Jr., *Kaisha: The Japanese Corporation* (New York; Basic Books, 1985), pp. 46–54.

31. Robert Bartley, *The Seven Fat Years—and How to Do it Again* (New York: Free Press, 1992), p. 12.

32. Robert Reich, *The Work of Nations* (New York: Alfred A. Knopf, 1991), p. 141.

33. Ibid.

2. The Credit Decision

1. The point is not that American accountants do not sometimes overlook bad news or misrepresent corporate financial health but that their doing so is regarded as a problem that requires *systemic* correcting. Congress has been involved, for example, in "a seven year effort to require whistle-blowing by independent accountants who detect fraud as they audit corporations," according to Andrew Taylor, "Panel OKs Bill Requiring CPAs to Report Fraud," *Congressional Weekly Report* (May 1, 1993), p. 1075.

2. Technically, the ministry told the banks they could report equity holdings at cost rather than market value; since most of the banks' portfolios had been acquired decades earlier at tiny fractions of the current market value, it became impossible for outsiders to gauge the actual conditions of the banks' capital cushions. See account in Chapter 9.

3. Robert J. Ballon and Iwao Tomita, *The Financial Behavior of Japanese Corporations* (New York and Tokyo: Kodansha International, 1988), p. 177.

4. The three agencies are the Japan Bond Research Institute, owned 100 percent by the *Nihon Keizai Shimbun*, the Nippon Investors Service, owned by a consortium of banks led by the Industrial Bank of Japan, and the Nippon Credit Rating Agency, led by the Long-Term Credit Bank of Japan, Sumitomo Trust, and Nippon Life.

5. Kuribayashi Yoshimitsu, *Ōkurashō: Fushin no Kōzu* (The Ministry of Finance: A Profile of Distrust) (Tokyo:

Kodansha, 1992), pp. 360–63. The author, now a free-lance journalist who spent much of his career covering the MOF, believes the greed and power lust of MOF bureaucrats is the source of what he contends is the growing distrust in Japan of this ministry. Chapter 6 of the book is a study of the influence of ex-MOF officials.

6. *Tōyō Keizai*, September 14, 1991, p. 20, carries a list of the positions held by the nine hundred or so members of the Ōkura Dōyūkai (retired MOF officials' organization).

7. Uchida Michio, " 'Dokusen' Ōkurashō Kenryoku no Kaitai" (Breaking the 'Monopoly' Power of the Finance Ministry), *Tōyō Keizai* (September 14, 1991), p. 16.

8. Tachibana Takashi, "Jōhō Wocchingu" (Media Watching—Regular Column), *Shūkan Gendai* (November 28, 1987), pp. 56–57.

9. Paul Krugman, *The Age of Diminished Expectations* (Cambridge, Mass.: MIT Press, 1990), p. 117n.

10. Mikuni Akio, "The Collapse in Japanese Financial Markets," occasional paper (Tokyo: Mikuni & Company, 1992), p. 1.

11. "Miwataseba Mina Ōkura OB" (We Find Retired MOF Officials Everywhere), *Nihon Keizai Shimbun,* (May 11, 1994), p. 2.

12. Uchihashi Katsuto, "Watakushi ga Shinbun o Shinjinai Riyū: *Yomirui; Nikkei* 'Sha setsu' no Kiken na Chōkō" (The Reasons I Don't Believe Newspapers: Dangerous Trends in "Editorials" of *Yomiuri* and *Nikkei*

Newspapers), *Shūkan Gendai* (January 1990), p. 101.

13. Karel van Wolferen has described the *kisha* clubs as coming "into their own in the war years, when censorship was official. . . . [They] help the journalist, since he or she need never worry about missing a vital development, and they provide the power-holders with their main means of co-ordinating media self-censorship. . . . Most Japanese journalists spend the entire day with fellow *kisha* club members, and generally have little contact with informants outside this environment. Their club makes collective decisions on what its members may or may not report, occasionally even on the tone of the reports." Op. cit., pp. 94–95.

14. "*Nikkei* Shimbun Sukūpu made no Butaiura" (Behind the Scenes of the *Nikkei*'s Scoop), *Shūkan Hoseki* (August 15, 1991), pp. 34–37.

15. "Black Monday Irai Shijō Nibanme no Kabuka Bōraku: *Nikkei* Hōdō Ōkisugita Hamon" (The Historical Second Drop in Stock Prices after Black Monday: The Excessive Effects of the *Nikkei*'s Reporting), *AERA* (April 17, 1990), pp. 14–16.

16. Gregory Millman, *The Vandal's Crown* (New York: Free Press, 1995), p. 155.

17. Rodney Clark, *The Japanese Company* (Tokyo: Charles E. Tuttle, 1987), pp. 74–75.

18. See discussion in Chalmers Johnson, *MITI and the Japanese Miracle: The Growth of Industrial Policy 1925–1975* (Stanford, Calif.: Stanford University Press, 1982), p. 303.

19. James M. Poterba's "Comparing the Cost of Capital in the United States and Japan: A Survey of Methods," *FRBNY Quarterly Review* (Winter 1991), pp. 21–32, is an overview of the academic literature on the subject. The article notes that "all of the studies conclude that the cost of capital is significantly higher in the United States than in Japan," but there is little agreement on what these costs actually are.

20. David Hale, *The Weekly Money Report* (Chicago: Kemper Financial Services, Inc., April 12, 1993).

21. Suzuki Yoshio, *The Japanese Financial System* (Oxford: Clarendon Press, 1989), p. 8. The author was the director of the Institute for Monetary and Economic Studies at the Bank of Japan.

22. Mikuni Akio, "Behind Japan's Economic Crisis," *New York Times* (February 1, 1993), op-ed page.

23. Sato Kazuo, "Saving and Investment," in *The Political Economy of Japan*, Vol. I, *The Domestic Transformation*, ed. Yamamura Kozo and Yasuba Yasukichi. (Stanford, Calif.: Stanford University Press, 1987), p. 173.

3. A Case of National Leverage
The Japanese Economic Miracle

1. Andrew Gordon describes the early struggles over the bonus system in *The Evolution of Labor Relations in Japan: Heavy Industry, 1853–1955* (Cambridge, Mass.: Harvard University Press, 1988), pp. 360–61.

2. The best account in English of Japan's secondary educational system and the crucial role it plays in sorting out Japanese boys for their ultimate positions in the economic hierarchy is Thomas P. Rohlen, *Japan's High Schools* (Berkeley and Los Angeles: University of California Press, 1983).

3. The classic account in English of middle-class Japanese daily life during the early years of the high-growth period—the years when Eiji would have been in grammar school—is Ezra F. Vogel, *Japan's New Middle Class* (Berkeley and Los Angeles: University of California Press, 1963).

4. So-called lifetime employment is not a legal arrangement but a kind of

norm to which the vast majority of all companies aspire. According to a 1993 Japan Labor Ministry survey, over 99 percent of all private companies with 300 or more employees claim to follow "lifetime" employment; the percentage drops to 95 in companies with 100 to 299 employees and to 85 for companies with 30 to 99 employees. In practice, "lifetime employment" means that companies will retain so-called *seisha-in* (company member) except for extraordinary situations (e.g., insubordination, criminal misconduct) until the normal retirement age, which has historically been the mid-fifties for men, the late twenties for women. Many companies rely, however, on considerable numbers of "part-time" workers (such people may in fact work full-time, but they are not considered *seisha-in* and thus not governed by "lifetime" employment protocols). Real "private-sector" job security in Japan is thus restricted to male *seisha-in* working for companies that do not fear bankruptcy. In 1992, according to the Labor Ministry, there were some 7,865,600 employees of companies with more than 1,000 workers. Of these, 68.7 percent were men, and of that percentage, 94.6 percent were *seisha-in*. Thus genuine bankable job security extends to only some 5,000,000 men in the private sector and another 4,500,000 men and women in the public sector, out of a total work force of some 65,000,000 people.

5. For the story of the Equal Opportunity Employment Act and the corporate reaction, see Frank Upham, *Law and Social Change in Postwar Japan* (Cambridge, Mass.: Harvard University Press, 1987), Chapter 4.

6. The household savings rate (household savings as a percentage of income) in Japan climbed steadily through the 1950s (earlier accumulated savings had been wiped out by the postwar hyperinflation), topping 15 percent by 1960, and it has never fallen below that number, even in the most economically straitened years. The rate peaked at 24 percent in 1974 and has been between 15 and 20 percent every year since 1978. In contrast, the household savings rate in the United States fell steadily through the 1970s to bottom out in the mid-1980s below 5 percent where it has remained ever since. If one is willing to wade through the obligatory equations and models, a useful discussion in English of Japan's household savings behavior through the early 1980s can be found in Sato Kazuo, op. cit., pp. 137–85. On page 162 Sato concludes that "the two major incentives for [Japanese] worker households to save are housing and retirement."

7. The book—Nakano Kōji, *Seihin no Shisō* (The Idea of Holy Poverty) (Tokyo: Sōshisha, 1992)—sold close to a million copies, unusual for an expensive hardback devoted to ruminations on the tea ceremony and ancient Japanese parables.

8. Gordon, op. cit., p. 28. In a biography of her grandfather the great Meiji finance minister Matsukata Masayoshi, Haru Matsukata Reischauer notes that on a trip to Europe in 1878, Matsukata was chided by an Englishman for the spendthrift habits of the Japanese. Determined that the Japanese would learn how to save, Matsukata studied the British postal savings system. Today the Japanese Postal Savings System is effectively the world's largest bank. See *Samurai and Silk: A Japanese and American Heritage* (Tokyo: Charles E. Tuttle, 1987), pp. 134–35.

9. Peter L. Berger, *The Capitalist Revolution: Fifty Propositions about Prosperity, Equality and Liberty* (New York: Basic Books, 1986), p. 144.

10. Hori Tsuneo, *Meiji Keizai Shisō-shi* (History of Meiji Economic Thought) (Tokyo: Nippon Keizai Hyōronsha, 1991), pp. 249–64, dis-

cusses the translation and the impact of List's ideas. Reischauer, op. cit., pp. 81–96, provides an overview in English on the debates in the 1870s and 1880s among the Japanese elite on the structure of the Japanese financial system. She notes that "throughout his life, Matsukata often referred to the protectionist policies of . . . Friedrich List as more suitable then for Japan than Adam Smith's ideas." For a specific discussion of the question of foreign financing, see E. H. Norman, *The Origins of the Modern Japanese State: Selected Writings of E. H. Norman*, ed. John Dower (New York: Pantheon Books, 1975), pp. 221–24.

11. Mark Mason, *American Multinationals and Japan: The Political Economy of Japanese Capital Controls, 1899–1980* (Cambridge, Mass.: Harvard University Press, 1992), pp. 107–08.

12. The character of the occupation in its early years made implementing this decision easier than it might otherwise have been, for it was, between 1945 and 1947, dominated by aging New Dealers fearful that rapacious multinationals would buy Japan up on the cheap. The occupation thus instituted "capital controls far stricter than those imposed by the Allied Occupation in Germany," writes Dennis Encarnation in *Rivals beyond Trade: America versus Japan in Global Competition* (Ithaca, N.Y.: Cornell University Press, 1992), p. 46.

13. A recent study by the research arm of Daiwa Securities was quoted in the *Asahi Shimbun,* (March 15, 1994), evening edition, as saying "the prices of daily commodities are more than double that of the U.S."

14. While the minimum investment size of long-term bank debentures was, at ¥10,000 (only $27 until 1971), low enough so that households could theoretically afford them, long-term bank branches were few in number. It was difficult in practical terms for households to buy them.

15. The incident is described in Johnson, op. cit., p. 247.

16. See discussion in Phyllis A. Genther, *A History of Japan's Government-Business Relationship: The Passenger Car Industry.* Michigan Papers in Japanese Studies No. 20 (Ann Arbor, Mich.: Center for Japanese Studies, University of Michigan, 1990), pp. 70–73.

17. The early 1950s debates over whether or not to have a passenger car industry are often confused with several later disputes between MITI and the auto companies. MITI wanted to reduce the number of players and acted as the go-between in the mid-sixties merger of Nissan and Prince Motors, but most of the firms balked at the proposed mergers. Several of the smaller firms also resisted MITI's attempts in 1961 to persuade them to specialize in certain vehicle sizes. And Mitsubishi Motors defied MITI's theretofore successful attempts to control foreign investment in the Japanese industry with its sensational announcement in 1969 of the tie-up with Chrysler, a development sometimes regarded as heralding the end of MITI's golden age. But the long history of disputes between the bureaucracy and the automobile industry should not blind one to the importance of access to cheap, centrally directed capital at the right junctures or the fundamental role of the bureaucracy in protecting the industry during its formative years. As Genther, op. cit., pp. 23–24, writes, "government officials never abandoned the most important form of assistance the domestic automakers received: direct or indirect protection from foreign competition until they had become internationally competitive in cost and quality." See also Michael Cusumano, *The Japanese Automobile Industry* (Cambridge, Mass.: Harvard University Press, 1985), particularly pp. 19–26. The account of the shock of the Mitsubishi-Chrysler announcement can be

found in Johnson, op. cit., pp. 286–89.

18. Johnson, op. cit., pp. 236–37.

19. A gripping account of the story of the Japanese computer industry is Marie Anchordoguy, *Computers Inc.: Japan's Challenge to IBM* (Cambridge, Mass.: Harvard University Press, 1989). About the so-called liberalization of this industry in the 1970s, Anchordoguy writes that "much of the fear that a gust of free trade was going to be allowed to blow through the long-protected market was hype, exaggerated to force the computer makers to get their own houses in order. MITI really had no intention of opening the computer industry to the vagaries of a free market. As Americans would begin to understand only more than a decade later, a free market, to the Japanese, means a market without such formal constraints as tariffs, quotas, and prohibitions on foreign investment; it has nothing to do with whether competitive foreign products are actually purchased. There was never any question in MITI's mind but that informal restraints would continue," p. 135.

20. Hamada Koichi and Horiuchi Akiyoshi, "The Political Economy of the Financial Market," in Yamamura and Yasuba, op. cit., p. 239.

21. J. Andrew Spindler, *The Politics of International Credit: Private Finance and Foreign Policy in Germany and Japan* (Washington, D.C.: Brookings Institution, 1984), p. 9. The writer notes: "German governments have hesitated to intervene directly to influence the behavior of German banks in specific transactions" (p. 14), while "the [Japanese] government has actively influenced the banking system's domestic allocation of capital through both careful supervision of the system and direct financial intermediation" (p. 94).

22. Mikuni Akio, remarks to the G-30 meeting, New York, September 24, 1992.

23. These three banks—the Industrial Bank of Japan, the Long-Term Credit Bank of Japan, and the Nippon Credit Bank—funded themselves through the issue of five- and seven-year fixed-rate debentures. No other institution was allowed to issue instruments that would compete with these debentures. Until at least the mid-1960s the MOF arranged for the purchase of the debentures and their coupons continue to be set by negotiation among the three banks, the MOF, and the BOJ. For a discussion of the postwar history of long-term bank funding, see Frank Packer, "The Role of the Long-Term Credit Banks within the Main Bank System," *Economic Development Institute of the World Bank Working Paper Number 94-6* (Washington, D.C: International Bank for Reconstruction and Development, 1994), pp. 7–12.

24. See, for example, Kent Calder, *Strategic Capitalism* (Princeton: Princeton University Press, 1993).

25. IBJ took on a critical role as a lead financier for key industrial firms that were only loosely, if at all, affiliated with the great *keiretsu*. These firms included such industrial giants as Nissan, Nippon Steel, and Hitachi. IBJ has also been Japan's leading orchestrator of mergers that typically happen in Japan to stave off bankruptcies by large companies or as MITI-organized rationalizations of the industrial structure. It is also usually IBJ bankers who are sent—with government blessing—to rescue important companies in trouble. The list of such firms includes Nippon Yakin Kogyo, a specialty steel manufacturer; Nittoku Metal Industry, a maker of small bulldozers and other industrial machinery; Daido Special Steel; the machine tool company Ikegai Tekko; Nissan Motors; Yamaichi Securities; and Japan Line, one of Japan's largest shipping companies. David Halberstam provides a riveting account of the career of the IBJ banker Kawamata

Katsuji, who was sent in 1947 to save Nissan and became its president in 1957. Kawamata was one of the key figures in the crushing of an independent Japanese labor movement when he broke a hundred-day strike in 1953 by Nissan's then-radical union. See *The Reckoning* (New York: William Morrow & Company, 1986), pp. 131–87.

26. The *Asahi Shimbun* contended that the real "scenario writer" of the merger was the Ministry of Finance. "Ukareru Ōkurasho; Meja Tanjyō; Mitsui, Taiyo Kobe Ginkō o Gappei" (Happy MOF: Major Birth; Merger of the Mitsui and Taiyo Kobe Banks)

(September 2, 1989), p. 9.

27. An exhaustive account of the mechanism of overloan has been provided by the former Bank of Japan official Suzuki Yoshio and can be found in English translation in his *Money and Banking in Contemporary Japan* (New Haven: Yale University Press, 1980). See particularly pp. 3–36 and 62–66.

28. See the discussion in van Wolferen, op. cit., pp. 384–86. Also see Suzuki, *Money and Banking . . .* , loc. cit., p. 16.

29. Milton Friedman, *Capitalism and Freedom* (Chicago: University of Chicago Press, 1962), p. 54.

4. Closing the Circle
Exports, Exchange Rates, and the 1970s

1. Robert C. Angel, *Explaining Economic Policy Failure: Japan in the 1969–1971 International Monetary Crisis* (New York: Columbia University Press, 1991), p. 38.

2. See the discussion of the theory of hegemonic stability in Robert Gilpin, *The Political Economy of International Relations* (Princeton: Princeton University Press, 1987), pp. 72–80.

3. Triffen wrote an influential book on the subject: Robert Triffen, *Gold and the Dollar Crisis* (New Haven: Yale University Press, 1960).

4. Paul Volcker and Gyohten Toyoo, *Changing Fortunes: The World's Money and the Threat to American Leadership* (New York: Times Books, 1992), p. 61.

5. Angel, op. cit., p. 272.

6. Van Wolferen, op. cit. Angel op. cit.

7. I. M. Destler, Fukui Haruhiro, and Sato Hideo, *The Textile Wrangle: Conflict in Japanese-American Relations, 1969–1971* (Ithaca, N.Y.: Cornell University Press, 1979), pp. 136–38.

8. Komiya Ryutaro and Suda Miyako, *Japan's Foreign Exchange Policy 1971–82*, tr. ed. Colin McKenzie (Sydney,

Australia: Allen & Unwin, 1991), p. 37.

9. Volcker and Gyohten, op. cit., p. 72.

10. Angel, op. cit., p. 252.

11. Volcker and Gyohten, op. cit., p. 97.

12. Ibid., p. 90.

13. Komiya and Suda, op. cit., p. 41.

14. Takahashi Kamekichi, "En o Saikiriage Sureba Keiki ni Daidageki; Nihon Keizai no Kaiko to Tenbō" (Should the Yen Be Revalued Again, It Would Deal a Severe Blow to the Economy; Retrospects and Prospects for Japan's Economy), *Tōyō Keizai* (January 13, 1973), pp. 46–50.

15. "Gaitae Shijō ni Miru En Saikiriage Fuan" (Foreign Exchange Market's Apprehension on the Prospect of Further Yen Revaluation), *Tōyō Keizai* (January 27, 1973), pp. 56–59.

16. Suzuki Toshio, writing in *Tōyō Keizai* (March 28, 1973), p. 43.

17. This account of the run on the yen draws heavily on Komiya and Suda, op. cit., pp. 76–96.

18. Ibid., p. 114.

19. Johnson, op. cit., p. 297.

20. Quoted in Komiya and Suda, op. cit., pp. 141–43.

21. Helmut Schmidt, quoted in the *New York Times* (January 26, 1977), p. 5.

22. Maruyama Masao, *Thought and Behavior in Modern Japanese Politics,* ed. Ivan Morris (London: Oxford University Press, 1963), p. 105. Chapter 3 in this seminal book features illuminating observations on the strikingly different psychologies of Germany's and Japan's wartime leaders.

23. Mikuni, "The Vitality of Japan . . ." loc. cit., p. 54.

24. Van Wolferen, op. cit., p. 403.

25. Robert Strauss, quoted in "U.S. and Japan Reach an Accord on Easing of Tensions in Trade," *New York Times* (January 14, 1978), p. 1.

26. "Gross saving of the corporate sector is the sum of provisions for capital consumption (depreciation) and retained profits (net saving). Capital consumption (as of 1985) has increased year by year due to expansion of depreciable assets. . . . Reflecting these trends . . . the corporate sector's net deficit of funds fell from about 7 percent of GNP in the early 1970's to slightly less than 3 percent in the second half of the 1970's. Though this net deficit expanded slightly in the early 1980's, it remained at the low level of just above 3 percent," writes Suzuki Yoshio in *The Japanese Financial System,* loc. cit., p. 8. Sato, op. cit., argues by implication that Japanese accounting practices of carrying assets at book rather than market value seriously understates depreciation expenses. Japan's economic administrators relied informally on the great discrepancy between book and market values to mask the actual financial condition of both corporations and banks right through the postwar period; until the end of the 1980s manipulation of these values was one of the key instruments of bureaucratized, informal credit allocation. The ultimate financial explanation for the prolonged recession of the 1990s is the disappearance of much of this discrepancy. See discussion in Chapter 9.

5. Weak Claims
Japanese Finance and the American Deficit

1. Albert M. Wojnilower, "Japan and the United States: Some Observations on Economic Policy," in *Japan and the United States Today: Exchange Rates, Macroeconomic Policies and Financial Market Innovations,* ed. Hugh T. Patrick and Tachi Ryuichiro (New York: Center on Japanese Economy and Business, Columbia University, 1986), p. 83.

2. David Stockman, *The Triumph of Politics* (London: Hodder and Stoughton, 1986), p. 79.

3. Ibid.

4. Ibid.

5. Ibid., p. 429.

6. "JAL's Battle against Red Ink Highlights Cost of Strong Yen," *Asian Wall Street Journal* August 10, 1994, p. 8.

7. *Economic Statistics Annual, 1993* (Tokyo: Research and Statistics Department, Bank of Japan, 1994), p. 125.

8. Ibid., p. 331.

9. Volcker and Gyohten, op. cit., pp. 178–79.

10. Stockman, op. cit., p. 284.

11. While Regan's autobiography— Donald T. Regan, *For the Record: From Wall Street to Washington* (San Diego and New York: Harcourt, Brace, Jovanovich, 1988)—does not, alas, discuss his experiences in financing the deficit and his views on the dollar, it does make clear his opinions of his colleagues. He writes (p. 153): "Stockman and his people . . . [had] a brassy confidence in their own expertise that would have gotten them fired for an excess of zeal from any group except the government or graduate school."

12. Joseph White and Aaron Wildavsky, *The Deficit and the Public Interest: The Search for Responsible Budgeting in the 1980's* (Berkeley and Los Angeles: University of California Press, 1989), p. 189.

13. Volcker and Gyohten, op. cit., p. 180.

14. U.S. Congress, Joint Economic Committee, *International Economic Policy,* hearings, 97th Congress, May 4, 1981, pp. 27–28.

15. I am grateful to Dr. Eric Hayden for bringing this paper to my attention.

16. "Foreign Exchange Value of the Dollar," *Joint Hearings before the Subcommittee on International Trade, Investment and Monetary Policy and the Subcommittee on Domestic Monetary Policy of the Committee on Banking, Finance, and Urban Affairs, House of Representatives, Ninety-eighth Congress, First Session.* Serial No. 98-48 (Washington, D.C.: U.S. Government Printing Office, 1984), p. 123.

17. I. M. Destler and C. Randall Henning, *Dollar Politics: Exchange Rate Policymaking in the United States* (Washington, D.C.: Institute for International Economics, 1989), p. 29.

18. Several years after these events *Tōyō Keizai* ran a long interview with Oba Tomomitsu, who had been vice minister for international affairs and thus Sprinkel's formal counterpart in 1983–84. Oba confirmed that Regan's table banging had happened more than once and that the whole episode of the sudden demands from Washington for financial liberalization had been both surprising and perplexing to MOF officials. "Tsūka

Gaikō no Seiji Keizaigaku" (The Political Economy of Foreign Exchange Policies), *Tōyō Keizai* May 22, 1987), pp. 6–11. Another (now-retired) senior MOF official whom I interviewed and who requested anonymity told me he and his colleagues regarded Sprinkel and Regan as "amateurish" in contrast with their successors, Richard Darman and James A. Baker III respectively.

19. "Teiryū" regular column, *Nihon Keizai Shimbun,* (October 15, 1983), p. 3.

20. "Report on Yen / Dollar Exchange Rate Issues by the Japanese Ministry of Finance—U.S. Department of the Treasury Working Group to Japanese Minister of Finance Noboru Takeshita and U.S. Secretary of the Treasury Donald T. Regan" (Washington: Department of the Treasury, May 1984).

21. Gyohten Toyoo, writing in Volcker and Gyohten, op. cit., p. 184.

22. Walter Mondale, "Transcript of Mondale Address Accepting Party Nomination," *New York Times* (July 20, 1994), p. A-12.

23. Mikuni Akio, "A New Era for Japanese Finance," *Asian Wall Street Journal* July 2–3, 1993), editorial page.

24. Van Wolferen op. cit., p. 148.

25. A major study in English of this pivotal figure is John Dower, *Empire and Aftermath: Yoshida Shigeru and the Japanese Experience, 1878–1954* (Cambridge, Mass.: Harvard University Press, 1979). See particularly Chapter 10.

6. Units of Account
The Plaza Accord

1. Hedrick Smith, *The Power Game: How Washington Works* (New York: Random House, 1988) discusses on p. 370 Baker's reasons for agreeing to the job switch with Regan. See also Lou Cannon, *President Reagan: The*

Role of a Lifetime (New York: Simon and Schuster, 1991), p. 557.

2. For Regan's account, see Regan, op. cit., pp. 218–31.

3. For example, Smith, op. cit., pp. 325–28. Or Peggy Noonan, *What I*

Saw at the Revolution: A Political Life in the Reagan Era (New York: Ballantine Books, 1990), Chapter 10. Or Cannon, op. cit., pp. 560–71.

4. Smith, op. cit., p. 313.

5. Ibid., p. 317.

6. The remark has been attributed to C. Fred Bergsten, although he denies having made it. It was, however, conventional wisdom in both Washington and Tokyo at the time that a rate of 180 was about what was needed to end the Japanese surpluses.

7. Destler and Henning, op. cit., p. 36.

8. Volcker and Gyohten op. cit., p. 234.

9. Funabashi Yoichi, Managing the Dollar: From the Plaza to the Louvre, 2d ed. (Washington, D.C.: Institute for International Economics, 1989), p. 4.

10. The incident is described in Clyde V. Prestowitz, Jr., Trading Places: How We Allowed Japan to Take the Lead (New York: Basic Books, 1988), p. 252.

11. Nakasone Yasuhiro, quoted in Fu-

nabashi, op. cit., p. 88.

12. Ibid., p. 11.

13. Ibid., p. 13.

14. Volcker and Gyohten, op. cit., p. 243.

15. Ibid.

16. C. Fred Bergsten, "The U.S.-Japan Economic Problem: Next Steps," in Patrick and Tachi, op. cit., p. 13.

17. The preeminent study in English of the Japanese government's budgeting procedures remains to this day John Creighton Campbell, Contemporary Japanese Budget Politics (Berkeley and Los Angeles: University of California Press, 1977).

18. Funabashi, op. cit., p. 61.

19. "Tokyo Summit no Gosan to Omoni" (The Misreading and Burden of the Tokyo Summit), Asahi Shimbun (May 7, 1986), p. 5.

20. "Shunjū" (column), Nihon Keizai Shimbun (May 8, 1986), p. 1.

21. Funabashi, op. cit., p. 156. See also Volcker and Gyohten, op. cit., p. 264.

22. Gyohten Toyoo, writing ibid., p. 265.

7. Coping with *Endaka*
Japan's "Bubble" Economy

1. "Speculative manias gather speed through expansion of money and credit or, perhaps, in some cases, get started because of an initial expansion of money and credit," writes Charles P. Kindleberger in his classic study Manias, Panics, and Crashes: A History of Financial Crises (New York: Basic Books, 1989), p. 57. These words open Chapter 4, which examines the links between rapid credit expansion and speculative manias.

2. See the discussion in Charles P. Kindleberger, The World in Depression, 1929–1939 (London: Penguin Books, 1987), pp. 53–54.

3. Tabuchi's statement about the MOF was not carried in Japanese news accounts of the press conference where he announced his resignation. But it was revealed a few days later when his successor "apologized" for Tabuchi's

remark. For example, "Nōmura Kabunushi Sōkai de no Tabuchi Zenshachō Hatsugen o Futeki Setsu to Tekkai de; Sonshitsu Hoten Mondai" (The Compensation Payment Problem: Denial of Inappropriate Remarks Made by Former President Tabuchi at Nomura Shareholders' Meeting), Asahi Shimbun (June 28, 1991), p. 1.

4. Quoted and translated by Taniguchi Tomohiko, "Japan's Banks and the 'Bubble' Economy' of the late 1980's," Monograph Series Number 4 (Princeton: Center of International Studies, Program on U.S.-Japan Relations, Princeton University, 1993), p. 9. Taniguchi is an editor of the business-financial journal Shūkan Nikkei Business, and his monograph is one of the best discussions I have seen of the bubble economy.

5. I am grateful to Dr. Kenneth Courtis for this observation.

6. Taniguchi, op. cit., p. 10.

7. Ibid., p. 6.

8. Press commentary was less critical of the report itself than of the damage to Japan's credibility done by raising expectations abroad that the idealistic recommendations in the report had any chance of being implemented. The eminent economist Komiya Ryutaro, writing in Japan's most prestigious business-financial weekly, described the report as a kind of "figment of the imagination" (*Tōyō Keizai* [June 14, 1986], p. 96), acknowledging that while the report did try to tackle substantive issues, it was of course emasculated by bureaucratic intervention. The commentator Doi Ayako noted in *Seiron* (May 1987), p. 46, that the report had "spoiled Japan's credibility" because of the false expectations it had raised.

9. The Bank of Japan's official discount rate—the key short-term interest rate—was cut five times between January 1986 and February 1987, dropping by half from the 5 percent where it had stood at the beginning of 1986 to 2.5 percent thirteen months later.

10. According to the Bank of Japan, wholesale prices in 1985 declined by 1.1 percent from 1984. In 1986 they declined 9.1 percent; in 1987, 3.8 percent, in 1988, 0.9 percent. In 1989, the last year of the bubble economy, wholesale prices finally rose by 2.5 percent. Meanwhile consumer prices, which had risen by 2 percent in 1985, rose in each of the following years by 0.6, 0.1, 0.7, and 2.3 percent respectively. This gap in the behavior of wholesale and consumer prices in and of itself demonstrates how little Japanese consumers benefited from the abrupt rise of the yen. While Japanese industry saw prices fall by some 15 percent in the late 1980s, Japanese consumers saw prices rise about 5 percent. Meanwhile M1 increased by 5, 6.9, 10.5, 8.4, and 4.1 percent in

each year between 1985 and 1989; the respective figures for M2 plus CDs are 8.4, 8.7, 10.4, 11.2, and 9.9 percent. See *Economic Statistics Annual, 1993* (Tokyo: Research and Statistics Department, Bank of Japan, 1994), p. 18 for prices, p. 39 for money supply numbers.

11. In 1986 Japan's imports totaled $126.4 billion. The largest categories were mineral fuels ($36.9 billion) and foodstuffs ($19.2 billion). Total manufactured imports were $52.8 billion, or 42 percent of the total import bill and 2.4 percent of Japan's gross domestic product that year. Source: Bank of Japan.

12. I am grateful to Mikuni Akio for bringing this to my attention. According to Bank of Japan statistics, lending by the city banks in 1986 was up by 14.4 percent over 1985 while nominal GDP grew 4.4 percent; in 1978 both percentages were an identical 9.7 percent over the respective 1977 figures.

13. See, for example, W. Carl Kester and Timothy A. Luehrman, "The Myth of Japan's Low-Cost Capital," *Harvard Business Review,* (May–June 1992), pp. 130–38.

14. Marie Anchordoguy, "Land Policy: A Public Policy Failure," in John O. Haley and Kozo Yamamura *Land Issues in Japan: A Policy Failure?,* ed. (Seattle: Society for Japanese Studies, University of Washington, 1992), p. 82. Anchordoguy's article is an excellent look at bureaucratic squabbling over land and the heavy costs it exacts on Japanese households.

15. Bill Sterling, an economist with Merrill Lynch, quoted in "Shaky Ground: Say Sayonara to the Great Boom in Japanese Real Estate," *Barron's* (August 27, 1990), p. 17.

16. Interview with Mikuni Akio.

17. See, for example, Christopher Wood, *The Bubble Economy: The Japanese Economic Collapse* (London: Sidgwick and Jackson, 1992), who writes, (p. 50) "It would not be an exaggeration

to say that Japan operates on a land standard. . ." or van Wolferen op. cit., p. 401, or Robert L. Cutts, "Japan's New Land Standard," *Journal of the American Chamber of Commerce in Japan,* vol. 27 (March 1990), or Brian Woodall "Politics of Land," in Haley and Yamamura, op. cit., p. 127. Woodall attributes the idea to the Japanese economist Tanaka Keiichi. The best discussion in English I have seen of the links among MOF-BOJ monetary policies, the land market, and the

workings of the bubble economy is Robert L. Cutts, "Power from the Ground Up: Japan's Land Bubble," *Harvard Business Review* (May–June 1990), pp. 164–72.

18. Wood, op. cit., p. 10. Wood was the *Economist'*s business-financial Tokyo correspondent during and immediately after the bubble years.

19. Wood, op. cit., makes this point very eloquently, particularly in the opening chapter.

20. Private letter, April 1994.

8. Saving the World

1. David Hale, "The Japanese Ministry of Finance and Dollar Diplomacy during the Late 1980's or How the University of Tokyo Law School Saved America from the University of Chicago Economics Department," unpublished paper (Chicago: Kemper Financial Services, Inc.), July 1989, p. 1.

2. Gilpin, op. cit., p. 72.

3. I am grateful to Alan Tonelson for this phrasing. Tonelson has written extensively on Washington's foreign policy community; see, for example, his "Beyond Left and Right," *National Interest* (Winter 1993–94), pp. 3–18.

4. The incident involved the forced departure of Professor Ivan Hall from Gakushuin University. Hall, a respected scholar of Japanese and American intellectual history, had been hired with assurances that he would be treated just like any Japanese full professor. When his contract was up for renewal, however, agitation by a few xenophobes on the faculty resulted in the renewal's being denied at the last moment. Hall threatened legal action, and the university capitulated, awarding a substantial severance package. The capitulation may have occurred because of publicity in the *Sankei Shimbun* and the *Los Angeles Times* within weeks of the marriage of one of the

university's most famous alumni, the crown prince.

5. These meetings were supposed to be a secret. When they came to light during the securities scandals of 1991, they were specifically defended on the ground they had helped contain the damage from Black Monday. "Ōkurashō ni Okeru Shōken Gyōkai no Jinmyaku no Jittai" (The Whole Picture of the Personal Connections between the Securities Industry and the MOF) *Tōyō Keizai* (September 14, 1991), pp. 18–22, discusses the monthly lunches and their role in communicating MOF guidance to the Big Four.

6. Albert J. Alletzhauser, *The House of Nomura: The Inside Story of the World's Most Powerful Company* (London: Bloomsbury Publishing Ltd., 1990), pp. 16–17.

7. An unsigned article in *Sentaku,* "Yonsha Kabushiki Buchō-kai" (The Four Firm Meeting of Equity Trading General Managers) (May 1988), pp. 126–29, maintains that the purchasing of NTT and Nippon Steel shares that afternoon was something directly agreed upon at the lunch. *Sentaku* is a self-consciously elite publication available only by subscription and noted for the quality of its analysis of the bureaucracy.

8. Richard Koo, "Japanese Investment in Dollar Securities after the Plaza Accord," supplement to "U.S. Foreign

Debt" *Hearing before the Joint Economic Committee, Congress of the United States, One Hundredth Congress, Second Session* (Washington, D.C.: U.S. Government Printing Office, 1989), p. 73.
9. Ibid., p. 75.
10. Ibid., p. 78.
11. David Hale, "Global Finance and the Retreat to Managed Trade," *Harvard Business Review* (January–February 1990), p. 152. Hale notes that "the

share of U.S. imports subject to some form of restraint increased from 12% in 1980 to 24% in 1989."
12. See discussion in Kindleberger, *The World...* loc. cit., pp. 49–54.
13. Two former Bush administration officials confirmed this incident for me. Both requested anonymity.
14. Tony Shale, "The Plot That Triggered Tokyo's Plunge," *Euromoney* (May 1990), pp. 32–36.

9. Bubble Jeopardy

1. The troubled Anbō Shinyōkumiai was merged with Kimitsu Shinyōkumiai. The costs of the bailout were met with a ¥3.3 billion loan from the Japanese government with repayment to be shared among Chiba Bank, the Chiba prefectural government, the National Association of Shinyōkumiai, and four healthy *shinyōkumiai*. Details from "Teirei Kensa Minaoshi: Anbō Shinyōkumiai Saiken Kogetsuki de Chibaken ga Hōshin" (Reconsideration of Regular Inspection: The Plans in Chiba Prefecture for the Anbo Shinyōkumiai Bad Debts), *Asahi Shimbun* (November 20, 1989—Chiba edition insert) and "Saihen no Kachū, Ōki na Hamon: Furyō Saiken wa 32 Oku En, Kyū Anbō Shinyōkumiai Hainin" (Large Problems from the Reconstruction: Bad Credits of ¥3.2 billion, Misfeasance at the Former Anbo Shinyokumiai), *Asahi Shimbun,* (June 22, 1991—Chiba edition insert).
2. The banks involved were Fuji, Sanwa, Mitsui Taiyo Kobe, and Tokai. "Ginkō Gappei / Chū: Koshi Tantan; Okusoku Tobikau Kinyūkai" (Bank Mergers—No. 2 in three-part series—Rumors and Watchfulness Abound in Banking Circles), *Mainichi Shimbun* (November 15, 1990), p. 9.
3. "Itoman Shachō Kainin o Kakusaku shita Sumi-gin Kensa no 'Nakami'"

(The [Real] Meaning of the Investigation of the Sumitomo Bank Which Planned to Fire Itoman's President), *Keizaikai* (May 12, 1991), p. 164.
4. William V. Rapp, an American investment banker in charge of Bank of America's Tokyo investment banking activities during the bubble years, has suggested that the MOF's decision to allow the business to take root was also affected by the minicrash in the Japanese government bond market of June 1987, when Nomura Securities and the Sanwa Bank were said to have cornered the so-called benchmark bond, the ten-year Japanese government security, changed every few months, that is one of the few genuinely liquid instruments in the Japanese government bond market. See William V. Rapp, "The Role of Foreign Firms in the Japanese Securities Industry in the 1980's," paper given at the conference on Development of Japan and Its Pacific Context, sponsored by Osaka University and Columbia University, June 1994, Osaka, Japan. By cornering this instrument, Nomura drove the yield below that of the Bank of Japan's official discount rate, threatening, as Mikuni Akio has suggested to me, the structure of short-term interest rates and the ability of the Bank of Japan effectively to subsidize the banks. The MOF may have hoped that derivatives would help prevent a repeat of the incident.

5. According to the *Nihon Keizai Shimbun,* in the fiscal year ending March 31, 1992, for example, foreign securities firms as a group made more money than the domestic industry. Salomon alone had pretax profits of ¥23.7 billion ($190 million) that year and earned more than any Japanese firm except Nomura itself. "92 nen 3 gatsuki, Gaikoku Shōken, Keijō-eki 5.6 bai; Saitei Torihiki Nobiru" (Period Ending March, 1992; Foreign Securities Houses' Ordinary Income Increases 5.6 times; Arbitrage Dealings Increase), *Nihon Keizai Shimbun* (June 21, 1992).

6. See account in Martin Mayer, *Nightmare on Wall Street: Salomon Brothers and the Corruption of the Marketplace* (New York: Simon and Schuster, 1993), pp. 227–28.

7. An account from the Singapore side of the pressure from Japan can be found in Millman, op. cit., pp. 129–34. An agreement was finally announced by the MOF and the Monetary Authority of Singapore in April 1992 for coordinated oversight to "prevent abrupt drops" on the Tokyo Stock Exchange and SIMEX, respectively. "Kabushiki Sakimono; Singapore to Kyōgi, Ōkurashō Kabuka Kyūraku Bōshi de Taisaku" (Stock Futures: Discussions with Singapore; Action [by] the MOF to Prevent Abrupt Stock Price Drop) *Nihon Keizai Shimbun* (July 11, 1992), p. 5.

8. Jesper Koll, quoted in "Authorities Sense Victory in Popping Asset Bubble," *Japan Times* (April 11, 1991).

9. "The Art of Not Learning from Experience," *Economist* (March 2, 1991), p. 81.

10. "Kabushiki Hyōkazon: 200 oku en Kosu, Hanwa-kō no Kugatsu Chūkanki; Ginkō kabu ga Chūshin" (Appraisal Loss in Stocks: More Than ¥20 Billion; September Semiannual Report of Hanwa Industries), *Nihon Keizai Shimbun* (October 12, 1990).

11. The C. Itoh–led bailout was financed by a ¥570 billion loan led by IBJ and the Nippon Credit Bank. "Asahi Jūken ga Saiken e: Tempō Tōhaigō; Chūko Bumon o Shukushō; Kariirekin 5,700 oku en" (Toward Asahi Juken's Reconstruction: Consolidates Branch Offices, Shrinks Condominium Resale Division, Borrows ¥570 billion), *Yomiuri Shimbun,* Osaka edition (August 7, 1991), p. 6.

12. "Kabushippai no Ikeda Bussan, Saimu Chōka wa 212 oku en ni mo" (Ikeda Bussan's Stock Market Losses: Excess Liabilities up to ¥21.2 billion), *Asahi Shimbun* (April 4, 1991), p. 8.

13. Among them, Nanatomi, Aoyama Building, and Kyowa.

14. Azabu Building, along with three other troubled companies, came to form the acronym "AIDS" of the Tokyo property market. The history of its stormy relationship with its bankers, led by Mitsui Trust, can be found in "Azabu Tatemono vs. Mitsui Shintaku no Jimetsu Sensō" (The Suicidal War of Azabu Building and Mitsui Trust), *Tōyō Keizai* (April 3, 1993), pp. 44–47.

15. The acquired *shinkin,* Sanwa Shinyō Kinko, had bad debts of ¥20 billion ($160 million) when the announcement of the merger was made in March. This was the first actual case of a take-over of a *shinkin* by a city bank, but newspaper reports, noting that the MOF had engineered the merger, speculated there would be more. For example, "Kyūzai Gappei no Zōka Hisshi: Keiei Sekinin Doko e—Tōkai Ginkō no Sanwa Shinkin Kyūshū" (Inevitable Increases in Bailout Mergers; Where Will Management Responsibility Lie?—Tokai Bank's Acquisition of the Sanwa Shinkin), *Asahi Shimbun,* (March 13, 1991), p. 9.

16. The company was in default on ¥350 billion in debt owed not only to its parent but to such heavyweights of Japanese banking as LTCB, Nippon Credit Bank, Yasuda Trust, Mitsui Trust, and Mitsubishi Trust. "Hok-

kaidō Saidaite Nonbank: Takuginkei no Esco Lease ga Keiei Akka," (Hokkaido's Biggest Nonbank: Business Troubles at Takugin-Related Esco Lease), *Asahi Shimbun* (May 22, 1991), p. 11.

17. "Shizushin Lease: Kōseihō Shinsei; Shizuoka Shinkin kei Nonbanku, Fusae Sōgaku 2,562 oku en." (Shizushin Lease: Applies [for Relief from Creditors] under Corporate Reorganization Law, Nonbank in the Shizuoka Shinkin Keiretsu, Total Debts ¥256.2 Billion), *Nihon Keizai Shimbun* (April 23, 1991).

18. Henny Sender, "Too Japanese to Fail?," *Institutional Investor,* International Edition (May 1991), p. 100.

19. The article that broke the news: "Nōmura Shōken ga Hōjin Sonshitsu 160 oku en Anaume; Saiken o Takane Kaimodo shi; Shōtori hō Ihan no Utagai" (Nomura Securities Deducts ¥16 Billion in Losses; [for] Securities Bought at High Prices; Violation of Securities Law Suspected), *Yomiuri Shimbun* (June 20, 1991), p. 1.

20. Takeuchi Michio, quoted in Uchida op. cit., p. 12.

21. Wood, op. cit., pp. 118–20, provides a useful discussion of the *eigyō tokkin* and the MOF's conflicting guidance.

22. Robert Zielinski and Nigel Holloway, *Unequal Equities: Power and Risk in Japan's Stock Market* (Tokyo and New York: Kodansha International, 1991), p. 45.

23. The MOF tried to place the blame back on the securities industry by leaking to the *Nihon Keizai Shimbun* the names of the large institutions that had received compensation payments. The names were printed in the July 29, 1991, issue. The leak forced the Big Four securities firms to acknowledge what they had been doing. See Chapter 2, n. 14.

24. Wood, op. cit., pp. 146–57, provides a detailed and riveting account of the IBJ scandal.

25. "Itoman Sōsa: Yama Kosu—Minamino Fumin Shinyōkumiai zen riji kaichō ra Kiso" (Itoman Investigation: Passes the Peak; Suit Brought Against Former Chairman Minamino of Fumin Shinyokumiai and Others), *Asahi Shimbun* (October 9, 1991), p. 1.

26. "Fujigin futan, ¥200,000,000; Osaka Fumin Shinkumi Saiken no Michi, Keiwashisō" (Fuji's Burden ¥200 Billion; Osaka Fumin Credit Union's Road to Reconstruction Seems Tough), *Asahi Shimbun* (September 14, 1991), p. 8.

27. "Fuji Ginkō no Zenkoku hachi shiten o Nukiuchi Kensa; Ichiren no Fusei kaimei e; Ōkurashō" (Sudden Inspection of Eight Fuji Bank Branches across the Country; Ministry of Finance Moves toward Digging Out Series of Scandals), *Asahi Shimbun* (October 3, 1991), p. 1.

28. "Apollo Lease o Shien; Taiyō Mitsui nado" (Help for Apollo Lease; from Mitsui Taiyo etc.), *Asahi Shimbun* (February 21, 1992) p. 8.

29. "America Cracks Down," *Economist* (January 18, 1992), p. 70. A detailed account of the activities of Japanese banks in California is Henny Sender, "Japan's California Comeuppance," *Institutional Investor,* International Edition (December 1991), pp. 105–10.

30. "Cosmo Shōken Skylark ni 360 oku en Baishō; Kaimodoshi Yakusoku Tsuki Torihiki" (Cosmo Securities ¥36 Billion Compensation to Skylark [Restaurant Chain]; Promised Buyback Deal), *Asahi Shimbun* (February 25, 1992), p. 1.

31. "Songai 700–800 oku en ni; Daiwa Shōken no Tobashi mondai" (Damage of ¥70–80 Billion; Daiwa Securities' *Tobashi* Problems), *Asahi Shimbun* March 11, 1992, evening edition, p. 1.

32. "Nissai Gin kei Nonbank Sansha, Entai Saiken icchōen kosu; Togin nado kara no Shien Taisei zukuri nankō" (Three NCB-Related Nonbanks, Nonperforming Loans over ¥1 Trillion; Difficulties in Bailout Plan from

the Likes of the City Banks), *Mainichi Shimbun* (July 13, 1992), p. 1.

33. "Jūtaku Kinyū Nana-sha no Shakuny-ūkin 14 chō en; Ginkō, Nōkyō-kei ga Taihan" (Seven Housing Companies Debt of ¥14 Trillion; Most Banks; Agriculture Unions Involved), *Asahi Shimbun* (July 17, 1992), p. 1.

34. Morita Akio, " 'Nihon-kata Keiei' ga Abunai" (Japanese-Style Management Is Dangerous), *Bungei Shunju*, (February 1992), pp. 94–103.

35. In the conference, Hata—undoubtedly at the behest of his nominal subordinates at the MOF—noted that the recession differed from the more conventional recessions of 1974 and 1986. Accordingly, extraordinary measures would be required, including bank accounting changes and stock market stabilization measures.

The conference was extensively reported in the Japanese media, including "Ōkurashō Kinyū Taisaku; Tōza Shinogi no Irokoku-Rigai Chōsei no Muzukashisa Shimesu" (MOF's Financial Actions; Just Dodging Immediate Problems—Indicates the Difficulty of Arranging Profits and Losses), *Asahi Shimbun* (August 19, 1992), p. 9.

36. In his farewell conference as prime minister, Miyazawa noted that his greatest regret was his government's failure to cope adequately with the destructive effects of the bubble economy. "Jibun no Pēsu de Dekita; Miyazawa Shushō Tainin no Ben." (He Did It at His Own Pace; Prime Minister Miyazawa's Remarks on Resignation), *Asahi Shimbun* (August 4, 1993), p. 7.

10. The Turn of the Screw

1. Bob Woodward, *The Agenda: Inside the Clinton White House* (New York: Simon and Schuster, 1994), p. 84. Woodward describes in relentless detail the crumbling of Clinton's campaign platform in the face of the accumulated deficits.

2. Ibid., p. 145.

3. James Fallows, *Looking at the Sun* (New York: Pantheon, 1994), p. 136.

4. See discussion in John Dower, "E. H. Norman, Japan, and the Uses of History," in Norman, loc. cit., pp. 44–45.

5. The key event was the 1951 hearings by the Senate Subcommittee on Internal Security on the subject of Communist influence at the Institute of Pacific Relations (IPR), then the principal international association for Asian studies. The hearings destroyed the IPR, and "wracked and eviscerated Asian studies in the United States." Ibid., p. 42.

6. Ibid., pp. 54–55.

7. The term "revisionist" to describe the shift in thinking on Japan was popu-

larized in an influential cover article for *Business Week:* Robert Neff, Paul Magnusson, and William J. Holstein, "Rethinking Japan: The New Harder Line toward Tokyo," *Business Week* (August 7, 1989), pp. 44–52. In a sidebar to that article, Fallows, van Wolferen, and Prestowitz were labeled "the triumvirate of revisionism."

8. Prestowitz, op. cit.

9. James Fallows, "Containing Japan" *Atlantic Monthly* (May 1989), pp. 40–54.

10. Van Wolferen, op. cit.

11. Neff et al., op. cit., p. 49.

12. Johnson, op. cit.

13. A selection of Maruyama's writings translated and edited by Ivan Morris was published as Maruyama Masao, *Thought and Behavior in Modern Japanese Politics* (London: Oxford University Press, 1963). Critics who attacked the revisionists as "Eurocentric" for pointing out the absence of transcendent standards of appeal in Japan or the lack of a responsible po-

litical center were betraying their ignorance of Japan's most important political thinker.

14. A selection of Norman's writings, including the essential "Japan's Emergence as a Modern State," was compiled and edited in Norman, op. cit. In a long essay that begins the book, John Dower describes the eclipse of Norman's work by modernization theory and the ideological straitjackets of the Cold War.

15. Remarks made at press conference, National Press Club, Tokyo, July 5, 1994.

16. "Prepared Remarks by the Vice President to the Council on Foreign Relations" Office of the Vice President, Office of the Press Secretary, April 27, 1992, p. 2.

17. The book has appeared in English as Ozawa Ichiro, *Blueprint for a New Japan: The Rethinking of a Nation* (New York: Kodansha International, 1994). In his review of the book in the *New York Times* ("Land of the Setting Sun," *New York Times Book Review* [September 11, 1994]) Steven R. Weisman, who had been bureau chief for the *Times* in Tokyo, wrote that it was "startling to read a populist manifesto from a longtime stalwart of Japan's ruling elite that actually echoes the analysis of the so-called revisionist critics of Japan in the United States." Eric Gower, who edited the English translation, remarked to me that "parts of Ozawa's book were like reading van Wolferen all over again."

18. John Makin, quoted in Pat Choate, *Agents of Influence: How Japan's Lobbyists in the United States Manipulate America's Political and Economic System* (New York: Alfred A. Knopf, 1990) p. 190.

19. Ibid., p. xi.

20. The reference is to a column by George Will, "Protected from Lexus," *Washington Post* (May 19, 1995), op-ed page. That Will's wife works as a lobbyist for the Japan Automobile Manufacturers' Association was noted in Howard Kurtz, "A Conflict of Wills?; Pundit Kept Quiet about Wife's Role as Lobbyist," *Washington Post* (May 23, 1995), p. D-1.

21. Arai Atsuko, "Yushutsu Rikkoku kara Bōeki Kuni ni Kaiki" (From an Exporting Nation to a Trading Nation), *Tōyō Keizai* (February 23, 1994), pp. 74–76, describes this mechanism. Arai is a researcher at Mikuni & Co. I am grateful to Mikuni Akio for bringing her work to my attention.

22. David Asher, "Dissecting the Yen Bubble: Price Keeping Operations and the Inflated Price of the Yen" (Washington, D.C.: Mike Mansfield Center for Pacific Affairs, 1995), p. 13.

23. Ibid.

24. In fairness, analysis of the reasons behind the high yen could be found from time to time in serious journals that laid the blame at the door of the MOF. *Sentaku*, in its October 1993 issue, argued that MOF policies to bail out the banks and support the stock market were directly responsible for the soaring of the yen. The article noted that this flew in the face of conventional wisdom and the explanations in the mass media. "Ōkurashō koso ga 'En daka Yūdō' no Genkyō" (MOF's Plans at the Root of 'Bringing about the High Yen'), pp. 74–76. Richard Koo, in his recent Japanese-language book *Yoi Endaka; Warui En-daka* (Good High Yen; Bad High Yen) (Tokyo: Tōyō Keizai Shimpōsha, 1994), argues that many in the bureaucracy quietly support the strong yen, believing it will help force an overhaul of Japanese industry. Mikuni Akio, *En no Sōkessan* (The Yen's Bottom Line) (Tokyo: Kodansha, 1993) maintains the strong yen is an inevitable outgrowth of Japan's economic methods.

25. Paul Krugman, *The Age of Diminished*

Expectations: U.S. Economic Policy in the 1990's (Cambridge, Mass.: MIT Press, 1990), p. 119n.

26. These ideas among economists are described in Paul Krugman, *Peddling Prosperity: Economic Sense and Nonsense in the Age of Diminished Expectations* (New York: W. W. Norton & Company, 1994), Chapter 9.

27. Krugman, opera cit.

28. An important survey of contemporary institutional economics is the two-volume *Evolutionary Economics*, ed. Marc. R. Tool (Armonk, N.Y., and London: M. E. Sharpe, Inc., 1988).

29. Hale, "Global Finance and the Retreat to Managed Trade" loc. cit.

30. "Numerical Targets Are Seen as Way to Keep Yen in Check," *Japan Times* (May 31, 1994), p. 3.

31. Jagdish Bhagwati, "Samurais No More," *Foreign Affairs*, vol. 73, no. 3 (May–June 1994), p. 10.

32. The one book-length study in English of this fascinating and admirable man is Sharon N. Nolte, *Liberalism in Modern Japan: Ishibashi Tanzan and His Teachers, 1905–1960* (Berkeley and Los Angeles: University of California Press, 1987). Nolte makes clear Ishibashi's intellectual debt to Keynes but does not discuss his direct contributions to the income doubling plan. For that, see Johnson, op. cit., pp. 229–30.

33. Explicit parallels were drawn between the Hosokawa and Konoe cabinets by Kubo Koushi, an editor of the conservative daily *Sankei Shimbun*, in an article, "Hosokawa Shin-Taisei no Kenryoku Kōzō" (The Power Structure of Hosokawa's New System), *Shokun* (October 1993), pp. 68–79. *Shokun* is a right-wing opinion magazine somewhat akin to the *National Review*.

34. The most important of these hints was in a speech made by Governor Mieno of the Bank of Japan on March 24, 1994, under the auspices of the *Yomiuri Shimbun*. In the speech Mieno said specifically that banks should think of themselves as private-sector institutions—in other words, that they were not immune to the risk of failure.

35. An article severely critical of the MOF's handling of the botched merger of the three Tohoku (northeast Honshu banks) was "Ōkura ga Tokuyō City Kyūzai o Gorioshi suru riyū; Shinhōshiki 'Heisei ginkō' no Tonza" (The Reason for MOF's Aggressive Pushing of the Rescue of Tokuyo City; Failure of the Newly Planned "Heisei Bank"), *Tōyō Keizai* (June 18, 1994).

36. See, for example, van Wolferen, op. cit., pp. 216–20.

37. Leon Hollerman, "The Headquarters Nation," *National Interest*, No 25 (Fall 1991), pp. 16–25.

38. "Ajia o muku Ōkurashō" (The MOF Turning Its Face to Asia), *Nikkei Business* (October 31, 1994), pp. 33–37. The article also discusses a supposedly growing consensus among the elite that Japan must consider greater involvement with Asia and less with the United States. Among the individuals mentioned were former Prime Ministers Takeshita Noboru and Hata Tsutomu, former MOF international affairs Vice Ministers Oba Tomomitsu and Gyohten Toyoo, current MITI Minister Hashimoto Ryutaro, and former MOF administrative Vice Ministers Chino Tadao and Nakahira Yukio. How much of this is serious and how much is simply intended as a warning to the United States are not clear; supporting the latter interpretation is the unusual step the magazine's editors took of mailing unsolicited copies to foreign journalists.

Conclusion
Seriousness and Accountability

1. Henry Kissinger, *Diplomacy* (New York: Simon and Schuster, 1994), p. 834.
2. Chalmers Johnson and E. B. Keehn, "A Disaster in the Making: Rational Choice and Asian Studies," *National Interest* (Summer 1994) p. 19, write: ". . . the competition between theory and area studies has come to an end—with the virtual defeat of the latter. In almost all graduate programs in economics and political science, doctoral students must force the data they have collected from non-Western civilizations into theoretical frameworks, such as rational choice, generated to explain American conditions."

Index